INTRODUCTION

Thirty-five years of the seventeenth century separate the earliest and latest plays in this volume, and changing times are clearly reflected in them. These plays set in England tell modern readers, with varying degrees of realism, much about life in the reigns of James I and Charles I.[1]

A Trick to Catch the Old One (first performed in 1606), by Thomas Middleton, derived its basic plot from folklore, but it is filled with contemporary satiric commentary on the ambitious capitalists (none specifically identifiable) who attempted to enlarge wealth and estates during the early years of the century. The play is exclusively urban in tone and interests; the characters regarded the country as little more than a locale from which eager people came to seize opportunities in London, or a region to which the affluent went to inspect their estates.

Like *A Trick to Catch the Old One*, *The Witch of Edmonton* (1621) is contemporary in tone; yet Thomas Dekker, John Ford and William Rowly divorced their collaborative drama from the sophistications and preoccupations of London. Edmonton is less than ten miles from the metropolis, but in this play the concerns of what is now a suburb of the city were largely rural, centring on farms, crops, livestock and long-enduring beliefs in magic and witchcraft. The Thorney plot in *The Witch of Edmonton* slightly touches social and economic aggrandizement, the principal subject of the earlier play, through old Thorney's ambitions to recoup a decayed fortune by a marriage between his son and the daughter of a wealthy yeoman.

In the English countryside some interest in witchcraft had long predated the seventeenth century, as men attempted to explain mysterious disasters associated with crop failures and with disease and death amongst both animals and people. In the three or four decades preceding 1621, responsibility for misfortune was

---

[1] Queen Elizabeth (d. 1603) was succeeded by her distant cousin James I (d. 1625), who was followed by his son Charles I. The Civil War (1642–9) climaxed his continuing struggle with Parliament. After Charles I's execution in 1649 and a period of confusion, England was ruled as a sternly Puritan Commonwealth under Oliver Cromwell until his death in 1658. During 1660 the monarchy was restored to power, the son of the late king ascending the throne as Charles II.

particularly directed towards old women, in reality harmless, but perhaps eccentric and suspect as the result of age or isolation.

The persecution of such women was probably no new thing; however, the number of such 'witches' grew in the sixteenth century, as the result of anti-Catholic suspicions, self-generating local hysteria and fuller court records and published information about witch trials, resulting from a series of harsh laws forbidding witchcraft. The county of Essex, very close to Edmonton, was notable for the number of witches executed—some sixty between 1558 and 1617. During this period Chelmsford was the scene of three witch trials that resulted in ten executions.[1] The trial of thirteen women at St Osyth in 1582 prompted Reginald Scot's *The Discoverie of Witchcraft* (1584).

Both *A Trick to Catch the Old One* and *The Witch of Edmonton* are thus immediate commentaries on aspects of Jacobean society: prejudice, acquisitiveness, ruthlessness, preoccupations with money and related status symbols, especially in connection with marriage.

A Jovial Crew (1641) stands apart from these earlier plays. Like them, Richard Brome's play is a part of its times, as the disparaging allusions to a commonwealth and puritan behaviour suggest, but much of the play looks back nostalgically, not to the cynicism of London of 1606 or the cruelty of Edmonton of 1621, but to a pastoral Elizabethan society. The kindly property-owner Oldrents of the last play in this volume is a sharp contrast to the land-hungry entrepreneurs of the first.

Despite some late-flowering blossoms of idealism in *A Jovial Crew*, the cankers of a real world are a blight in paradise. Hints of contemporary disease appear in the prefatory poetry and prose, where the writers allude to their troubles and insecurities in the years previous to the Civil War.

At the beginning of the play Squire Oldrents lives in an apparently idyllic, timeless society, surrounded by the security of dutiful children, loyal friends, devoted servants and an obsequious crew of beggars in the barn. Yet the ruthlessness referred to above infects every phase of his life. Almost everyone on whom the squire depends for assurance rebels against the conventional code of behaviour. In the final act, however, Brome re-established tradition, with familiar, old-fashioned devices like a long lost son and a series of happy marriages. The play sets in juxtaposition pastoral charm and ominous realism. Marriage is unquestionably

[1] In 1645, twenty-four years after the time of the events in the play, nineteen more women were hanged at Chelmsford for witchcraft.

In this volume

Thomas Middleton
A TRICK TO CATCH THE OLD ONE

Thomas Dekker, John Ford, William Rowley
THE WITCH OF EDMONTON

Richard Brome
A JOVIAL CREW

Jacobean and Caroline Comedies

Edited with an Introduction by
ROBERT G. LAWRENCE

*Associate Professor of English
at the University of Victoria, British Columbia*

J. M. Dent & Sons Ltd, London

COLLEGE LIBRARY
CARYSFORT PARK
BLACKROCK DUBLIN

CONTENTS

an important subject in these three plays, each revealing seventeenth-century attitudes towards matrimony.

A Trick to Catch the Old One is essentially a marriage game of a commercial variety frequently played during this period. Theodorus Witgood is a trickster of necessity. Having casually let his estates slip into the hands of his usurer-uncle, he must get them back in order to make a conventional marriage; he persuades his former mistress, the Courtesan, to collaborate with him in deceiving the uncle. The game is complicated by the avaricious activities of several of Uncle Lucre's associates, whose greed makes it possible for Witgood to turn their connivance back on them. Middleton's satiric contempt for these men is clear, but he made Witgood a largely sympathetic figure, by means of a quantity of good will in him (i.e. his kindly treatment of the Courtesan).

Frank Thorney, the centre of the marriage plot in *The Witch of Edmonton*, is by contrast so entirely lacking in goodwill that his manipulations result in two pathetic deaths. Frank's father encourages something like a *mariage de convenance* between his son and Susan Carter subsequent to Frank's secret marriage to the pregnant Winnifride. Frank's resentment of his situation, despite his willing participation in it, leads to the murder of Susan; however, conventional justice ultimately triumphs in Frank's punishment.

Nothing like this hard edge appears in Brome's handling of the marriage theme in *A Jovial Crew*. Brome saw wedlock as a stabilizing force, and the relationships amongst his central youthful figures promise this. In addition to the two engaged couples who appear early in the play, the dramatist establishes two contrasting situations related to marriage. In Act III, the unhappy Amie has little prospect of marital happiness with either Talboy or Martin, but a further romantic development gives her every prospect of marital joy. In Act V the revelation of a discreditable episode from Squire Oldrents's past, a refusal to carry a romantic liaison to a formal fulfilment, accounts for a long-enduring unhappiness in him. The attitudes towards marriage of all the playwrights represented in this volume are extended logically to the theme of loyalty.

Witgood's loyalty towards his Courtesan is a distinctive part of his character, and her enthusiastic participation in the trick to catch an old one is a corollary to that kind of integrity. Two other examples of loyalty in this play may be noted in Audrey's fidelity to her master, the repulsive Dampit, and Walkadine Hoard's determination to remain steadfast to his bride subsequent to the embarrassing revelation of her true identity and her poverty.

Romantic constancy also dominates Susan Carter's relationship with her unworthy husband, Frank Thorney, in *The Witch of Edmonton*. In sharp and purposeful contrast is the black dog's ultimate desertion of Mother Sawyer, who had poured out so much affection upon the devil's agent.

Loyalty and disloyalty are set in clear opposition to each other in *A Jovial Crew*. Brome approached loyalty largely through its converse, notably in Springlove, whose wanderlust made him intermittently faithless to his employer, Squire Oldrents, and in Amie, who rebelled against her guardian's choice of husband. As well, Oldrents's failure, years before, to accept responsibility for his actions led to complex reverberations.

Each play in this collection has a serious theme behind the comic, satiric or critical elements; at the centre of each is social stability, under attack in the seventeenth century by various forces of irrationality or by aggressive economic and political powers. The humorous and the didactic have long been associated in English drama and other literary forms; thus, it is no accident that the authors of these two comedies and the tragicomedy should have been concerned with justice. Middleton chose not to be dogmatic about this subject, and although the sternest of moralists may not approve of the playwright's benign attitude towards Witgood, chagrin covers the tricksters who are caught by their covetousness. Obviously the authors of *The Witch of Edmonton* had an impassioned care for justice and brought into ironic juxtaposition, on their separate ways to the scaffold, Frank Thorney, who, prompted by self-interest, cruelly murdered his wife, and the pitiful Mother Sawyer, accused of diabolical activities by her reactionary neighbours. Justice operates on various levels in *A Jovial Crew;* it is characteristic of Brome's apparent tolerance that he allowed all his true lovers to be united and failed to condemn Justice Clack.

The principal themes of these three plays, written over three hundred years ago, are surprisingly modern. Variations on the marriage game are of unquestioned relevance in the twentieth century—misrepresentations are not unknown, an interest in money and possessions is often closely related to matrimony, and rebellion against a conventional marriage is common enough.

A metaphorical blindness in the forms of arrogance and

prejudice, easily recognized in this century, is a part of each play here. In *A Trick to Catch the Old One* the blindness takes the familiar guise of self-deception in Lucre, Walkadine Hoard, Dampit and the creditors.

The most obvious example of a comparable imperceptiveness in *A Jovial Crew* is Justice Clack. In him Brome developed a timeless picture of biased legal judgement: 'Have I not broke my own rule, which is to punish before I examine, and so have the law the surer o' my side?' (V, i, 30–32). Yet the contributions to the comedy by the garrulous old man do not represent serious social criticism; rather, they are a part of the Jonsonian humour tradition.[1]

The insensitivity and prejudice behind the pathetic story of Mother Sawyer give it an enduring impact. Each act of *The Witch of Edmonton* develops an ironic tone through the mixture of comic and tragic elements; however, in the witchcraft plot these elements progress from the casual teasing of the eccentric old woman and the magic games of her familiar spirit, the black dog, to Dekker's indictment of the inhumanity and irrationality that condemned her to death. Modern history has recorded many comparable deaths.

The earliest published versions of the plays have provided the basis of the present editions. Only *A Trick to Catch the Old One* was published (in 1608) close to the time of its first stage production. The others had to wait until the hungry days of the theatreless Commonwealth prompted publication, *A Jovial Crew* in 1652 and *The Witch of Edmonton* in 1658.

Spelling and punctuation have been conservatively modernized, with square brackets indicating material not in the original editions. Obsolete words or phrases which were used frequently in the plays are clarified in the glossary; others appear in footnotes.

The editor is particularly indebted to the Library of the British Museum, which made available the quarto texts, and to the staff for generous assistance in clarifying obscure allusions; he is also indebted to the University of Victoria for research and stenographic assistance, and to the Canada Council for financial aid.

1973. ROBERT G. LAWRENCE.

[1] This tradition influenced the characterization of other persons in this play, as well as several in *A Trick to Catch the Old One* and *The Witch of Edmonton*: Dampit the extortioner and 'plain Dunstable' Mr Carter, amongst others.

SELECT BIBLIOGRAPHY

GENERAL

E. K. Chambers, *The Elizabethan Stage*, 4 vols., 1923.

L. C. Knights, *Drama and Society in the Age of Jonson*, 1937.

G. E. Bentley, *The Jacobean and Caroline Stage*, 7 vols., 1949–68. Invaluable.

T. M. Parrott and R. H. Ball, *A Short View of Elizabethan Drama*. New York, 1958.

A. Nicoll, *British Drama*, 1962.

U. Ellis-Fermor, *The Jacobean Drama*. New York, 1964. A particularly useful critical study.

J. A. Bastiaenen, *The Moral Tone of Jacobean and Caroline Drama*. New York, 1966.

G. H. Blayney, 'Enforcement of Marriage in English Drama', *Philological Quarterly*, XXXVIII (1959), pp. 459–72.

MIDDLETON

R. H. Barker, *Thomas Middleton*, 1958.

M. C. Bradbrook, *The Growth and Structure of Elizabethan Comedy*, 1962.

B. Gibbons, *Jacobean City Comedy*, 1968.

D. M. Holmes, *The Art of Thomas Middleton*, 1970.

A. R. Stonex, 'The Usurer in Elizabethan Drama', *PMLA*, XXXI (1916), pp. 190–210.

G. Williams, 'The Cuckoo, the Welsh Ambassador', *Modern Language Review*, LI (1956), pp. 223–5.

R. Levin, 'The Dampit Scenes in *A Trick to Catch the Old One*', *Modern Language Quarterly*, XXV (1964), pp. 140–52.

DEKKER, FORD, ROWLEY

H. J. Rowley, *The Problem of John Ford*. Cambridge, 1955.

C. Leech, *John Ford and the Drama of his Time*, 1957.

R. H. Robbins, *An Encyclopaedia of Witchcraft and Demonology*. New York, 1959. An interesting book.

K. M. Briggs, *Pale Hecate's Team*, 1962. On witchcraft in the seventeenth century.

M. J. Sargeaunt, *John Ford*. New York, 1966.

G. R. Price, *Thomas Dekker*. New York, 1969.

E. S. West, 'The Significance of *The Witch of Edmonton*', *Criterion*, XVII (1937), pp. 23–32.

L. L. Brodwin, 'The Domestic Tragedy of Frank Thorney in *The Witch of Edmonton*', *Studies in English Literature*, VII (1967), pp. 311–28.

BROME

H. F. Allen, *A Study of the Comedies of Richard Brome*, 1912.

C. E. Andrews, *Richard Brome, a Study of his Life and Works*. New Haven, 1913.

R. J. Kaufmann, *Richard Brome, Caroline Playwright*, 1961. The most useful biographical and critical study.

R. Brome, *A Jovial Crew*, ed. A. Haaker. University of Nebraska Press, 1968.

J. W. Crowther, 'The Literary History of Brome's *A Joviall Crew*', *Studies in English Renaissance Literature*, ed. W. F. McNeir, 1960.

Unless otherwise stated the place of publication of books is London.

A TRICK TO CATCH THE OLD ONE

THOMAS MIDDLETON

(baptized 18th April 1580–1627)

Born in London: studied at Queen's College, Oxford. Wrote pageants, masques, and pamphlets; was City Chronologer (1620–7). A varied dramatic achievement: comedies, among them *A Trick to Catch the Old One*, *A Chaste Maid in Cheapside;* tragedies, *Women Beware Women*, *The Changeling* (with Rowley); and a political satire, *A Game at Chess*. Buried at Newington Butts, 4th July.

A TRICK TO CATCH THE OLD ONE (1606)

This is one of Middleton's most admirable plays for economy, vitality and effective integration of action, character and theme. It is short, only 2210 lines, with a straightforward development of situation, complication and resolution. The three tangential Dampit scenes hardly qualify as a subplot; their principal function is to underline the basic theme of corruption. The play evolves, with seemingly uncontrived artistry, out of Witgood's understandable desire to regain possession of the property which his uncle, Pecunious Lucre, had deviously acquired. Although Witgood is not a model young man, Middleton was clearly more in sympathy with him than with anyone else in the play; thus one responds positively to Witgood's cleverness in foiling the selfish ambitions of Lucre and Walkadine Hoard and in reaching a satisfactory settlement of relationships with his fiancée, Joyce, and his erstwhile mistress, the Courtesan.

Although Witgood occupies the central situation, with reference to the original motivation and its consequences, it is the courtesan-widow who holds the key position in terms of the rhythm and structural pattern of the play. To the audience she remains consistently the Courtesan throughout, but to Lucre and Walkadine Hoard she is, until the denouement, an affluent widow, who represents a potential advantage and profit to both. The Courtesan contributes further to the structural unity of *A Trick to Catch the Old One* by her intimate involvement with the marriage theme. First, she is inevitably a foil for Joyce, the virtuous girl of his own class whom Witgood wishes to marry. Second, in her role as a rich widow, the Courtesan arouses almost simultaneously the interest of four men, Lucre, Walkadine Hoard, Sam Freedom and Moneylove, all of whom plot to win her for her fortune.

The fundamental subject of this play, the corrupting power of money, touches every character, but it reaches a climax of intensity in the actions and characterization of Dampit, the extortioner. He is the ultimate extension of everything that Lucre, the Hoard brothers, and their hangers-on stand for. In his study of Dampit, Middleton used effectively the technique of self-revelation. Dampit is frankly a sycophant and a usurer,

3

proud of having risen from nothing to £10,000 a year. His skill in padding his expense accounts has a very modern ring: 'Twenty pound a year have I brought in for boat-hire, and I ne'er stepped into boat in my life' (I, iv, 66–67). Dampit reveals a progressive deterioration. Early in the play there is a passing reference to his drinking habits, in the middle of the action he is drunk, and by late in Act IV, lying in his bed, he is dribbling wine down his face and talking disjointedly, apparently dying of acute alcoholism.

Middleton's prose and verse styles in *A Trick to Catch the Old One* are distinguished by their natural, conversational tone. Little intrusive roughness of rhythm is evident, but the verse is very eccentric, almost flippant, with casual shifts from poetry to prose and back again within the same speech. The line lengths of poetry are uneven, with many lines shorter or longer than normal, including the frequent use of extra light stresses within the line.

The most outstanding aspect of verbal artistry in *A Trick to Catch the Old One* is the author's use of irony, a characteristic feature of his plays. Undoubtedly the ironies in this play were intensified in the original stage production by a children's company, through the youthful mimicry of adult activity. Although the play is full of verbal ironies, situational irony is more important. The dominant example is the Courtesan's appearance as a wealthy widow. In a succession of scenes a reader derives great pleasure from the machinations of several zealous men to win her, with an ironic climax in the self-congratulatory soliloquy of Walkadine Hoard as he privately catalogues his bride's riches and property (IV, iv, 1–21). The background manipulations of Witgood to advance the Courtesan are not of fundamental importance; Middleton made his ironic point by having the self-interested and self-righteous defeat themselves.

One of the plot devices treated with skilful irony is that of 'bread upon the waters'. For instance, Lucre contributes with little urging to the payment of Witgood's debts (II, i, 245–249) in order to ingratiate himself with his nephew, the potential possessor of the rich widow. This is followed by Witgood's persuading his greedy creditors that greater wealth will accrue to them if they hold back their bills until he has secured his widow (III, i, 42–49).

The recurrent, timeless theme of the power of money reinforces the self-interest which dominates Lucre and Walkadine Hoard in their relationships with everyone. Middleton developed a clever irony through their gratuitous efforts to take advantage of each other, perversely contributing to their defeat. Although both men are usurers, they are not extravagant dramatic caricatures of the general type (Barabas, Shylock, Volpone, etc.); Lucre and Walkadine Hoard show something like normality in their behaviour, fitting smoothly and ironically into the broadly realistic way-of-the-world atmosphere of the play.

Social pretensions are a part of the lives of both Lucre and Walkadine Hoard. Lucre refers to his wife's rise in status: 'Thy first husband married thee out of an alderman's kitchen. . . . Here's none but friends. Most of our beginnings must be wink'd at' (IV, ii, 72–75). Walkadine Hoard is conscious of status symbols in a very modern way. In Act IV he daydreams of the prospect of a triumphant procession with his bride towards her large country estates, accompanied by distinguished friends in velvet cassocks and gold chains, with ten servants 'in watchet liveries and orange-tawny capes'.

Middleton left only two secondary figures, Joyce and the Courtesan, relatively uncontaminated by pretentiousness and greed. Joyce strengthens an awareness of Witgood's better nature. She has little direct association with the subject of money, but is willing enough to participate in the tricking of an old one (her uncle, Walkadine Hoard) so that she will be able to marry Witgood. The Courtesan is the most likeable and intelligent of the many women of doubtful virtue in Middleton's plays. She is first represented as having been the victim of Witgood's lust and later as the potential victim of Walkadine Hoard's covetousness. By her declaration to Hoard, 'I promise you I ha' nothing, sir' (III, ii, 94), she absolves herself, at least technically, from complicity in the trick.

Middleton provided Witgood with a degree of sincerity in his reformation and with a recognition that he must be as unscrupulous in his methods of achieving his objectives as the two old scoundrels are in taking advantage of him; thus, even though one of them is his uncle, Witgood must set a trap, allowing the greedy old men to step into it of their own volition.

Although *A Trick to Catch the Old One* reveals several echoes of Ben Jonson's early plays, especially *Volpone,* no specific source for *A Trick* can be traced. Middleton could easily have drawn from many stories in folklore, fiction and drama that dealt with a credulous old man being hoaxed by a shrewd young man. This subject evidently greatly appealed to the playwright, for *A Mad World, my Masters, Michaelmas Term, A Trick to Catch the Old One, The Roaring Girl* and *A Chaste Maid in Cheapside,* all published within a few years of 1608, have very similar plots. It is possible too that Middleton's frequent involvements with the law, as a result of the tangled business affairs of his mother and step-father, influenced his jaundiced view of lawyers like Harry Dampit.

The first edition of *A Trick to Catch the Old One*, the authority for the present text, was published in 1608, about two years after its original stage production by the Children of Paul's. A reissue, with revised title-page, appeared in the same year, and a second edition, with few substantive changes, came out in 1616.

A TRICK TO CATCH THE OLD ONE

by Thomas Middleton
1606
[*Dramatis Personae*

Theodorus Witgood, *scapegrace nephew to Pecunious Lucre*
Pecunious Lucre [1]
Walkadine Hoard, *uncle to Joyce*
Onesiphorus Hoard, *brother to Walkadine Hoard*
Limber ⎫
Kix [2]
Sir Tristram Lamprey ⎬ *friends to Walkadine Hoard*
Spitchcock [3]
Moneylove ⎭
Harry Dampit [4] ⎫
Gulf ⎭ *usurers*
Sam Freedom, *stepson to Lucre*
Sir Lancelot
Host
Three Creditors
George, *servant to Lucre*
Arthur, *servant to Walkadine Hoard*
Gentlemen, *friends to Lucre*
Drawer, Vintner, Scrivener, Sergeants, Boys, Servants
Courtesan
Mistress Lucre
Joyce, *beloved of Witgood*
Lady Foxstone
Audrey, *servant to Dampit*

Scene: Leicestershire and London]

---

[1] This name and others like it are echoes from the morality plays.   [2] A dry stalk.   [3] A fried or broiled eel.   [4] He is referred to in the play as 'Old Harry,' a nickname for the devil; 'Dampit' suggests 'damned pit' (IV, v, 2), i.e. Hell.

[ACT I SCENE 1]

[A town in Leicestershire]

Enter Witgood, *a gentleman, solus*

WIT. All's gone! Still thou'rt a gentleman, that's all. But a poor
one, that's nothing. What milk brings thy meadows forth now?
Where are thy goodly uplands and thy downlands? All sunk
into that little pit, lechery. Why should a gallant pay but two
shillings for his ord'nary [1] that nourishes him, and twenty times
two for his brothel [2] that consumes him? But where's Long-acre? [3]
In my uncle's conscience, which is three years' voyage about.
He that sets out upon his conscience ne'er finds the way home
again; he is either swallowed in the quicksands of law-quillets [4]
or splits upon the piles of a *praemunire*; [5] yet these old fox-
brain'd and ox-brow'd uncles have still defences for their avarice
and apologies for their practices, and will thus greet our follies:

> He that doth his youth expose
> To brothel, drink, and danger,
> Let him that is his nearest kin
> Cheat him before a stranger.

And that's his uncle; 'tis a principle in usury. I dare not visit the
city; there I should be too soon visited by that horrible plague,
my debts, and by that means I lose a virgin's love, her portion,
and her virtues. Well, how should a man live now that has no
living? Hum. Why, are there not a million of men in the world
that only sojourn upon their brain and make their wits their
mercers? [6] And am I but one amongst that million and cannot
thrive upon't? Any trick out of the compass of law [7] now would
come happily to me.

Enter Courtesan

COURT. My love!

WIT. My loathing! Hast thou been the secret consumption of my
purse, and now com'st to undo my last means, my wits? Wilt
leave no virtue in me, and yet thou ne'er the better?

[1] The ordinary meal regularly provided at an inn or a tavern.
[2] Prostitute.   [3] A conventional name for an estate.   [4] Legal techni-
calities.   [5] A writ.   [6] Rely upon their intelligence and make their
shrewdness their dealers.   [7] Not punishable by law.

9

30   Hence, courtesan, round-webb'd tarantula,
       That dryest the roses in the cheeks of youth.
       COURT. I have been true unto your pleasure, and all your lands
       Thrice rack'd [1] was never worth the jewel
       Which I prodigally gave you, my virginity.
       Lands mortgag'd may return, and more esteem'd,
       But honesty [2] once pawn'd is ne'er redeem'd.
       WIT. Forgive; I do thee wrong
       To make thee sin and then to chide thee for't.
       COURT. I know I am your loathing now; farewell.
40   WIT. Stay, best invention,[3] stay.
       COURT. I that have been the secret consumption of your purse,
       shall I stay now to undo your last means, your wits? Hence,
       courtesan, away.
       WIT. I prithee make me not mad at my own weapon.[4] Stay—a
       thing few women can do, I know that, and therefore they had
       need wear stays—be not contrary. Dost love me? Fate has so
       cast it that all my means I must derive from thee.
       COURT. From me? Be happy then;
       What lies within the power of my performance
       Shall be commanded of thee.
50   WIT.   Spoke like
       An honest drab, i' faith; it may prove something.
       What trick is not an embryo at first,
       Until a perfect shape come over it?
       COURT. Come, I must help you. Whereabouts left you?
       I'll proceed.
       Though you beget, 'tis I must help to breed.
       Speak. What is't? I'd fain conceive it.
       WIT. So, so, so. Thou shalt presently take the name and form
       upon thee of a rich country widow, four hundred a year valiant,[5]
60   in woods, in bullocks, in barns, and in rye stacks. We'll to
       London and to my covetous uncle.
       COURT. I begin to applaud thee; our states being both desperate,
       they are soon resolute.[6] But how for horses?
       WIT. Mass, that's true. The jest will be of some continuance.
       Let me see. Horses now, a bots [7] on 'em! Stay. I have acquain-
       tance with a mad host,[8] never yet bawd to thee. I have rins'd
       the whoreson's gums in mull-sack many a time and often; put

---

[1] Rented at exorbitant rates.   [2] Virtue.   [3] Device.   [4] i.e. the words
with which I have attacked you.   [5] Worth.   [6] Decided.   [7] An
expletive; lit., a parasitic disease.   [8] A merry innkeeper; publicans were
sometimes procurers.

but a good tale into his ear now so it come off cleanly, and there's
horse and man for us, I dare warrant thee.

COURT. Arm your wits then
Speedily. There shall want nothing in me,
Either in behaviour, discourse, or fashion,
That shall discredit your intended purpose.
I will so artfully disguise my wants
And set so good a courage on my state[1]
That I will be believed.

WIT. Why, then, all's furnish'd. I shall go nigh to catch that old
fox mine uncle, though he make but some amends for my
undoing. Yet there's some comfort in't: He cannot otherwise
choose, though it be but in hope to cozen me again, but supply
any hasty want that I bring to town with me. The device well
and cunningly carried, the name of a rich widow and four
hundred a year in good earth will so conjure up a kind of usurer's
love in him to me that he will not only desire my presence, which
at first shall scarce be granted him—I'll keep off a' purpose—
but I shall find him so officious to deserve, so ready to supply.
I know the state of an old man's affection so well: If his
nephew be poor indeed, why he lets God alone with him, but if
he be once rich, then he'll be the first man that helps him.

COURT. 'Tis right the world;[2] for in these days an old man's love
to his kindred is like his kindness to his wife, 'tis always done
before he comes at it.

WIT. I owe thee for that jest. Begone. Here's all my wealth.
Prepare thyself. Away. I'll to mine host with all possible haste,
and, with the best art and most profitable form, pour the sweet
circumstance into his ear, which shall have the gift to turn all
the wax to honey.   [*Exit* Courtesan.]
How now? Oh, the right worshipful seniors of our country.
                                            [*Stands aside*]

[*Enter* Three Gentlemen][3]

1 GENT. Who's that?
2 GENT. Oh, the common rioter. Take no note of him.
WIT. [*Aside*] You will not see me now; the comfort is
Ere it be long you will scarce see yourselves.   [*Exit.*]
1 GENT. I wonder how he breathes; h'as consum'd all
Upon that courtesan.

[1] Put up a good front.   [2] So it is the world over.   [3] Onesiphorus
Hoard, Limber, and Kix, but not so identified until later (I, i, 112; V, ii,
44–64).

2 GENT.   We have heard so much.

1 GENT. You have heard all truth; his uncle and my brother[1]
Have been these three years mortal adversaries.
Two old tough spirits, they seldom meet but fight,
Or quarrel when 'tis calmest. I think their anger
Be the very fire that keeps their age alive.

110 2 GENT. What was the quarrel, sir?

1 GENT. Faith, about a purchase,[2] fetching over[3] a young heir.
Master Hoard, my brother, having wasted much time in beating[4]
the bargain, what did me old Lucre but, as his conscience
mov'd him, knowing the poor gentleman, stepp'd in between
'em and cozen'd him himself.

2 GENT. And was this all, sir?

1 GENT. This was e'en it, sir. Yet for all this, I know no reason
but the match might go forward betwixt his wife's son[5] and my
niece. What though there be a dissension between the two old
120 men, I see no reason it should put a difference between the two
younger. 'Tis as natural for old folks to fall out as for young to
fall in. A scholar comes a-wooing to my niece; well, he's wise,
but he's poor. Her son comes a-wooing to my niece; well, he's a
fool, but he's rich.

2 GENT. Ay, marry, sir.

1 GENT. Pray now, is not a rich fool better than a poor philosopher?

2 GENT. One would think so, i' faith.

1 GENT. She now remains at London with my brother, her
130 second uncle, to learn fashions, practise music. The voice
between her lips, and the viol between her legs, she'll be fit for a
consort[6] very speedily. A thousand good pound is her portion;
if she marry, we'll ride up and be merry.

3 GENT. A match, if it be a match.   *Exeunt.*

---

[1] Pecunious Lucre and Walkadine Hoard.   [2] Profit.   [3] Getting the
better of.   [4] Striking.   [5] Sam Freedom, son of Lucre's wife by a
former marriage.   [6] A pun on a musical performance and spouse.

[ACT I SCENE 2]

[*A town in Leicestershire*]

Enter at one door Witgood; *at the other*, Host

WIT. Mine host?

HOST. Young Master Witgood.

WIT. I have been laying [1] all the town for thee.

HOST. Why, what's the news, Bully [2] Had-land?

WIT. What geldings are in the house of thine own? Answer me to that first.

HOST. Why, man, why?

WIT. Mark me what I say. I'll tell thee such a tale in thine ear that thou shalt trust me spite of thy teeth, furnish me with some money willy-nilly, and ride up with me thyself *contra voluntatem et professionem.* [3]

HOST. How! Let me see this trick, and I'll say thou hast more art than a conjurer.

WIT. Dost thou joy in my advancement?

HOST. Do I love sack and ginger?

WIT. Comes my prosperity desiredly to thee?

HOST. Come forfeitures to a usurer, fees to an officer, punks to an host, and pigs to a parson [4] desiredly? Why, then, la!

WIT. Will the report of a widow of four hundred a year, boy, make thee leap and sing and dance and come to thy place again?

HOST. Wilt thou command me now? I am thy spirit; conjure me into any shape.

WIT. I ha' brought her from her friends, turn'd back the horses by a sleight. Not so much as one amongst her six men, goodly, large, yeomanly fellows, will she trust with this her purpose; by this light, all unmann'd; regardless of her state, neglectful of vainglorious ceremony, all for my love. Oh, 'tis a fine little voluble tongue, mine host, that wins a widow.

HOST. No, 'tis a tongue with a great [5] T, my boy, that wins a widow.

WIT. Now, sir, the case stands thus, good mine host; if thou lov'st my happiness, assist me.

HOST. Command all my beasts i' th' house.

WIT. Nay, that's not all neither; prithee, take truce with thy joy and listen to me. Thou know'st I have a wealthy uncle i' th' city, somewhat the wealthier by my follies. The report of this

---

[1] Searching.   [2] 'Good fellow'.   [3] Against your wish and declaration.
[4] i.e. his tithes.   [5] Capital.

fortune, well and cunningly carried, might be a means to draw
some goodness from the usuring rascal, for I have put her in
hope already of some estate that I have, either in land or money.
40 Now if I be found true in neither, what may I expect but a
sudden breach of our love, utter dissolution of the match, and
confusion of my fortunes for ever?

HOST. Wilt thou but trust the managing of thy business with me?

WIT. With thee? Why, will I desire to thrive in my purpose?
Will I hug four hundred a year? I that know the misery of
nothing? Will that man wish a rich widow, that has ne'er a hole
to put his head in? With thee, mine host? Why, believe it, sooner
with thee than with a covey of counsellors.

HOST. Thank you for your good report. I' faith, sir, and if I
50 stand you not in stead, why, then, let an host come off *hic et haec
hostis*,[1] a deadly enemy to dice, drink, and venery. Come,
where's this widow?

WIT. Hard at Park End.

HOST. I'll be her serving-man for once.

WIT. Why, there we let off together. Keep full time; my thoughts
were striking then just the same number.

HOST. I knew't. Shall we then see our merry days again?

WIT. Our merry nights, which ne'er shall be more seen. *Exeunt.*

[ACT I SCENE 3]

[*A street in London*]

Enter at several doors old Lucre *and old* [Walkadine] Hoard,
gentlemen [Lamprey, Spitchcock, Sam Freedom, *and* Moneylove]
coming between them to pacify 'em

LAMP. Nay, good Master Lucre, and you, Master Hoard, anger
is the wind which you're both too much troubled withal.

W. HOARD.[2] Shall my adversary thus daily affront me, ripping
up the old wound of our malice, which three summers could not
close up? Into which wound the very sight of him drops
scalding lead instead of balsamum?

---

[1] A meaningless alliterative phrase, to pun on 'host' and enemy'.
[2] Q speech prefixes identify Walkadine and Onesiphorus Hoard as 'Hoo' or
'Hoord' and 'Ony'. Here they will be referred to as W. and O. Hoard.

LUCRE. Why, Hoard, Hoard, Hoard, Hoard, Hoard! May I not pass in the state of quietness to mine own house? Answer me to that, before witness, and why? I'll refer the cause to honest, even-minded gentlemen, or require the mere indifferences[1] of the law to decide this matter. I got the purchase,[2] true; was't not any man's case? Yes. Will a wise man stand as a bawd, whilst another wipes his nose[3] of the bargain? No, I answer, no, in that case.

LAMP. Nay, sweet Master Lucre.

W. HOARD. Was it the part of a friend? No; rather of a Jew. Mark what I say: When I had beaten the bush to the last bird, or, as I may term it, the price to a pound, then, like a cunning usurer, to come in the evening of the bargain and glean all my hopes in a minute; to enter, as it were, at the back door of the purchase, for thou ne'er cam'st the right way by it!

LUCRE. Hast thou the conscience to tell me so, without any impeachment to thyself?

W. HOARD. Thou that canst defeat[4] thy own nephew, Lucre, lap[5] his lands into bonds, and take the extremity of thy kindred's forfeitures because he's a rioter, a wastethrift,[6] a brothel-master, and so forth—what may a stranger expect from thee but *vulnera dilacerata*,[7] as the poet says, dilacerate dealing?

LUCRE. Upbraid'st thou me with 'nephew'? Is all imputation laid upon me? What acquaintance have I with his follies? If he riot, 'tis he must want it; if he surfeit, 'tis he must feel it; if he drab it, 'tis he must lie by't. What's this to me?

W. HOARD. What's all to thee? Nothing, nothing; such is the gulf of thy desire and the wolf of thy conscience. But be assured, old Pecunious Lucre, if ever fortune so bless me that I may be at leisure to vex thee, or any means so favour me that I may have opportunity to mad thee, I will pursue it with that flame of hate, that spirit of malice, unrepressed wrath, that I will blast thy comforts.

LUCRE. Ha, ha, ha!

LAMP. Nay, Master Hoard, you're a wise gentleman.

W. HOARD. I will so cross thee—

LUCRE. And I thee.

W. HOARD. So without mercy fret thee—

LUCRE. So monstrously oppose thee—

W. HOARD. Dost scoff at my just anger? Oh, that I had as much power as usury has over thee!

---

[1] Absolute impartialities.   [2] Advantage.   [3] Cheats him.   [4] Defraud.
[5] Enfold.   [6] Squanderer.   [7] Mangled wounds.

LUCRE. Then thou wouldst have as much power as the devil has over thee!

50 W. HOARD. Toad!

LUCRE. Aspic!

W. HOARD. Serpent!

LUCRE. Viper!

SPITCH. Nay, gentlemen, then we must divide you perforce.

LAMP. When the fire grows too unreasonable hot, there's no better way than to take off the wood.

Exeunt [Lamprey, Spitchcock, Lucre *and* W. Hoard].

Manent Sam [Freedom] *and* Moneylove

SAM. A word, good signior.

MONEY. How now, what's the news?

SAM. 'Tis given me to understand that you are a rival of mine in
60   the love of Mistress Joyce, Master Hoard's niece. Say me ay, say me no.

MONEY. Yes, 'tis so.

SAM. Then look to yourself; you cannot live long. I'm practising every morning; a month hence I'll challenge you.

MONEY. Give me your hand upon't. There's my pledge I'll meet you!   *Strikes him. Exit.*

SAM. Oh! Oh! What reason had you for that, sir, to strike before the month? You knew I was not ready for you, and that made you so crank.[1] I am not such a coward to strike again, I warrant
70   you; my ear has the law of her side, for it burns horribly. I will teach him to strike a naked face, the longest day of his life. 'Slid, it shall cost me some money, but I'll bring this box into the Chancery.[2]   *Exit.*

[ACT I SCENE 4]

[*A street in London*]

Enter Witgood *and the* Host

HOST. Fear you nothing, sir, I have lodg'd her in a house of credit, I warrant you.

WIT. Hast thou the writings?[3]

---

[1] Bold.   [2] The highest court of justice.   [3] The manufactured evidence for the widow's wealth; see II, i, 34.

HOST. Firm, sir.

[*Enter* Dampit *and* Gulf, *who stand apart*]

WIT. Prithee, stay, and behold two [of] the most prodigious rascals that ever slipp'd into the shape of men: Dampit, sirrah, and young Gulf, his fellow caterpillar.[1]

HOST. Dampit? Sure, I have heard of that Dampit.

WIT. Heard of him? Why, man, he that has lost both his ears may hear of him;[2] a famous infamous trampler[3] of time (his own phrase). Note him well. That Dampit, sirrah, he in the uneven beard and the serge[4] cloak, is the most notorious, usuring, blasphemous, atheistical, brothel-vomiting rascal that we have in these latter times now extant, whose first beginning was the stealing of a mastie[5] dog from a farmer's house.

HOST. He look'd as if he would obey the commandment[s] well, when he began first with stealing.

WIT. True. The next town he came at, he set the dogs together by th'ears.

HOST. A sign he should follow the law, by my faith.

WIT. So it followed, indeed; and being destitute of all fortunes, stak'd his mastie against a noble,[6] and by great fortune his dog had the day. How he made it up ten shillings I know not, but his own boast is that he came to town with but ten shillings in his purse, and now is credibly worth ten thousand pound.

HOST. How the devil came he by it?

WIT. How the devil came he not by it? If you put in[7] the devil once, riches come with a vengeance. H'as been a trampler of the law, sir, and the devil has a care of his footmen. The rogue has spied me now; he nibbled me finely once too. [*Aside*] A pox search you.—Oh, Master Dampit! [*Aside*] The very loins of thee!—Cry you mercy, Master Gulf; you walk so low[8] I promise you I saw you not, sir.

GULF. He that walks low walks safe, the poets tell us.

WIT. [*Aside*] And nigher Hell by a foot and a half than the rest of his fellows—But my old Harry!

DAMPIT. My sweet Theodorus!

WIT. 'Twas a merry world when thou cam'st to town with ten shillings in thy purse.

---

[1] Extortioner.   [2] Both the totally deaf and the criminal (with cropped ears) are likely to know of the notorious Dampit.   [3] An opprobrious term for an attorney.   [4] A durable cloth often worn by the poor.   [5] Mastiff.   [6] A gold coin worth thirty-four pence in modern British decimal currency.   [7] Introduce.   [8] Humbly.

40 DAMPIT. And now worth ten thousand pound, my boy. Report
it: Harry Dampit, a trampler of time; say he would be up in a
morning and be here with his serge gown, dash'd[1] up to the
hams in a cause, have his feet stink about Westminster Hall,
and come home again; see the galleons, the galleasses,[2] the
great armadas of the law; then there be hoys[3] and petty vessels,
oars and scullers of the time; there be picklocks of the time too.
Then would I be here; I would trample up and down like a mule;
now to the judges: 'May it please your reverend, honourable
fatherhoods'; then to my counsellor: 'May it please your
50 worshipful patience'; then to the examiner's office: 'May it
please your mastership's gentleness'; then to one of the clerks:
'May it please your worshipful lousiness', for I find him scrub-
bing in his codpiece; then to the hall again; then to the chamber
again—
WIT. And when to the cellar again?[4]
DAMPIT. E'en when thou wilt again. Tramplers of time,
motions[5] of Fleet Street, and visions[6] of Holborn; here I have
fees of one, there I have fees of another; my clients come about
me, the fooliaminy and coxcombry[7] of the country. I still
60 trash'd[8] and trotted for other men's causes; thus was poor Harry
Dampit made rich by others' laziness, who, though they would
not follow their own suits, I made 'em follow me with their
purses.
WIT. Didst thou so, old Harry?
DAMPIT. Ay, and I sous'd 'em with bills of charges, i' faith;
twenty pound a year have I brought in for boat-hire, and I
ne'er stepp'd into boat in my life.
WIT. Tramplers of time!
DAMPIT. Ay, tramplers of time, rascals of time, bull-beggars.[9]
70 WIT. Ah, thou'rt a mad old Harry! Kind Master Gulf, I am bold
to renew my acquaintance.
GULF. I embrace it, sir.   *Music.*   *Exeunt.*

---

[1] Bespattered.   [2] Heavy vessels, larger than galleons.   [3] Small coastal
ships.   [4] An allusion to Dampit's drinking habits.   [5] Puppet-shows.
[6] Apparitions (?).   [7] Coined words.   [8] Bustled.   [9] Bugbears.

Incipit ACT II [SCENE 1]

[Lucre's *house*]

Enter Lucre

LUCRE. My adversary ever more twits me with my nephew; forsooth, my nephew, Why may not a virtuous uncle have a dissolute nephew? What though he be a brotheller, a waste-thrift, a common surfeiter, and, to conclude, a beggar? Must sin in him call up shame in me? Since we have no part in their follies, why should we part in their infamies? For my strict hand towards his mortgage, that I deny not; I confess I had an uncle's pen'worth. Let me see, half in half,[1] true. I saw neither hope of his reclaiming nor comfort in his being, and was it not then better bestow'd upon his uncle than upon one of his aunts? I need not say 'bawd', for everyone knows what 'aunt' stands for in the last[2] translation.

[*Enter* Servant]

Now, sir?

SERV. There's a country serving-man, sir, attends to speak with your worship.

LUCRE. I'm at best leisure now; send him in to me. [*Exit* Servant.]

Enter Host, *like a serving-man*

HOST. Bless your venerable worship.

LUCRE. Welcome, good fellow.[3]

HOST [*Aside*] He calls me thief at first sight, yet he little thinks I am an host.

LUCRE. What's thy business with me?

HOST. Faith, sir, I am sent from my mistress to any sufficient gentleman indeed, to ask advice upon a doubtful point. 'Tis indifferent, sir, to whom I come, for I know none, nor did my mistress direct me to any particular man, for she's as mere a stranger here as myself; only I found your worship within, and 'tis a thing I ever lov'd, sir, to be dispatch'd as soon as I can.

LUCRE. [*Aside*] A good blunt honesty; I like him well.—What is thy mistress?

HOST. Faith, a country gentlewoman, and a widow, sir. Yester-day was the first flight[4] of us, but now she intends to stay until a little term[5] business be ended.

LUCRE. Her name, I prithee.

---

[1] Fifty per cent profit.   [2] Most recent.   [3] A cant term for a thief.
[4] Excursion (away from home).   [5] An allusion to term time, a period when the courts sat.

HOST. It runs there in the writings, sir, among her lands, Widow Medlar.[1]

LUCRE. Medlar? Mass, have I ne'er heard of that widow?

HOST. Yes, I warrant you, have you, sir; not the rich widow in Staffordshire?

40 LUCRE. Cuds me,[2] there 'tis, indeed. Thou hast put me into memory. There's a widow indeed! Ah, that I were a bachelor again.

HOST. No doubt your worship might do much then, but she's fairly promis'd to a bachelor already.

LUCRE. Ah, what is he, I prithee?

HOST. A country gentleman too, one whom your worship knows not, I'm sure; h'as spent some few follies in his youth, but marriage, by my faith, begins to call him home. My mistress loves him, sir, and love covers faults, you know. One Master Witgood, if ever you have heard of the gentleman.

50 LUCRE. Ha! Witgood, say'st thou?

HOST. That's his name indeed, sir. My mistress is like to bring him to a goodly seat yonder; four hundred a year, by my faith.

LUCRE. But, I pray, take me with you.[3]

HOST. Ay, sir.

LUCRE. What countryman might this young Witgood be?

HOST. A Leicestershire gentleman, sir.

LUCRE. [Aside] My nephew. By th' mass, my nephew. I'll fetch out more of this, i' faith; a simple country fellow, I'll work't out of him.—And is that gentleman, say'st thou, presently to marry 60 her?

HOST. Faith, he brought her up to town, sir; h'as the best card in all the bunch[4] for't, her heart; and I know my mistress will be married ere she go down.[5] Nay, I'll swear that, for she's none of those widows that will go down first and be married after; she hates that, I can tell you, sir.

LUCRE. By my faith, sir, she is like to have a proper gentleman and a comely; I'll give her that gift.

HOST. Why, does your worship know him, sir?

LUCRE. I know him? Does not all the world know him? Can a 70 man of such exquisite qualities be hid under a bushel?

---

[1] Lucre and Walkadine Hoard (later) were both obtuse and greedy, evidenced by their failure to recognize a popular joke which associated this apple-like fruit, eaten when over-ripe, with sexuality. In *Women Beware Women* Middleton associated medlar and whore (IV, ii, 97–9).
[2] Probably a corruption of 'God save me'.   [3] Let me understand you.
[4] Pack.   [5] A pun on 'return to the country' and 'engage in a sexual relationship'.

HOST. Then your worship may save me a labour, for I had charge given me to inquire after him.

LUCRE. Inquire of him? If I might counsel thee, thou shouldst ne'er trouble thyself further. Inquire of him of no more but of me; I'll fit[1] thee. I grant he has been youthful, but is he not now reclaim'd? Mark you that, sir. Has not your mistress, think you, been wanton in her youth? If men be wags, are there not women wagtails?[2]

HOST. No doubt, sir.

0 LUCRE. Does not he return wisest that comes home whipp'd with his own follies?

HOST. Why, very true, sir.

LUCRE. The worst report you can hear of him, I can tell you, is that he has been a kind gentleman, a liberal, and a worthy; who but lusty Witgood, thrice-noble Witgood?

HOST. Since your worship has so much knowledge in him, can you resolve[3] me, sir, what his living might be? My duty binds me, sir, to have a care of my mistress' estate. She has been ever a good mistress to me, though I say it. Many wealthy suitors

0 has she nonsuited[4] for his sake; yet, though her love be so fix'd, a man cannot tell whether his nonperformance may help to remove it, sir. He makes us believe he has lands and living.

LUCRE. Who? Young Master Witgood? Why believe it, he has as goodly a fine living out yonder—what do you call the place?

HOST. Nay, I know not, i' faith.

LUCRE. Hum. See like a beast, if I have not forgot the name. Pooh! And out yonder again, goodly grown woods and fair meadows—Pax[5] on't, I can ne'er hit of that place neither. He? Why, he's Witgood of Witgood Hall; he, an unknown thing?

00 HOST. Is he so, sir? To see how rumour will alter! Trust me, sir, we heard once he had no lands, but all lay mortgag'd to an uncle he has in town here.

LUCRE. Push! 'Tis a tale, 'tis a tale.

HOST. I can assure you, sir, 'twas credibly reported to my mistress.

LUCRE. Why, do you think, i' faith, he was ever so simple to mortgage his lands to his uncle, or his uncle so unnatural to take the extremity of such a mortgage?

HOST. That was my saying[6] still, sir.

10 LUCRE. Pooh! Ne'er think it.

[1] Answer.   [2] Profligates.   [3] Assure.   [4] Rejected.   [5] Pox.
[6] Report.

HOST. Yet that report goes current.

LUCRE. Nay, then, you urge me.

Cannot I tell that best that am his uncle.

HOST. How, sir! What have I done?

LUCRE. Why, how now? In a sound,[1] man?

HOST. Is your worship his uncle, sir?

LUCRE. Can that be any harm to you, sir?

HOST. I do beseech you, sir, do me the favour to conceal it. What a beast was I to utter so much! Pray, sir, do me the
120 kindness to keep it in. I shall have my coat pull'd o'er my ears [2] an't should be known; for the truth is, an't please your worship, to prevent much rumour and many suitors, they intend to be married very suddenly and privately.

LUCRE. And dost thou think it stands with my judgment to do them injury? Must I needs say the knowledge of this marriage comes from thee? Am I a fool at fifty-four? Do I lack subtlety now, that have got all my wealth by it? There's a leash[3] of angels[4] for thee. Come, let me woo thee. Speak. Where lie [5] they?

130 HOST. So I might have no anger, sir,—

LUCRE. Passion of me, not a jot. Prithee, come.

HOST. I would not have it known it came by my means.

LUCRE. Why, am I a man of wisdom?

HOST. I dare trust your worship, sir, but I'm a stranger to your house, and to avoid all intelligencers I desire your worship's ear.

LUCRE. [Aside] This fellow's worth a matter of trust.—Come, sir. [Host whispers] Why now, thou'rt an honest lad. [Aside] Ah, sirrah nephew!

HOST. Please you, sir, now I have begun with your worship,
140 when shall I attend for your advice upon that doubtful point? I must come warily now.

LUCRE. Tut, fear thou nothing.

Tomorrow's evening shall resolve[6] the doubt.

HOST. The time shall cause my attendance.   *Exit.*

LUCRE. Fare thee well. There's more true honesty in such a country serving-man than in a hundred of our cloak companions.[7] I may well call 'em companions, for since blue coats [8] have been turn'd into cloaks, we can scarce know the man from the master. George!

---

[1] Swoon.   [2] Preparatory for whipping.   [3] Set of three.   [4] Gold coins worth fifty pence each.   [5] Lodge.   [6] Remove.   [7] A sneer at the new custom of servants wearing livery-cloaks.   [8] The traditional garb of servants.

[*Enter* George]

150 GEORGE. Anon, sir.

LUCRE. List hither. [*Whispers*] Keep the place secret. Commend
me to my nephew. I know no cause, tell him, but he might see
his uncle.

GEORGE. I will, sir.

LUCRE. And, do you hear, sir?
Take heed you use him with respect and duty.

GEORGE. [*Aside*] Here's a strange alteration. One day he must be
turn'd out like a beggar, and now he must be call'd in like a
knight.   *Exit.*

160 LUCRE. Ah, sirrah, that rich widow! Four hundred a year!
Beside, I hear she lays claim to a title of a hundred more.
This falls unhappily that he should bear a grudge to me now,
being likely to prove so rich. What is't, trow, that he makes me a
stranger for? Hum, I hope he has not so much wit to apprehend
that I cozened him; he deceives me then. Good Heaven, who
would have thought it would ever have come to this pass?
Yet he's a proper gentleman, i' faith, give him his due. Marry,
that's his mortgage, but that I ne'er mean to give him. I'll
make him rich enough in words, if that be good; and if it
170 come to a piece of money, I will not greatly stick for't. There
may be hope some of the widow's lands too may one day fall
upon me, if things be carried wisely.

[*Enter* George]

Now, sir, where is he?

GEORGE. He desires your worship to hold him excused; he has
such weighty business it commands him wholly from all men.

LUCRE. Were those my nephew's words?

GEORGE. Yes, indeed, sir.

LUCRE. [*Aside*] When men grow rich they grow proud too, I
perceive that. He would not have sent me such an answer once
180 within this twelvemonth; see what 'tis when a man's come to his
lands.—Return to him again, sir; tell him his uncle desires his
company for an hour. I'll trouble him but an hour, say; 'tis for
his own good, tell him, and—do you hear, sir?—put 'worship'
upon him. Go to, do as I bid you. He's like to be a gentleman
of worship very shortly.

GEORGE. [*Aside*] This is good sport, i' faith.   *Exit.*

LUCRE. Troth, he uses his uncle discourteously now. Can he tell
what I may do for him? Goodness may come from me in a minute that comes not in seven year again. He knows my humour;

190 I am not so usually good. 'Tis no small thing that draws
kindness from me; he may know that, and[1] he will. The chief
cause that invites me to do him most good is the sudden astonish-
ing of old Hoard, my adversary. How pale his malice will look
at my nephew's advancement! With what a dejected spirit he
will behold his fortunes, whom but last day he proclaimed rioter,
penurious makeshift, despised brothel-master! Ha, ha! 'Twill
do me more secret joy than my last purchase, more precious
comfort than all these widows' revenues.—

Enter [George *and*] Witgood

Now, sir.

200 GEORGE. With much entreaty he's at length come, sir.   [*Exit.*]

LUCRE. Oh, nephew, let me salute you, sir; you're welcome,
nephew.

WIT. Uncle, I thank you.

LUCRE. Y'ave a fault, nephew: You're a stranger here. Well,
Heaven give you joy!

WIT. Of what, sir?

LUCRE. Ha, we can hear.
You might have known your uncle's house, i' faith,
You and your widow. Go to, you were to blame,

210 If I may tell you so without offence.

WIT. How could you hear of that, sir?

LUCRE.   Oh, pardon me!
It was your will to have it kept from me, I perceive now.

WIT. Not for any defect of love, I protest, uncle.

LUCRE. Oh, 'twas unkindness,[2] nephew. Fie, fie, fie!

WIT. I am sorry you take it in that sense, sir.

LUCRE. Pooh! You cannot colour it, i' faith, nephew.

WIT. Will you but hear what I can say in my just excuse, sir?

LUCRE. Yes, faith, will I, and welcome.

WIT. You that know my danger i' th' city, sir, so well, how great
220 my debts are, and how extreme my creditors, could not out of
your pure judgment, sir, have wish'd us hither.

LUCRE. Mass, a firm reason indeed.

WIT. Else my uncle's house, why, 't 'ad been the only make-
match—

LUCRE. Nay, and thy credit.

WIT. My credit? Nay, my countenance![3] Push! Nay, I know,
uncle, you would have wrought it so. By your wit you would
have made her believe in time the whole house had been mine—

---

[1] If.   [2] Unnaturalness.   [3] Favour.

LUCRE. Ay, and most of the goods too.

230 WIT. La, you there. Well, let 'em all prate what they will, there's nothing like the bringing of a widow to one's uncle's house.

LUCRE. Nay, let nephews be ruled as they list, they shall find their uncle's house the most natural place when all's done.

WIT. There they may be bold.

LUCRE. Life, they may do anything there, man, and fear neither beadle [1] nor sum'ner. [2] An uncle's house, a very Cole Harbour! [3] Sirrah, I'll touch thee near now. Hast thou so much interest [4] in thy widow that by a token thou couldst presently send for her?

WIT. Troth, I think I can, uncle.

240 LUCRE. Go to, let me see that.

WIT. Pray, command one of your men hither, uncle.

LUCRE. George!

[Enter George]

GEORGE. Here, sir.

LUCRE. Attend my nephew. [*Witgood and* George *speak apart*] [*Aside*] I love a' life to prattle with a rich widow; 'tis pretty, methinks, when our tongues go together, and then to promise much and perform little. I love that sport a' life, i' faith, yet I am in the mood now to do my nephew some good, if he take me handsomely.—   [*Exit George.*]

250 What, have you dispatch'd?

WIT. I ha' sent, sir.

LUCRE. Yet I must condemn you of unkindness, nephew.

WIT. Heaven forbid, uncle!

LUCRE. Yes, faith, must I. Say your debts be many, your creditors importunate, yet the kindness of a thing is all, nephew; you might have sent me close word on't, without the least danger or prejudice to your fortunes.

WIT. Troth, I confess it, uncle; I was to blame there, but indeed my intent was to have clapp'd it up suddenly, and so have broke

260 forth like a joy to my friends and a wonder to the world. Beside, there's a trifle of a forty-pound [5] matter towards the setting of me forth. My friends should ne'er have known on't; I meant to make shift for that myself.

LUCRE. How, nephew! Let me not hear such a word again, I beseech you. Shall I be beholding to you?

[1] Parish constable.   [2] A minor official who summoned people to court. [3] A group of tenements near London Bridge, traditionally considered a haven for debtors and other law-breakers. It was also notorious for hasty marriages.   [4] Claim upon.   [5] An allusion to Witgood's debts, which were in fact considerably larger.

WIT. To me? Alas, what do you mean, uncle?

LUCRE. I charge you, upon my love. You trouble nobody but myself.

WIT. Y'ave no reason for that, uncle.

270 LUCRE. Troth, I'll ne'er be friends with you while you live and you do.

WIT. Nay, and you say so, uncle. Here's my hand; I will not do't—

LUCRE. Why, well said. There's some hope in thee when thou wilt be ruled. I'll make it up fifty, faith, because I see thee so reclaimed. Peace, here comes my wife with Sam, her tother husband's son.

[Enter Wife *and* Sam Freedom]

WIT. Good aunt,—

SAM. Cousin Witgood! I rejoice in my salute; you're most
280 welcome to this noble city, govern'd with the sword in the scabbard.[1]

WIT. [*Aside*] And the wit in the pommel![2]—Good Master Sam Freedom, I return the salute.

LUCRE. By the mass, she's coming, wife; let me see now how thou wilt entertain[3] her.

WIFE. I hope I am not to learn, sir, to entertain a widow; 'tis not so long ago since I was one myself.

[Enter Courtesan]

WIT. Uncle,—

LUCRE. She's come indeed.

290 WIT. My uncle was desirous to see you, widow, and I presum'd to invite you.

COURT. The presumption was nothing, Master Witgood. Is this your uncle, sir?

LUCRE. Marry am I, sweet widow, and his good uncle he shall find me. Ay, by this smack that I give thee, thou'rt welcome. Wife, bid the widow welcome the same way again.

SAM. [*Aside*] I am a gentleman now too, by my father's occupation, and I see no reason but I may kiss a widow by my father's copy.[4] Truly, I think the charter is not against it; surely these
300 are the words: 'The son, once a gentleman, may revel it, though his father were a dauber'.[5] 'Tis about the fifteenth page. I'll to her.

---

[1] i.e. peaceably.   [2] With as much intelligence as is in the knob on the hilt of a sword.   [3] Receive.   [4] Copyhold, right.   [5] Plasterer.

[*Attempts to kiss the* Courtesan *and is repulsed*]

LUCRE. Y'are not very busy now; a word with thee, sweet
widow.

SAM. [*Aside*] Coad's nigs![1] I was never so disgrac'd since the hour
my mother whipp'd me!

LUCRE. Beside, I have no child of mine own to care for; she's my
second wife, old, past bearing. Clap sure to him, widow; he's
like to be my heir, I can tell you.

310 COURT. Is he so, sir?

LUCRE. He knows it already, and the knave's proud on't. Jolly
rich widows have been offer'd him here i' th' city, great mer-
chants' wives, and do you think he would once look upon 'em?
Forsooth, he'll none. You are beholding to him i' th' country
then, ere we could be; nay, I'll hold a wager, widow, if he were
once known to be in town, he would be presently sought after;
nay, and happy were they that could catch him first.

COURT. I think so.

LUCRE. Oh, there would be such running to and fro, widow, he
320 should not pass the streets for 'em; he'd be took up in one great
house or other presently. Faugh, they know he has it and must
have it. You see this house here, widow? This house and all
comes to him! Goodly rooms ready furnish'd, ceil'd with plaster
of Paris, and all hung about with cloth of arras.[2] Nephew!

WIT. Sir?

LUCRE. Show the widow your house. Carry her into all the rooms
and bid her welcome. You shall see, widow. [*Aside*] Nephew,
strike all sure above and thou be'st a good boy. Ah,—

WIT. Alas, sir, I know not how she would take it.

330 LUCRE. The right way, I warrant 'ee. A pox! Art an ass? Would
I were in thy stead. Get you up! I am asham'd of you.

[*Exeunt* Witgood *and* Courtesan.]

[*Aside*] So, let 'em agree as they will now. Many a match has been
struck up in my house i' this fashion. Let 'em try all manner of
ways, still there's nothing like an uncle's house to strike the
stroke in. I'll hold my wife in talk a little.—Now, Jenny, your
son there goes a-wooing to a poor gentlewoman but of a
thousand[3] portion; see my nephew, a lad of less hope, strikes at
four hundred a year in good rubbish.[4]

WIFE. Well, we must do as we may, sir.

340 LUCRE. I'll have his money ready told for him again[5] he come

---

[1] An obscure oath, perhaps equivalent to 'God's nails'.   [2] A richly
figured tapestry.   [3] i.e. a thousand pound.   [4] Used facetiously.
[5] Against the time that.

down. Let me see too. By th' mass, I must present the widow
with some jewel, a good piece of plate, or such a device; 'twill
hearten her on well. I have a very fair standing cup,[1] and a good
high standing cup will please a widow above all other pieces.

Exit.

WIFE. Do you mock us with your nephew? I have a plot in my
head, son; i' faith, husband, to cross you.

SAM. Is it a tragedy plot or a comedy plot, good mother?

WIFE. 'Tis a plot shall vex him. I charge you, of my blessing, son
Sam, that you presently withdraw the action of your love from
350   Master Hoard's niece.

SAM. How, mother!

WIFE. Nay, I have a plot in my head, i' faith. Here, take this
chain of gold and this fair diamond. Dog me the widow home to
her lodging, and at thy best opportunity fasten 'em both upon
her. Nay, I have a reach [2] I can tell you. Thou art known what
thou art, son, among the right worshipful, all the twelve companies.[3]

SAM. Truly, I thank 'em for it.

WIFE. He? He's a scab to thee! And so certify her thou hast two
360   hundred a year of thyself, besides thy good parts, a proper
person and a lovely. If I were a widow I could find it in my heart
to have thee myself, son, ay, from 'em all.

SAM. Thank you for your good will, mother, but indeed I had
rather have a stranger. And if I woo her not in that violent
fashion, that I will make her be glad to take these gifts ere I
leave her, let me never be called the heir of your body.

WIFE. Nay, I know there's enough in you, son, if you once come
to put it forth.

SAM. I'll quickly make a bolt or a shaft on't.[4]   *Exeunt.*

[1] A cup with a base and sometimes a stem.   [2] Scheme.   [3] The trade
guilds of London.   [4] To use either a heavy arrow or a slender one; i.e.
proverbially, to accept the venture.

[ACT II SCENE 2]

[*A street in London*]

Enter Moneylove *and* [W.] Hoard

MONEY. Faith, Master Hoard, I have bestowed many months in the suit of your niece, such was the dear love I ever bore to her virtues, but since she hath so extremely denied me, I am to lay out for my fortunes elsewhere.

W. HOARD. Heaven forbid but you should, sir; I ever told you my niece stood otherwise affected.

MONEY. I must confess you did, sir; yet in regard of my great loss of time and the zeal with which I sought your niece, shall I desire one favour of your worship?

10 W. HOARD. In regard of those two, 'tis hard, but you shall, sir.

MONEY. I shall rest grateful. 'Tis not full three hours, sir, since the happy rumour of a rich country widow came to my hearing.

W. HOARD. How! A rich country widow?

MONEY. Four hundred a year, landed.

W. HOARD. Yea?

MONEY. Most firm, sir, and I have learn'd her lodging. Here my suit begins, sir: If I might but entreat your worship to be a countenance[1] for me and speak a good word—for your words will pass—I nothing doubt but I might set fair for the widow;

20 nor shall your labour, sir, end altogether in thanks—two hundred angels—[2]

W. HOARD. So, so. What suitors has she?

MONEY. There lies the comfort, sir; the report of her is yet but a whisper, and only solicited by young riotous Witgood, nephew to your mortal adversary.

W. HOARD. Ha! Art certain he's her suitor?

MONEY. Most certain, sir, and his uncle very industrious to beguile the widow and make up the match.

W. HOARD. [*Aside*] So! Very good.

30 MONEY. Now, sir, you know this young Witgood is a spendthrift, dissolute fellow.

W. HOARD. A very rascal.

MONEY. A midnight surfeiter.

W. HOARD. The spume of a brothel-house.

MONEY. True, sir; which being well told in your worship's phrase may both heave him out of her mind, and drive a fair way for me to the widow's affections.

[1] Support.   [2] Approximately one hundred pounds.

W. HOARD. Attend me about five.

MONEY. With my best care, sir.   *Exit.*

40 W. HOARD. Fool, thou hast left thy treasure with a thief,
To trust a widower with a suit in love!
Happy revenge, I hug thee. I have not only the means laid before
me extremely to cross my adversary and confound the last hopes
of his nephew, but thereby to enrich my state, augment my
revenues, and build mine own fortunes greater. Ha, ha!
I'll mar your phrase, o'erturn your flatteries,
Undo your windings, policies, and plots,
Fall like a secret and dispatchful[1] plague
On your secured comforts. Why, I am able
50 To buy three of Lucre, thrice outbid him,
Let my out-monies[2] be reckon'd and all.   *[Moves aside.]*

Enter three Creditors

1 CRED. I am glad of this news.

2 CRED. So are we, by my faith.

3 CRED. Young Witgood will be a gallant again now.

W. HOARD. *[Aside]* Peace!

1 CRED. I promise you, Master Cockpit, she's a mighty rich
widow.

2 CRED. Why, have you ever heard of her?

1 CRED. Who, widow Medlar? She lies open to much rumour.

60 3 CRED. Four hundred a year, they say, in very good land.

1 CRED. Nay, tak't of my word, if you believe that, you believe
the least.

2 CRED. And to see how close he[3] keeps it!

1 CRED. Oh, sir, there's policy in that, to prevent better suitors.

3 CRED. He owes me a hundred pound, and I protest I ne'er
look'd for a penny.

1 CRED. He little dreams of our coming; he'll wonder to see his
creditors upon him.   *Exeunt* [Creditors].

W. HOARD. Good, his creditors. I'll follow. This makes for me.
70 All know the widow's wealth, and 'tis well known
I can estate her fairly, ay, and will.
In this one chance shines a twice-happy fate;
I both deject my foe and raise my state.   *Music. Exit.*

---

[1] Consuming.   [2] Funds invested.   [3] Witgood.

Incipit ACT III [SCENE 1]

[*A street in London*]

[*Enter*] Witgood *with his* Creditors

WIT. Why, alas, my creditors, could you find no other time to undo me but now? Rather your malice appears in this than the justness of the debt.

1 CRED. Master Witgood, I have forborne my money long.

WIT. I pray, speak low, sir. What do you mean?

2 CRED. We hear you are to be married suddenly to a rich country widow.

WIT. What can be kept so close but you creditors hear on't? Well, 'tis a lamentable state that our chiefest afflicters should
10 first hear of our fortunes. Why, this is no good course, i' faith, sirs. If ever you have hope to be satisfied, why do you seek to confound the means that should work it? There's neither piety, no, nor policy in that. Shine favourably now, why I may rise and spread again, to your great comforts.

1 CRED. He says true, i' faith.

WIT. Remove me now, and I consume for ever.

2 CRED. Sweet gentleman!

WIT. How can it thrive which from the sun you sever?

3 CRED. It cannot indeed.

20 WIT. Oh, then, show patience; I shall have enough
To satisfy you all.

1 CRED.   Ay, if we could
Be content, a shame take us.

WIT.   For, look you,
I am but newly sure [1] yet to the widow,
And what a rend might this discredit make!
Within these three days will I bind you lands
For your securities.

1 CRED.   No, good Master Witgood;
Would 'twere as much as we dare trust you with.

WIT. I know you have been kind; however, now
Either by wrong report or false incitement,
30 Your gentleness is injur'd; in such
A state as this a man cannot want foes.
If on the sudden he begin to rise,
No man that lives can count his enemies.

[1] Betrothed.

You had some intelligence, I warrant ye,
From an ill-willer.

2 CRED. Faith, we heard you brought up a rich widow, sir, and
were suddenly to marry her.

WIT. Ay. Why, there it was; I knew 'twas so. But since you are
so well resolv'd [1] of my faith towards you, let me be so much

40   favour'd of you, I beseech you all—

ALL. Oh, it shall not need, i' faith, sir,—

WIT. As to lie still awhile and bury my debts in silence, till I be
fully possess'd of the widow. For the truth is, I may tell you as
my friends—

ALL. Oh, oh, oh!

WIT. I am to raise a little money in the city towards the setting
forth of myself, for mine own credit and your comfort. Now if
my former debts should be divulg'd, all hope of my proceedings
were quite extinguish'd.

50   1 CRED. [To Witgood] Do you hear, sir? I may deserve your
custom hereafter. Pray, let my money be accepted before a
stranger's. Here's forty pound I receiv'd as I came to you;
if that may stand you in any stead, make use on't. Nay, pray,
sir, 'tis at your service.

WIT. [To 1 Creditor] You do so ravish me with kindness that
I'm constrain'd to play the maid [2] and take it.

1 CRED. [To Witgood] Let none of them see it, I beseech you.

WIT. [Aside] Faugh!

1 CRED. [To Witgood] I hope I shall be first in your remem-
60   brance
After the marriage rites.

WIT. [To 1 Creditor] Believe it firmly.

1 CRED. So.—What, do you walk, sirs?

2 CRED. I go. [To Witgood] Take no care, sir, for money to
furnish you. Within this hour I'll send you sufficient.—Come,
Master Cockpit, we both stay for you.

3 CRED. I ha' lost a ring, i' faith; I'll follow you presently.
[Exeunt 1 and 2 Creditors.]
But you shall find it, sir. I know your youth and expenses have
disfurnish'd you of all jewels. There's a ruby of twenty pound
price, sir; bestow it upon your widow. What, man! 'Twill call

70   up her blood to you. Beside, if I might so much work with you,
I would not have you beholding to those blood-suckers for
any money.

---

[1] Assured.   [2] Be coy.

WIT. Not I, believe it.

3 CRED. Th'are a brace of cutthroats.

WIT. I know 'em.

3 CRED. Send a note of all your wants to my shop, and I'll supply you instantly.

WIT. Say you so? Why, here's my hand then; no man living shall do't but thyself.

80 3 CRED. Shall I carry it away from 'em both then?

WIT. I' faith, shalt thou.

3 CRED. Troth, then, I thank you, sir.

WIT. Welcome, good Master Cockpit.   *Exit* [3 Creditor].
Ha, ha, ha! Why, is not this better now than lying abed? I perceive there's nothing conjures up wit sooner than poverty, and nothing lays it down sooner than wealth and lechery. This has some savour yet. Oh that I had the mortgage from mine uncle as sure in possession as these trifles, I would forswear brothel at noonday and muscadine and eggs[1] at midnight!

Enter Courtesan

90 COURT. Master Witgood, where are you?

WIT. Holla!

COURT. Rich news!

WIT. Would 'twere all in plate!

COURT. There's some in chains and jewels. I am so haunted with suitors, Master Witgood, I know not which to dispatch first.

WIT. You have the better term,[2] by my faith!

COURT. Among the number,
One Master Hoard, an ancient gentleman.

WIT. Upon my life, my uncle's adversary!

100 COURT. It may well hold so, for he rails on you,
Speaks shamefully of him.

WIT.   As I could wish it.

COURT. I first denied him, but so cunningly
It rather promis'd him assured hopes
Than any loss of labour.

WIT.   Excellent.

COURT. I expect him every hour, with gentlemen
With whom he labours to make good his words,
To approve[3] you riotous, your state consum'd,
Your uncle—

---

[1] Reputed to be aphrodisiac in effect.   [2] The period when the law courts sat, a profitable one for London prostitutes.   [3] Confirm.

WIT. Wench, make up thy own fortunes now; do thyself a good
110 turn once in thy days. He's rich in money, movables, and lands.
Marry him. He's an old doting fool, and that's worth all. Marry
him. 'Twould be a great comfort to me to see thee do well, i' faith.
Marry him. 'Twould ease my conscience well to see thee well
bestow'd. I have a care of thee, i' faith.

COURT. Thanks, sweet Master Witgood.

WIT. I reach at farther happiness. First, I am sure it can be no
harm to thee, and there may happen goodness to me by it.
Prosecute it well. Let's send up for our wits, now we require
their best and most pregnant assistance.

120 COURT. Step in. I think I hear 'em.   *Exeunt.*

[ACT III SCENE 2]

[*The* Courtesan's *lodgings*]

Enter [W.] Hoard *and* Gentlemen,[1] *with the* Host [*as*] *serving-man.*

W. HOARD. Art thou the widow's man? By my faith, sh'as a company of proper men then.

HOST. I am the worst of six, sir, good enough for blue coats.[2]

W. HOARD. Hark hither. I hear say thou art in most credit with
her.

HOST. Not so, sir.

W. HOARD. Come, come, thou'rt modest. There's a brace of
royals;[3] prithee, help me to th' speech of her.

HOST. I'll do what I may, sir, always saving myself harmless.[4]

10 W. HOARD. Go to. Do't, I say. Thou shalt hear better from me.

HOST. [*Aside*] Is not this a better place than five mark[5] a year
standing wages? Say a man had but three such clients in a day,
methinks he might make a poor living on't. Beside, I was never
brought up with so little honesty to refuse any man's money.
Never! What gulls there are a' this side the world! Now know I
the widow's mind, none but my young master comes in her
clutches. Ha, ha, ha!   *Exit.*

---

[1] Perhaps Lamprey and Spitchcock.   [2] i.e. to be ordinary servants.
[3] Gold coins, worth about 75 pence.   [4] 'Provided that I remain out
of trouble.'   [5] The amount of £3.34; a mark (67 pence) did not exist
as a coin.

W. HOARD. Now, my dear gentlemen, stand firmly to me.
   You know his [1] follies and my worth.

1 GENT.   We do, sir.

20 2 GENT. But, Master Hoard, are you sure he is not i' th' house
   now?

W. HOARD. Upon my honesty, I chose this time
   A' purpose, fit. The spendthrift is abroad.
   Assist me; here she comes.

             [Enter Courtesan.]

                    Now, my sweet widow.

COURT. Y'are welcome, Master Hoard.

W. HOARD. [*To* Gentlemen] Dispatch,[2] sweet gentlemen, dis-
   patch.—
   I am come, widow, to prove those my words
   Neither of envy sprung nor of false tongues,

30   But such as their [3] deserts and actions
   Do merit and bring forth; all which these gentlemen,
   Well known and better reputed, will confess.

COURT. I cannot tell
   How my affections may dispose of me,
   But surely if they find him so desertless
   They'll have that reason to withdraw themselves.
   And therefore, gentlemen, I do entreat you,
   As you are fair in reputation,
   And in appearing form, so shine in truth.

40   I am a widow, and, alas, you know
   Soon overthrown; 'tis a very small thing
   That we withstand, our weakness is so great.
   Be partial unto neither, but deliver,
   Without affection,[4] your opinion.

W. HOARD. And that will drive it home.

COURT. Nay, I beseech your silence, Master Hoard;
   You are a party.

W. HOARD.   Widow, not a word!

1 GENT. The better first to work you to belief,
   Know neither of us owe him [5] flattery,

50   Nor tother [6] malice, but unbribed censure,[7]
   So help us our best fortunes.

COURT.   It suffices.

---

[1] Witgood's.   [2] Hasten.   [3] Witgood and Lucre's.   [4] Prejudice.
[5] Walkadine Hoard.   [6] Witgood.   [7] Judgment.

1 GENT. That Witgood is a riotous, undone man,
Imperfect both in fame and in estate,
His debts wealthier than he, and executions[1]
In wait for his due body, we'll maintain
With our best credit and our dearest blood.
COURT. Nor land nor living, say you? Pray, take heed
You do not wrong the gentleman.
1 GENT.   What we speak
Our lives and means are ready to make good.
60 COURT. Alas, how soon are we poor souls beguil'd!
2 GENT. And for his uncle,—
W. HOARD.   Let that come to me.
His uncle, a severe extortioner,
A tyrant at a forfeiture, greedy of others'
Miseries, one that would undo his brother,
Nay, swallow up his father if he can,
Within the fathoms of his conscience.
1 GENT. Nay, believe it, widow,
You had not only match'd yourself to wants,
But in an evil and unnatural stock.
70 W. HOARD. [To Gentlemen] Follow hard, gentlemen, follow
hard!
COURT. Is my love so deceiv'd? Before you all
I do renounce him; on my knees I vow
He ne'er shall marry me.

[Witgood *looks in*]

WIT. [*Aside*] Heaven knows he never meant it!
W. HOARD. [To Gentlemen] There, take her at the bound.
1 GENT. Then, with a new and pure affection,
Behold yon gentleman, grave, kind, and rich,
A match worthy yourself. Esteeming him,
80 You do regard[2] your state.
W. HOARD. [To 1 Gentleman] I'll make her a jointure,[3] say.
1 GENT. He can join land to land and will possess you
Of what you can desire.
2 GENT.   Come, widow, come.
COURT. The world is so deceitful.
1 GENT.   There, 'tis deceitful,
Where flattery, want, and imperfection lies.
But none of these in him. Push!

---

[1] Seizures of goods.   [2] Look to.   [3] Property held jointly by a husband and wife, customarily with provision for inheritance by the widow.

COURT.   Pray, sir,—

1 GENT. Come, you widows are ever most backward when you
should do yourselves most good; but were it to marry a chin not
worth a hair [1] now, then you would be forward enough. Come,
clap hands, a match.

W. HOARD. With all my heart, widow. Thanks, gentlemen;
I will deserve [2] your labour, and thy love.

COURT. Alas, you love not widows but for wealth.
I promise you I ha' nothing, sir.

W. HOARD.   Well said, widow,
Well said! Thy love is all I seek, before
These gentlemen.

COURT.   Now I must hope the best.

W. HOARD. My joys are such they want to be express'd.

COURT. But, Master Hoard, one thing I must remember you of
before these gentlemen, your friends: How shall I suddenly
avoid the loathed soliciting of that perjur'd Witgood and his
tedious, dissembling uncle, who this very, very day hath
appointed a meeting for the same purpose too, where, had not
truth come forth, I had been undone, utterly undone?

W. HOARD. What think you of that, gentlemen?

1 GENT. 'Twas well devis'd.

W. HOARD. Hark thee, widow, train [3] out young Witgood single; [4]
hasten him thither with thee, somewhat before the hour, where,
at the place appointed, these gentlemen and myself will wait
the opportunity, where by some sleight, removing him from
thee, we'll suddenly enter and surprise thee, carry thee away by
boat to Cole Harbour, [5] have a priest ready, and there clap it up
instantly. How lik'st it, widow?

COURT. In that it pleaseth you, it likes me well.

W. HOARD. I'll kiss thee for those words. Come, gentlemen;
Still must I live a suitor to your favours,
Still to your aid beholding.

1 GENT.   We're engag'd, sir;
'Tis for our credits now to see't well ended.

W. HOARD. 'Tis for your honours, gentlemen. Nay, look to't.
Not only in joy, but I in wealth excel.
No more sweet widow, but sweet wife, farewell.

COURT. Farewell, sir.   *Exeunt* [W. Hoard *and* Gentlemen].

Enter Witgood

---

[1] i.e. a youth.   [2] Requite.   [3] Entice.   [4] Alone.
[5] See II, i, 236, and note.

wit. Oh for more scope! I could laugh eternally.
Give you joy, Mistress Hoard! I promis['d] your fortune was
good, forsooth; y'ave fell upon wealth enough, and there's
young gentlemen enow can help you to the rest. Now it requires
our wits. Carry thyself but heedfully now, and we are both—

[Enter Host]

host. Master Witgood, your uncle—
wit. Cuds me! Remove thyself awhile; I'll serve for him.

[Exeunt Courtesan and Host.]

Enter Lucre

lucre. Nephew, good morrow, nephew.
130 wit. The same to you, kind uncle.
lucre. How fares the widow? Does the meeting hold?
wit. Oh, no question of that, sir.
lucre. I'll strike the stroke then for thee; no more days.[1]
wit. The sooner the better, uncle. Oh, she's mightily followed.
lucre. And yet so little rumour'd.
wit. Mightily! Here comes one old gentleman, and he'll make
her a jointure of three hundred a year, forsooth; another wealthy
suitor will estate his son in his lifetime, and make him weigh
down the widow; here's a merchant's son will possess her with
140 no less than three goodly lordships[2] at once, which were all
pawns to his father.
lucre. Peace, nephew, let me hear no more of 'em; it mads me.
Thou shalt prevent[3] 'em all. No words to the widow of my
coming hither. Let me see, 'tis now upon nine; before twelve,
nephew, we will have the bargain struck. We will, faith, boy.

[Exit.]

wit. Oh, my precious uncle!

[ACT III SCENE 3]

[W. Hoard's *house*]

Enter [W.] Hoard *and his* Niece[4]

w. hoard. Niece, sweet niece, prithee have a care to my house.
I leave all to thy discretion. Be content to dream awhile;
I'll have a husband for thee shortly. Put that care upon me,

---

[1] No further extensions of time (usually for the payment of debts).
[2] Manors.   [3] Forestall.   [4] i.e. Joyce.

wench, for in choosing wives and husbands I am only fortunate;
I have that gift given me.   *Exit.*

NIECE. But 'tis not likely you should choose for me,
Since nephew to your chiefest enemy
Is he whom I affect. But, O forgetful,
Why dost thou flatter thy affections so,
With name of him that for a widow's bed
Neglects thy purer love? Can it be so,
Or does report dissemble?

[*Enter* George]

How now, sir?
GEORGE. A letter, with which came a private charge.
NIECE. Therein I thank your care.   [*Exit* George]
                      I know this hand.   *Reads*
'Dearer than sight, what the world reports of me yet believe
not. Rumour will alter shortly. Be thou constant. I am still the
same that I was in love, and I hope to be the same in fortunes.
                          Theodorus Witgood.'
I am resolv'd.[1] No more shall fear or doubt
Raise their pale powers to keep affection out.   *Exit.*

[ACT III SCENE 4]

[*An inn*]

Enter, with a Drawer, [W.] Hoard *and two* Gentlemen [2]

DRAWER. You're very welcome, gentlemen. Dick, show these
gentlemen the Pom'granate [3] there.
W. HOARD. Hist!
DRAWER. Up those stairs, gentlemen.
W. HOARD. Pist, drawer!
DRAWER. Anon, sir.
W. HOARD. Prithee, ask at the bar if a gentlewoman came not in
lately.
DRAWER. William, at the bar! Did you see any gentlewoman
come in lately? Speak you ay, speak you no?

[1] Assured.   [2] Perhaps Lamprey and Spitchcock.   [3] It was then usual
to give rooms names instead of numbers.

WITHIN. No, none came in yet but Mistress Florence.

DRAWER. He says none came in yet, sir, but one Mistress
Florence.

W. HOARD. What is that Florence? A widow?

DRAWER. Yes, a Dutch[1] widow.

W. HOARD. How!

DRAWER. That's an English drab, sir. Give your worship good
morrow.   [*Exit.*]

W. HOARD. A merry knave, i' faith! I shall remember 'a Dutch
20   widow' the longest day of my life.

1 GENT. Did not I use most art to win the widow?

2 GENT. You shall pardon me for that, sir; Master Hoard knows
I took her at best 'vantage.

W. HOARD. What's that, sweet gentlemen, what's that?

2 GENT. He will needs bear me down that his art only wrought
with the widow most.

W. HOARD. Oh, you did both well, gentlemen, you did both well,
I thank you.

1 GENT. I was the first that mov'd her.

W. HOARD.   You were, i' faith.

30   2 GENT. But it was I that took her at the bound.

W. HOARD. Ay, that was you; faith, gentlemen, 'tis right.

1 GENT. I boasted least, but 'twas I join'd their hands.

W. HOARD. By th' mass, I think he did. You did all[2] well,
Gentlemen, you did all well. Contend no more.

1 GENT. Come, yon room's fittest.

W. HOARD.   True, 'tis next the door. *Exeunt.*

Enter [Drawer,] Witgood, Courtesan, *and* Host

DRAWER. You're very welcome. Please you to walk upstairs;
cloth's laid, sir.

COURT. Upstairs? Troth, I am weary, Master Witgood.

WIT. Rest yourself here awhile, widow. We'll have a cup of
40   muscadine in this little room.

DRAWER. A cup of muscadine? You shall have the best, sir.

WIT. But, do you hear, sirrah?

DRAWER. Do you call? Anon, sir.

WIT. What is there provided for dinner?

DRAWER. I cannot readily tell you, sir. If you please, you may
go into the kitchen and see yourself, sir. Many gentlemen of
worship do use to do it, I assure you, sir.   [*Exit.*]

---

[1] At that time an opprobrious word.   [2] Everything.

HOST. A pretty familiar, priggin'[1] rascal! He has his part without
  book.

WIT. Against you are ready to drink to me, widow, I'll be present
  to pledge you.

COURT. Nay, I commend your care; 'tis done well of you. [*Exit*
  Alas, what have I forgot?   Witgood.]

HOST. What, mistress?

COURT. I slipp'd my wedding ring off when I wash'd, and left it
  at my lodging. Prithee, run. I shall be sad without it.
                                                    [*Exit* Host.]

  So, he's gone. Boy!

                      [*Enter* Boy]

BOY. Anon, forsooth.

COURT. Come hither, sirrah. Learn secretly if one Master Hoard,
  an ancient gentleman, be about house.

BOY. I heard such a one nam'd.

COURT. Commend me to him.   [*Exit* Boy.]

            Enter [W.] Hoard *with* Gentlemen

W. HOARD. I'll do thy commendations.

COURT. Oh, you come well. Away! To boat! Begone!

W. HOARD. Thus wise men are reveng'd, give two for one.
                                                       Exeunt.

            Enter Witgood *and* Vintner

WIT. I must request
  You, sir, to show extraordinary care.
  My uncle comes with gentlemen, his friends,
  And 'tis upon a making.[2]

VINT.   Is it so?
  I'll give a special charge, good Master Witgood.
  May I be bold to see her?

WIT.   Who, the widow?
  With all my heart, i' faith. I'll bring you to her.

VINT. If she be a Staffordshire gentlewoman, 'tis much if I know
  her not.

WIT. How now? Boy! Drawer!

VINT. Hie!

                      [*Enter* Boy]

BOY. Do you call, sir?

WIT. Went the gentlewoman up that was here?

BOY. Up, sir? She went out, sir.

                    ¹ Dishonest.   ² Matchmaking.

80 WIT. Out, sir?

BOY. Out, sir. One Master Hoard, with a guard of gentlemen, carried her out at back door a pretty while since, sir.

[*Exit* Boy.]

WIT. Hoard? Death and darkness! Hoard?[1]

Enter Host

HOST. The devil of ring I can find!

WIT. How now? What news? Where's the widow?

HOST. My mistress? Is she not here, sir?

WIT. More madness yet!

HOST.   She sent me for a ring.

WIT. A plot, a plot! To boat! She's stole away.

HOST. What?

Enter Lucre *with* Gentlemen[2]

90 WIT. Follow! Inquire! Old Hoard, my uncle's adversary,—

[*Exit* Host.]

LUCRE. Nephew, what's that?

WIT.   Thrice-miserable wretch!

LUCRE. Why, what's the matter?

VINT.   The widow's borne away, sir.

LUCRE. Ha! Passion of me! A heavy welcome, gentlemen.

1 GENT. The widow gone?

LUCRE. Who durst attempt it?

WIT. Who but old Hoard, my uncle's adversary?

LUCRE. How!

WIT. With his confederates.

LUCRE. Hoard, my deadly enemy! Gentlemen, stand to me.
100   I will not bear it. 'Tis in hate of me
      That villain seeks my shame, nay, thirsts[3] my blood.
      He owes me mortal malice.
      I'll spend my wealth on this despiteful plot,
      Ere he shall cross me and my nephew thus.

WIT. So maliciously!

Enter Host

LUCRE. How now, you treacherous rascal?

HOST. That's none of my name, sir.

WIT. Poor soul, he knew not on't.

LUCRE. I'm sorry. I see then 'twas a mere[4] plot.

HOST. I trac'd 'em nearly,—

---

[1] Witgood's distress is feigned; see III, i, 109–114.   [2] Friends to Lucre; not named.   [3] Longs for.   [4] Absolute.

LUCRE.   Well?

10 HOST.   And hear for certain
They have took [1] Cole Harbour.

LUCRE.   The devil's sanctuary!
They shall not rest. I'll pluck her from his arms.
Kind and dear gentlemen,
If ever I had seat within your breasts,—

1 GENT. No more, good sir. It is a wrong to us
To see you injur'd. In a cause so just
We'll spend our lives, but we will right our friends.

LUCRE. Honest and kind! Come, we have delay'd too long.
Nephew, take comfort; a just cause is strong.

WIT. That's all my comfort, uncle. *Exeunt* [Lucre, Gentlemen
                                         and Host].

20   Ha, ha, ha!
Now may events fall luckily and well;
He that ne'er strives, says wit, shall ne'er excel.   *Exit.*

[ACT III SCENE 5]

[Dampit's *house*]

Enter Dampit, *the usurer, drunk*

DAMPIT. When did I say my prayers? In anno '88, when the
great armada was coming, and in anno '99,[2] when the great
thund'ring and lightning was. I pray'd heartily then, i' faith, to
overthrow Povey's [3] new buildings. I kneel'd by my great iron
chest, I remember.

[*Enter* Audrey]

AUDREY. Master Dampit, one may hear you before they see you.
You keep sweet hours, Master Dampit. We were all abed three
hours ago.

DAMPIT. Audrey?

AUDREY. Oh, y'are a fine gentleman!

---

[1] Reached.   [2] Probably an error for '89, when a great storm occurred.
[3] Evidently a business rival. Povey owned a wooden building in Saint Paul's
Churchyard, *c.* 1605; it was soon pulled down because it contravened
building regulations.

DAMPIT. So I am, i' faith, and a fine scholar. Do you use to go
to bed so early, Audrey?

AUDREY. Call you this early, Master Dampit?

DAMPIT. Why, is't not one of clock i' th' morning? Is not that
early enough? Fetch me a glass of fresh beer.

AUDREY. Here, I have warm'd your nightcap for you, Master
Dampit.

DAMPIT. Draw it on then, I am very weak truly. I have not eaten
so much as the bulk of an egg these three days.

20 AUDREY. You have drunk the more, Master Dampit.

DAMPIT. What's that?

AUDREY. You mought and you would, Master Dampit.

DAMPIT. I answer you, I cannot. Hold your prating. You prate
too much and understand too little. Are you answered? Give
me a glass of beer.

AUDREY. May I ask you how you do, Master Dampit?

DAMPIT. How do I? I' faith, naught.

AUDREY. I ne'er knew you do otherwise.

DAMPIT. I eat not one penn'ort' of bread these two years. Give
30 me a glass of fresh beer, I am not sick, nor I am not well.

AUDREY. Take this warm napkin about your neck, sir, whilst I
help you make you unready.[1]

DAMPIT. How now, Audrey-prater,[2] with your scurvy devices,
what say you now?

AUDREY. What say I, Master Dampit? I say nothing but that you
are very weak.

DAMPIT. Faith, thou hast more cony-catching[3] devices than all
London.

AUDREY. Why, Master Dampit, I never deceiv'd you in all my life.

40 DAMPIT. Why was that? Because I never did trust thee.

AUDREY. I care not what you say, Master Dampit.

DAMPIT. Hold thy prating. I answer thee, thou art a beggar, a
quean, and a bawd. Are you answer'd?

AUDREY. Fie, Master Dampit! A gentleman, and have such
words!

DAMPIT. Why, thou base drudge of infortunity,[4] thou kitchen-
stuff drab of beggary, roguery, and coxcombry, thou caver-
nesed[5] quean of foolery, knavery, and bawdreaminy,[6] I'll tell
thee what, I will not give a louse for thy fortunes.

50 AUDREY. No, Master Dampit, and there's a gentleman comes

---

[1] Undress you.   [2] A coined word, analogous to 'Margery-prater', a cant
term for a hen.   [3] Cheating.   [4] Misfortune.   [5] A coined word;
hollow (?).   [6] A coined word; licentiousness.

a-wooing to me, and he doubts [1] nothing but that you will get me from him.

DAMPIT. I? If I would either have thee or lie with thee for two thousand pound, would I might be damn'd! Why, thou base, impudent quean of foolery, flattery, and coxcombry, are you answer'd?

AUDREY. Come, will you rise and go to bed, sir?

DAMPIT. Rise and go to bed too, Audrey. How does Mistress Proserpine? [2]

AUDREY. Fooh!

DAMPIT. She's as fine a philosopher of a stinkard's wife as any within the liberties.[3] Faugh, faugh, Audrey!

AUDREY. How now, Master Dampit?

DAMPIT. Fie upon't, what a choice of stinks here is! What hast thou done, Audrey? Fie upon't, here's a choice of stinks indeed! Give me a glass of fresh beer, and then I will to bed.

AUDREY. It waits for you above, sir.

DAMPIT. Fooh, I think they burn horns [4] in Barnard's Inn.[5] If ever I smell'd such an abominable stink, usury forsake me.

[*Exit.*]

AUDREY. They be the stinking nails of his trampling feet, and he talks of burning of horns.   *Exit.*

Incipit ACT IV [SCENE 1]

[*A house at Cole Harbour*]

Enter, at Cole Harbour, [W.] Hoard, *the* Widow, *and* Gentlemen,[6]
he married now

1 GENT. Join hearts, join hands,
 In wedlock's bands;
 Never to part,
 Till death cleave your heart.
 You shall forsake all other women;
 You, lords, knights, gentlemen, and yeomen.

---

[1] Fears.   [2] Dampit identifies Audrey with Persephone, a resident of earth for one half of the year and consort of Pluto in the infernal regions during the other half.   [3] Suburban areas outside the jurisdiction of civic authorities, frequented by prostitutes and other persons of ill repute.
[4] Either to create a smell for medicinal purposes or for use as fertilizer.
[5] One of the inns of court (a law school).   [6] Spitchcock and Lamprey.

What my tongue slips
Make up with your lips.

w. HOARD. Give you joy, Mistress Hoard; let the kiss come
about.

10   Who knocks? Convey my little pig-eater [1] out.

LUCRE. [*Within*] Hoard!

w. HOARD. Upon my life, my adversary, gentlemen!

LUCRE. [*Within*] Hoard, open the door or we will force it ope.
Give us the widow.

w. HOARD.   Gentlemen, keep 'em out.

LAMP. He comes upon his death that enters here.

LUCRE. [*Within*] My friends, assist me.

w. HOARD.   He has assistants, gentlemen.

LAMP. Tut! Nor him nor them, we in this action fear.

LUCRE. [*Within*] Shall I in peace speak one word with the widow?

COURT. Husband and gentlemen, hear me but a word.

w. HOARD. Freely, sweet wife.

20   COURT.   Let him in peaceably;
You know we're sure from any act of his.

w. HOARD. Most true.

COURT. You may stand by and smile at his old weakness.
Let me alone to answer him.

w. HOARD.   Content.
'Twill be good mirth, i' faith. How think you, gentlemen?

LAMP. Good gullery!

w. HOARD.   Upon calm conditions, let him in.

LUCRE. [*Within*] All spite and malice—

LAMP.   Hear me, Master Lucre.
So you will vow a peaceful entrance
With those your friends, and only exercise

30   Calm conference with the widow, without fury,
The passage shall receive you.

LUCRE. [*Within*]   I do vow it.

LAMP. Then enter and talk freely. Here she stands.

Enter Lucre [, *his* friends, *and* Host]

LUCRE. Oh, Master Hoard, your spite has watch'd [2] the hour.
You're excellent at vengeance, Master Hoard.

w. HOARD. Ha, ha, ha!

LUCRE. I am the fool you laugh at.
You are wise, sir, and know the seasons. Well,
Come hither, widow.   [*They speak apart*]
            Why, is it thus?

[1] A term of endearment.   [2] Awaited.

Oh, you have done me infinite disgrace
And your own credit no small injury.
Suffer mine enemy so despitefully
To bear you from my nephew? Oh, I had
Rather half my substance had been forfeit
And begg'd by some starv'd rascal.

COURT. Why, what would you wish me do, sir?
I must not overthrow my state for love;
We have too many precedents for that.
From thousands of our wealthy undone widows
One may derive some wit. I do confess
I lov'd your nephew; nay, I did affect him
Against the mind and liking of my friends,
Believ'd his promises, lay here in hope
Of flatter'd living and the boast of lands.
Coming to touch his wealth and state indeed,
It appears dross. I find him not the man;
Imperfect, mean, scarce furnish'd of his needs.
In words, fair lordships; in performance, hovels.
Can any woman love the thing that is not?

LUCRE. Broke you for this?

COURT.   Was it not cause too much?
Send to inquire his state. Most part of it
Lay two years mortgag'd in his uncle's hands.

LUCRE. Why, say it did. You might have known my mind;
I could have soon restor'd it.

COURT. Ay. Had I but seen any such thing perform'd,
Why, 'twould have tied my affection and contain'd
Me in my first desires. Do you think, i' faith,
That I could twine such a dry oak as this,
Had promise in your nephew took effect?

LUCRE. Why, and there's no time pass'd, and rather than
My adversary should thus thwart my hopes,
I would—

COURT. Tut! Y'ave been ever full of golden speech.
If words were lands, your nephew would be rich.

LUCRE. Widow, believe it, I vow by my best bliss,
Before these gentlemen, I will give in
The mortgage to my nephew instantly,
Before I sleep or eat.

1 GENT.[1]   We'll pawn our credits,

[1] A friend to Lucre.

Widow, what he speaks shall be perform'd
In fullness.

LUCRE.   Nay, more. I will estate him
80   In farther blessings: He shall be my heir.
I have no son.
I'll bind myself to that condition.

COURT. When I shall hear this done I shall soon yield
To reasonable terms.

LUCRE.   In the mean season,
Will you protest, before these gentlemen,
To keep yourself as you are now at this present?

COURT. I do protest, before these gentlemen,
I will be as clear then as I am now.

LUCRE. I do believe you. Here's your own honest servant;
I'll take him along with me.

90   COURT.   Ay, with all my heart.

LUCRE. He shall see all perform'd, and bring you word.

COURT. That's all I wait for.

W. HOARD. What, have you finish'd, Master Lucre? Ha, ha, ha,
ha!

LUCRE. So, laugh, Hoard, laugh at your poor enemy, do.
The wind may turn; you may be laugh'd at too!
Yes, marry, may you, sir. Ha, ha, ha!
                        Exeunt [Lucre, *his* friends, *and* Host].

W. HOARD. Ha, ha, ha! If every man that swells in malice
Could be reveng'd as happily as I,
100   He would choose hate and forswear amity.
What did he say, wife, prithee?

COURT. Faith, spoke to ease his mind.

W. HOARD. Oh, oh, oh!

COURT. You know now, little to any purpose.

W. HOARD. True, true, true.

COURT. He would do mountains now.

W. HOARD. Ay, ay, ay, ay.

LAMP. Y'ave struck him dead, Master Hoard.

SPITCH. Ay, and his nephew desperate.

110   W. HOARD. I know't, sirs, ay.
Never did man so crush his enemy.   *Exeunt.*

[ACT IV SCENE 2]

[Lucre's *house*]

Enter Lucre *with* Gentlemen [1] [*and* Host], *meeting* Sam Freedom

LUCRE. My son-in-law, Sam Freedom, where's my nephew?

SAM. O man in lamentation,[2] father!

LUCRE. How!

SAM. He thumps his breast like a gallant dicer that has lost his doublet, and stands in's shirt to do penance.

LUCRE. Alas, poor gentleman!

SAM. I warrant you may hear him sigh in a still evening to your house at Highgate.

LUCRE. I prithee, send him in.

SAM. Were it to do a greater matter, I will not stick[3] with you, sir, in regard you married my mother. [*Exit.*]

LUCRE. Sweet gentlemen, cheer him up. I will but fetch the mortgage and return to you instantly. *Exit.*

1 GENT. We'll do our best, sir. See where he comes,
E'en joyless and regardless of all form.

[*Enter* Witgood]

2 GENT. Why, how, Master Witgood! Fie! You a firm scholar and an understanding gentleman, and give your best parts to passion?

1 GENT. Come, fie!

WIT. Oh, gentlemen,—

1 GENT. Sorrow of me, what a sigh was there, sir!
Nine such widows are not worth it.

WIT. To be borne from me by that lecher, Hoard!

1 GENT. That vengeance is your uncle's, being done
More in despite to him than wrong to you,
But we bring comfort now.

WIT. I beseech you, gentlemen,—

2 GENT. Cheer thyself, man; there's hope of her, i' faith.

WIT. Too gladsome to be true.

Enter Lucre

LUCRE.   Nephew, what cheer?
Alas, poor gentleman, how art thou chang'd!
Call thy fresh blood into thy cheeks again.
She comes—

---

[1] Friends to Lucre.   [2] A variant on an old ballad, 'O man in desperation'
(Peele, *An Old Wives' Tale*, I, i, 20).   [3] Haggle.

WIT.   Nothing afflicts me so much
But that it is your adversary, uncle,
And merely [1] plotted in despite of you.
LUCRE. Ay, that's it mads me, spites me. I'll spend my wealth ere
he shall carry her so, because I know 'tis only to spite me. Ay, this
is it. Here, nephew, before these kind gentlemen, I deliver in your
mortgage, my promise to the widow. See, 'tis done. Be wise.
You're once more master of your own; the widow shall perceive
40   now you are not altogether such a beggar as the world reputes
you. You can make shift to bring her to three hundred a year, sir.
1 GENT. By'r lady, and that's no toy, sir.
LUCRE.   A word, nephew.
1 GENT. Now you may certify [2] the widow.
LUCRE. You must conceive it aright, nephew, now.
To do you good, I am content to do this.
WIT. I know it, sir.
LUCRE. But your own conscience can tell I had it
Dearly enough of you.
WIT.   Ay, that's most certain.
LUCRE. Much money laid out, beside many a journey
50   To fetch the rent. I hope you'll think on't, nephew.
WIT. I were worse than a beast else, i' faith.
LUCRE. Although to blind the widow and the world,
I out of policy do't, yet there's a conscience, nephew.
WIT. Heaven forbid else!
LUCRE.   When you are full possess'd,
'Tis nothing to return it.
WIT. Alas, a thing quickly done, uncle.
LUCRE. Well said. You know I give it you but in trust.
WIT. Pray let me understand you rightly, uncle:
You give [3] it me but in trust?
60   LUCRE. No.
WIT.   That is, you trust me with it.
LUCRE. True, true.
WIT. [Aside] But if ever I trust you with it again,
Would I might be truss'd up for my labour.
LUCRE. You can all witness, gentlemen, and you, sir yeoman.
HOST. My life for yours, sir, now. I know my mistress' mind too
well towards your nephew. Let things be in preparation, and
I'll train [4] her hither in most excellent fashion.   *Exit.*
LUCRE. A good old boy.—Wife! Jenny!

[1] Absolutely.   [2] Assure.   [3] Witgood evidently emphasizes this word.
[4] Entice.

Enter Wife

wife. What's the news, sir?

lucre. The wedding day's at hand! Prithee, sweet wife, express
thy housewifery. Thou'rt a fine cook, I know't; thy first
husband married thee out of an alderman's kitchen. Go to!
He rais'd thee for raising of paste.[1] What! Here's none but
friends. Most of our beginnings must be wink'd at. Gentlemen,
I invite you all to my nephew's wedding against Thursday
morning.

1 gent. With all our hearts, and we shall joy to see
Your enemy so mock'd.

lucre. He laugh'd at me, gentlemen; ha, ha, ha.

Exeunt [Lucre, Wife, *and* Gentlemen].

wit. He has no conscience, faith, would laugh at them.
They laugh at one another.
Who then can be so cruel? Troth, not I;
I rather pity now than aught envy.
I do conceive such joy in mine own happiness,
I have no leisure yet to laugh at their follies.
Thou soul of my estate,[2] I kiss thee,
I miss life's comfort when I miss thee.
Oh, never will we part again,
Until I leave the sight of men.
We'll ne'er trust conscience of our kin,
Since cozenage brings that title in.   [*Exit.*]

[ACT IV SCENE 3]

[*Outside* Witgood's *house*]

Enter three Creditors

1 cred. I'll wait these seven hours, but I'll see him caught.

2 cred. Faith, so will I.

3 cred. Hang him, prodigal! He's stripp'd of the widow.

1 cred. A' my troth, she's the wiser; she has made the happier
choice, and I wonder of what stuff those widows' hearts are
made of, that will marry unfledg'd boys, before comely thrum-
chinn'd[3] gentlemen.

[1] Dough.   [2] i.e. the mortgage.   [3] Bearded; the thrum is the fringe of
a piece of weaving.

Enter a Boy

BOY. News, news, news!

1 CRED. What, boy?

10   BOY. The rioter is caught!

1 CRED. So, so, so, so. It warms me at the heart.
I love a' life to see dogs upon men.
Oh, here he comes.

Enter Witgood *with sergeants*

WIT. My last joy was so great it took away the sense of all future
afflictions. What a day is here o'ercast! How soon a black tempest rises!

1 CRED. Oh, we may speak with you now, sir. What's become of
your rich widow? I think you may cast your cap at[1] the widow,
may you not, sir?

20   2 CRED. He, a rich widow? Who, a prodigal, a daily rioter, and
a nightly vomiter? He, a widow of account? He, a hole i' th'
Counter![2]

WIT. You do well, my masters, to tyrannize over misery, to
afflict the afflicted. 'Tis a custom you have here amongst you.
I would wish you never leave it, and I hope you'll do as I bid you.

1 CRED. Come, come, sir; what say you extempore now to your
bill of a hundred pound? A sweet debt for frotting[3] your doub-
lets.

2 CRED. Here's mine of forty.

30   3 CRED. Here's mine of fifty.

WIT. Pray, sirs, you'll give me breath?

1 CRED. No, sir, we'll keep you out of breath still. Then we shall
be sure you will not run away from us.

WIT. Will you but hear me speak?

2 CRED. You shall pardon us for that, sir. We know you have
too fair a tongue of your own; you overcame us too lately, a
shame take you. We are like to lose all that for want of witnesses.
We dealt in policy then. Always when we strive to be most
politic we prove most coxcombs, *non plus ultra*.[4] I perceive by

40   us, we're not ordain'd to thrive by wisdom, and therefore we
must be content to be tradesmen.

WIT. Give me but reasonable time, and I protest I'll make you
ample satisfaction.

1 CRED. Do you talk of reasonable time to us?

---

[1] Give up.   [2] A debtors' prison in London.   [3] Rubbing with perfume,
to remove perspiration odours and stains.   [4] The ultimate, normally *ne
plus ultra*.

WIT. 'Tis true, beasts know no reasonable time.

2 CRED. We must have either money or carcass.

WIT. Alas, what good will my carcass do you?

3 CRED. Oh, 'tis a secret delight we have amongst us. We that
are used to keep birds in cages have the heart to keep men in
prison, I warrant you.

WIT. [*Aside*] I perceive I must crave a little more aid from my
wits: Do but make shift for me this once, and I'll forswear ever
to trouble you in the like fashion hereafter. I'll have better employment for you and I live.—You'll give me leave, my masters,
to make trial of my friends, and raise all means I can?

1 CRED. That's our desires, sir.

Enter Host

HOST. Master Witgood?

WIT. Oh, art thou come?

HOST. May I speak one word with you in private, sir?

WIT. No, by my faith, canst thou. I am in Hell here, and the devils
will not let me come to thee.

CITIZENS.[1] Do you call us devils? You shall find us puritans!
Bear him away. Let 'em talk as they go. We'll not stand to
hear 'em. Ah, sir, am I a devil? I shall think the better of myself
as long as I live. A devil, i' faith!   *Exeunt.*

[ACT IV SCENE 4]

[W. Hoard's *house*]

Enter [W.] Hoard

W. HOARD. What a sweet blessing hast thou, Master Hoard,
above a multitude! Wilt thou never be thankful? How dost
thou think to be bless'd another time? Or dost thou count this the
full measure of thy happiness? By my troth, I think thou dost.
Not only a wife large in possessions, but spacious in content.
She's rich, she's young, she's fair, she's wise. When I wake,
I think of her lands; that revives me. When I go to bed, I dream
of her beauty, and that's enough for me. She's worth four
hundred a year in her very smock, if a man knew how to use it.
But the journey will be all, in troth, into the country; to ride to

[1] i.e. the three creditors, talking at once.

her lands in state and order, following my brother and other
worshipful gentlemen, whose companies I ha' sent down for
already, to ride along with us in their goodly decorum [1] beards,
their broad velvet cassocks,[2] and chains of gold twice or thrice
double. Against which time I'll entertain [3] some ten men of mine
own into liveries, all of occupations [4] or qualities.[5] I will not keep
an idle man about me. The sight of which will so vex my adversary Lucre, for we'll pass by his door of purpose, make a little
stand for [the] nonce,[6] and have our horses curvet before the
20 window. Certainly he will never endure it, but run up and hang
himself presently.

[*Enter* Servant]

How now, sirrah? What news? Any that offer their service to
me yet?

SERV. Yes, sir, there are some i' th' hall that wait for your
worship's liking, and desire to be entertain'd.

W. HOARD. Are they of occupation?

SERV. They are men fit for your worship, sir.

W. HOARD. Say'st so? Send 'em all in. [*Exit* Servant] To see ten
30 men ride after me in watchet [7] liveries with orange-tawny capes,
'twill cut his comb,[8] i' faith.

Enter all [, Tailor, Barber, Perfumer, Falconer, *and* Huntsman]
How now? Of what occupation are you, sir?

TAILOR. A tailor, an't please your worship.

W. HOARD. A tailor? Oh, very good. You shall serve to make all
the liveries.—What are you, sir?

BARBER. A barber, sir.

W. HOARD. A barber? Very needful. You shall shave all the
house, and if need require, stand for a reaper i' th' summer
time.—You, sir?

40 PERF. A perfumer.

W. HOARD. I smell'd you before. Perfumers, of all men, had
need carry themselves uprightly, for if they were once knaves
they would be smell'd out quickly.—To you, sir?

FALC. A falc'ner, an't please your worship.

W. HOARD. Sa ho, sa ho, sa ho![9]—and you, sir?

HUNT. A huntsman, sir.

W. HOARD. There, boy, there, boy, there, boy.[10] I am not so old
but I have pleasant days to come. I promise you, my masters,

---

[1] Dignified.   [2] Long, loose coats.   [3] Employ.   [4] Employments.
[5] Accomplishments.   [6] Temporarily.   [7] Light blue.   [8] Humiliate.
[9] A hawking or hunting call.   [10] A hunting call.

I take such a good liking to you that I entertain you all. I put
you already into my countenance,[1] and you shall be shortly in
my livery. But especially you two, my jolly falc'ner and my
bonny huntsman, we shall have most need of you at my wife's
manor houses i' th' country. There's goodly parks and cham-
pion[2] grounds for you. We shall have all our sports within ourselves. All the gentlemen a' th' country shall be beholding to us
and our pastimes.

FALC. And we'll make your worship admire,[3] sir.

W. HOARD. Say'st thou so? Do but make me admire, and thou
shalt want for nothing.—My tailor?

TAILOR. Anon, sir.

W. HOARD. Go presently in hand with the liveries.

TAILOR. I will, sir.

W. HOARD. My barber.

BARBER. Here, sir.

W. HOARD. Make 'em all trim fellows, louse 'em well, especially
my huntsman, and cut all their beards of the Polonian[4] fashion.
—My perfumer?

PERF. Under your nose, sir.

W. HOARD. Cast a better savour upon the knaves, to take away
the scent of my tailor's feet and my barber's lotium water.[5]

PERF. It shall be carefully perform'd, sir.

W. HOARD. But you, my falc'ner and huntsman, the welcom'st
men alive, i' faith!

HUNT. And we'll show you that, sir, shall deserve your worship's favour.

W. HOARD. I prithee, show me that. Go, you knaves all, and
wash your lungs i' th' buttery, go.

[*Exeunt* Tailor, Barber, Perfumer, Falconer, *and* Huntsman.]
By th' mass, and well remem'bred. I'll ask my wife that question.
Wife! Mistress Jane Hoard!

Enter Courtesan, *alter'd in apparel*

COURT. Sir, would you with me?

W. HOARD. I would but know, sweet wife, which might stand
best to thy liking, to have the wedding dinner kept here or i' th'
country?

COURT. Hum. Faith, sir, 'twould like me better here. Here you
were married, here let all rites be ended.

---

[1] Favour.   [2] i.e. champaign; unenclosed.   [3] Marvel.   [4] Polish; i.e. close-
trimmed except for a long forelock.   [5] A preparation used on the hair,
based on urine.

W. HOARD. Could a marquess[1] give a better answer? Hoard,
bear thy head aloft, thou'st a wife will advance it.

[*Enter* Host *with a letter*]

What haste comes here now? Yes, a letter, some dreg of my
adversary's malice. Come hither. What's the news?

90 HOST. A thing that concerns my mistress, sir.

W. HOARD. Why, then it concerns me, knave.

HOST. Ay, and you, knave, too—cry your worship mercy. You
are both like to come into trouble, I promise you, sir: a precontract.[2]

W. HOARD. How! A precontract, say'st thou?

HOST. I fear they have too much proof on't, sir. Old Lucre, he
runs mad up and down, and will to law as fast as he can. Young
Witgood, laid hold on by his creditors, he exclaims upon you
a' tother side, says you have wrought his undoing by the
100 injurious detaining of his contract.

W. HOARD. Body a' me!

HOST. He will have utmost satisfaction.
The law shall give him recompense he says.

COURT. [*Aside*] Alas, his creditors so merciless! My state being
yet uncertain, I deem it not unconscionable to further him.

HOST. True, sir,—

W. HOARD. Wife, what says that letter? Let me construe it.

COURT. Curs'd be my rash and unadvised words!
I'll set my foot upon my tongue
110 And tread my inconsiderate grant to dust.

[*Stamps on the letter*]

W. HOARD. Wife,—

HOST. [*Aside*] A pretty shift, i' faith. I commend a woman when
she can make away a letter from her husband handsomely, and
this was cleanly done, by my troth.

COURT. I did, sir.
Some foolish words I must confess did pass,
Which now litigiously he fastens on me.

W. HOARD. Of what force? Let me examine 'em.

COURT. Too strong, I fear. Would I were well freed of him.

120 W. HOARD. Shall I compound?[3]

COURT. No, sir, I'd have it done some nobler way
Of your side. I'd have you come off with honour;

---

[1] Marchioness.   [2] A formal agreement to marry; here a supposititious
precontract between the widow and Witgood, an arrangement that may
nullify Hoard's marriage to the girl.   [3] Bargain.

Let baseness keep with them. Why, have you not
The means, sir? The occasion's offer'd you.

w. hoard. Where? How, dear wife?

court. He is now caught by his creditors. The slave's needy, his
debts petty. He'll rather bind himself to all inconveniences
than rot in prison. By this only means you may get a release
from him. 'Tis not yet come to his uncle's hearing. Send
30 speedily for the creditors. By this time he's desperate; he'll set
his hand to anything. Take order for his debts or discharge 'em
quite. A pax on him! Let's be rid of a rascal.

w. hoard. Excellent!
Thou dost astonish me.—Go, run, make haste!
Bring both the creditors and Witgood hither.

host. [*Aside*] This will be some revenge yet.   [*Exit.*]

w. hoard. In the mean space I'll have a release drawn.—
Within there!

[*Enter* Servant]

serv. Sir?

40 w. hoard. Sirrah, come take directions. Go to my scrivener.[1]
[*Speaks aside to* Servant]

court. [*Aside*] I'm yet like those whose riches lie in dreams;
If I be wak'd, they're false. Such is my fate,
Who ventures deeper than the desperate state.
Though I have sinn'd, yet could I become new,
For where I once vow, I am ever true.

w. hoard. Away! Dispatch! On my displeasure, quickly!
[*Exit* Servant.]
Happy occasion! Pray Heaven he be in the right vein now to set
his hand to't, that nothing alter him. Grant that all his follies
may meet in him at once, to besot him enough.
50 I pray for him, i' faith, and here he comes.

[*Enter* Witgood *and* Creditors]

wit. What would you with me now, my uncle's spiteful adversary?

w. hoard. Nay, I am friends.

wit.   Ay, when your mischief's spent.

w. hoard. I heard you were arrested.

wit.   Well, what then?
You will pay none of my debts I am sure.

w. hoard. A wise man cannot tell.

[1] Notary.

There may be those conditions 'greed upon
May move me to do much.

WIT.   Ay, when?
'Tis thou, perjured woman! Oh, no name
160   Is vild [1] enough to match thy treachery,
That art the cause of my confusion.

COURT.   Out, you
Penurious slave!

W. HOARD.   Nay, wife, you are too froward.[2]
Let him alone. Give losers leave to talk.

WIT. Shall I remember thee of another promise
Far stronger than the first?

COURT.   I'd fain know that.

WIT. 'Twould call shame to thy cheeks.

COURT.   Shame?

WIT.   Hark in your ear.
[*To* Courtesan] Will he come off, think'st thou, and pay my
debts roundly?

COURT. [*To* Witgood] Doubt nothing. There's a release a-draw-
170   ing and all, to which you must set your hand.

WIT. [*To* Courtesan] Excellent!

COURT. [*To* Witgood] But methinks, i' faith, you might have
made some shift to discharge this yourself, having in the mortgage, and never have burden'd my conscience with it.

WIT. [*To* Courtesan] A' my troth, I could not, for my creditors'
cruelties extend to the present.

COURT. [*To* Witgood] No more.—Why, do your worst for that,
I defy you.

WIT. Y'are impudent! I'll call up witnesses.

180 COURT. Call up thy wits, for thou hast been devoted
To follies a long time.

W. HOARD.   Wife, y'are too bitter.
Master Witgood, and you, my masters, you shall hear a mild
speech come from me now, and this it is: 'Thas been my fortune,
gentlemen, to have an extraordinary blessing pour'd upon me a'
late, and here she stands. I have wedded her and bedded her,
and yet she is little the worse. Some foolish words she hath
pass'd to you in the country, and some peevish [3] debts you owe
here in the city. Set the hare's head to the goose-giblet.[4] Release
you her of her words, and I'll release you of your debts, sir.

190 WIT. Would you so? I thank you for that, sir. I cannot blame
you, i' faith.

---

[1] Vile.   [2] Presumptuous.   [3] Trifling.   [4] Proverbial: 'Give tit for tat'.

W. HOARD. Why, are not debts better than words, sir?

WIT. Are not words promises, and are not promises debts, sir?

W. HOARD. [*Aside*] He plays at back-racket[1] with me.

1 CRED. Come hither, Master Witgood, come hither. Be rul'd by fools once.

2 CRED. We are citizens and know what belong[s] to't.

1 CRED. Take hold of his offer. Pax on her! Let her go. If your debts were once discharg'd, I would help you to a widow
200   myself worth ten of her.

3 CRED. Mass, partner, and now you remember me on't, there's Master Mulligrub's[2] sister newly fall'n a widow.

1 CRED. Cuds me, as pat as can be. There's a widow left for you; ten thousand in money, beside plate, jewels, *et cetera*. I warrant it a match. We can do all in all with her. Prithee, dispatch. We'll carry thee to her presently.

WIT. My uncle will ne'er endure me when he shall hear I set my hand to a release.

2 CRED. Hark, I'll tell thee a trick for that. I have spent five
210   hundred pound in suits in my time, I should be wise. Thou'rt now a prisoner; make a release. Take't of my word, whatsoever a man makes as long as he is in durance, 'tis nothing in law, not thus much.   [*Snaps his fingers*]

WIT. Say you so, sir?

3 CRED. I have paid for't, I know't.

WIT. Proceed then. I consent.

3 CRED. Why, well said.

W. HOARD. How now, my masters, what have you done with him?

1 CRED. With much ado, sir, we have got him to consent.
220 W. HOARD. Ah, ah, ah! And what came his debts to now?

1 CRED. Some eight score odd pound, sir.

W. HOARD. Naw, naw, naw, naw. Tell me the second time. Give me a lighter sum. They are but desperate debts, you know, ne'er call'd in but upon such an accident. A poor, needy knave, he would starve and rot in prison. Come, come, you shall have ten shillings in the pound, and the sum down roundly—

1 CRED. You must make it a mark,[3] sir.

W. HOARD. Go to, then. Tell your money in the meantime; you shall find little less there. [*Gives them money*] —Come, Master
230 Witgood, you are so unwilling to do yourself good now.

---

[1] Gives a sharp return (as in tennis). [2] An unpleasant character in Marston's *Dutch Courtesan* (1605); a mulligrub is a state of the spleen. A few copies of Q have 'Mulgrave's'. [3] A value of sixty-seven pence.

[*Enter* Scrivener]

Welcome, honest scrivener. Now you shall hear the release read.

SCRIV. 'Be it known to all men by these presents [1] that I, Theodorus Witgood, gentleman, sole nephew to Pecunious Lucre, having unjustly made title and claim to one Jane Medlar, late widow of Anthony Medlar, and now wife to Walkadine Hoard, in consideration of a competent sum of money to discharge my debts, do for ever hereafter disclaim any title, right, estate, or interest in or to the said widow, late in the occupation [2]

240 of the said Anthony Medlar and now in the occupation of Walkadine Hoard; as also neither to lay claim, by virtue of any former contract, grant, promise or demise, [3] to any of her manor[s], manor houses, parks, groves, meadow grounds, arable lands, barns, stacks, stables, dove holes, and cony burrows, together with all her cattle, [4] money, plate, jewels, borders, [5] chains, bracelets, furnitures, hangings, movables, or immovables. In witness whereof, I, the said Theodorus Witgood, have interchangeably [6] set to my hand and seal before these presents, [7] the day and date above written.'

250 WIT. What a precious fortune hast thou slipp'd here, like a beast as thou art!

W. HOARD. Come, unwilling heart, come.

WIT. Well, Master Hoard, give me the pen; I see 'Tis vain to quarrel with our destiny.

W. HOARD. Oh, as vain a thing as can be. You cannot commit a greater absurdity, sir. So, so, give me that hand now. Before all these presents, I am friends for ever with thee.

WIT. Troth, and it were pity of my heart now if I should bear you any grudge, i' faith.

260 W. HOARD. Content. I'll send for thy uncle against the wedding dinner. We will be friends once again.

WIT. I hope to bring it to pass myself, sir.

W. HOARD. How now? Is't right, [8] my masters?

1 CRED. 'Tis something wanting, sir, yet it shall be sufficient.

W. HOARD. Why, well said. A good conscience makes a fine show nowadays. Come, my masters, you shall all taste of my wine ere you depart.

ALL. We follow you, sir. [*Exeunt* W. Hoard, Scrivener, *and* Courtesan.]

---

[1] This document.   [2] Use.   [3] Conveyance.   [4] Chattels.   [5] Decorative work on the edge of a garment.   [6] Reciprocally.   [7] Witnesses. [8] Is the sum of money correct?

WIT. [*Aside*] I'll try these fellows now.—A word, sir. What, will
70   you carry me to that widow now?
1 CRED. Why, do you think we were in earnest, i' faith? Carry
     you to a rich widow? We should get much credit by that! A
     noted rioter, a contemptible prodigal! 'Twas a trick we have
     amongst us to get in our money. Fare you well, sir.
                                         Exeunt [Creditors].
WIT. Farewell and be hang'd, you short pig-hair'd, ram-headed
     rascals! He that believes in you shall ne'er be sav'd, I warrant
     him. By this new league I shall have some access unto my love.

                      She is above

NIECE. Master Witgood!
WIT. My life!
80 NIECE. Meet me presently. That note directs you. I would not be
     suspected. Our happiness attends us. Farewell.   [*Exit.*]
WIT. A word's enough.   [*Exit.*]

                    [ACT IV SCENE 5]
                   [Dampit's *bedroom*]

          Dampit *the usurer in his bed,* Audrey *spinning by*

[AUDREY.] *Song.*
     Let the usurer cram him, in interest that excel,
     There's pits enow to damn him before he comes to Hell.
     In Holborn some, in Fleet Street some,
     Where'er he come, there's some, there's some.[1]
DAMPIT. *Trahe, trahito,*[2] draw the curtain. Give me a sip of
     sack more.

              Enter Gentlemen[3] [*, who stand apart*]

LAMP. Look you, did not I tell you he lay like the devil in
     chains,[4] when he was bound for a thousand year?
SPITCH. But I think the devil had no steel bedstaffs. He goes
10   beyond him for that.

---

[1] From a lyric by Thomas Ravenscroft, in *Melismata* (1611).
[2] Imperative forms of 'draw', i.e. the curtains and a drink.
[3] Lamprey and Spitchcock.   [4] Revelation, xx, 1–3; see below, IV, v,
153. Dampit's bed was apparently hung with chains and fitted with rods,
perhaps intended to control him when he was drunk.

LAMP. Nay, do but mark the conceit [1] of his drinking. One must wipe his mouth for him with a muckinder.[2] Do you see, sir?

SPITCH. Is this the sick trampler? Why, he is only bedrid with drinking.

LAMP. True, sir. He spies us.

DAMPIT. What, Sir Tristram? You come and see a weak man here, a very weak man.

LAMP. If you be weak in body, you should be strong in prayer, sir.

20 DAMPIT. Oh, I have pray'd too much, poor man.

LAMP. [*To* Spitchcock] There's a taste of his soul for you.

SPITCH. [*To* Lamprey] Faugh! Loathsome!

LAMP. I come to borrow a hundred pound of you, sir.

DAMPIT. Alas, you come at an ill time. I cannot spare it, i' faith. I ha' but two thousand i' th' house.

AUDREY. Ha, ha, ha!

DAMPIT. Out, you gernative quean,[3] the mullipood [4] of villainy, the spinner of concupiscency!

Enter other Gentleman [5] [*and* Boy]

LANC. Yea, gentlemen, are you here before us? How is he now?

30 LAMP. Faith, the same man still. The tavern bitch has bit him i' th' head.

LANC. We shall have the better sport with him. Peace.—And how cheers Master Dampit now?

DAMPIT. Oh, my bosom Sir Lancelot, how cheer I? Thy presence is restorative.

LANC. But I hear a great complaint of you, Master Dampit, among gallants.

DAMPIT. I am glad of that, i' faith. Prithee, what?

LANC. They say you are wax'd proud a' late, and if a friend visit
40 you in the afternoon, you'll scarce know him.

DAMPIT. Fie, fie! Proud? I cannot remember any such thing. Sure, I was drunk then.

LANC. Think you so, sir?

DAMPIT. There 'twas, i' faith. Nothing but the pride of the sack, and so certify 'em. Fetch sack, sirrah.

BOY. [*Aside*] A vengeance sack you once!

AUDREY. Why, Master Dampit, if you hold on as you begin and lie a little longer, you need not take care how to dispose your wealth; you'll make the vintner your heir.

---

[1] Artifice.   [2] Handkerchief.   [3] Peevish strumpet.   [4] A coined word, perhaps combining mulligrub (a splenetic mood) and pode (a toad).
[5] Lancelot.

DAMPIT. Out, you babliaminy,[1] you unfeather'd cremitoried[2] quean, you cullisance[3] of scabiosity![4]

AUDREY. Good words, Master Dampit, to speak before a maid and a virgin!

DAMPIT. Hang thy virginity upon the pole of carnality.

AUDREY. Sweet terms! My mistress shall know 'em.

LAMP. [*Aside*] Note but the misery of this usuring slave. Here he lies, like a noisome dunghill, full of the poison of his drunken blasphemies, and they to whom he bequeaths all grudge him the very meat that feeds him, the very pillow that eases him. Here may a usurer behold his end. What profits it to be a slave in this world and a devil i' th' next?

DAMPIT. Sir Lancelot, let me buss thee, Sir Lancelot. Thou art the only friend that I honour and respect.

LANC. I thank you for that, Master Dampit.

DAMPIT. Farewell, my bosom Sir Lancelot.

LANC. [*Aside*] Gentlemen, and you love me, let me step behind you, and one of you fall a-talking of me to him.

LAMP. [*Aside*] Content.—Master Dampit.

DAMPIT. So, sir?

LAMP. Here came Sir Lancelot to see you e'en now.

DAMPIT. Hang him, rascal!

LAMP. Who, Sir Lancelot?

DAMPIT. Pythagorical[5] rascal!

LAMP. Pythagorical?

DAMPIT. Ay. He changes his cloak when he meets a sergeant.

LANC. [*Aside*] What a rogue's this!

LAMP. I wonder you can rail at him, sir; he comes in love to see you.

DAMPIT. A louse for his love! His father was a combmaker. I have no need of his crawling love. He comes to have longer day,[6] the superlative rascal.

LANC. [*Aside*] 'Sfoot, I can no longer endure the rogue.—Master Dampit, I come to take my leave once again, sir.

DAMPIT. Who? My dear and kind Sir Lancelot? The only gentleman of England. Let me hug thee. Farewell, and a thousand.[7]

LAMP. [*Aside*] Compos'd of wrongs and slavish flatteries.

LANC. [*Aside*] Nay, gentlemen, he shall show you more tricks yet. I'll give you another taste of him.

---

[1] A coined word; chatterer.   [2] A coined word; perhaps 'burned out'.
[3] Badge (from 'cognizance').   [4] A coined word, suggestive of a scabby or syphilitic condition.   [5] An allusion to the Pythagorean doctrine of the transmigration of souls; the logic of the remark is made clear immediately below.   [6] An extension of time to pay a debt.   [7] i.e. farewells.

LAMP. [*Aside*] Is't possible?

90 LANC. [*Aside*] His memory is upon departing.

DAMPIT. Another cup of sack!

LANC. [*Aside*] Mass, then 'twill be quite gone. Before he drink that, tell him there's a country client come up, and here attends for his learned advice.

LAMP. [*Aside*] Enough.

DAMPIT. One cup more, and then let the bell toll. I hope I shall be weak enough by that time.

LAMP. Master Dampit.

DAMPIT. Is the sack spouting?

100 LAMP. 'Tis coming forward, sir.

[*Enter* Boy *with sack*]

Here's a countryman, a client of yours, waits for your deep and profound advice, sir.

DAMPIT. A coxcombry?[1] Where is he? Let him approach. Set me up a peg higher.

LAMP. You must draw near, sir.

DAMPIT. Now, goodman fooliaminy, what say you to me now?

LANC. Please your good worship, I am a poor man, sir,—

DAMPIT. What make you in my chamber then?

LANC. I would entreat your worship's device[2] in a just and
110 honest cause, sir.

DAMPIT. I meddle with no such matters. I refer 'em to Master No-man's office.

LANC. I had but one house left me in all the world, sir, which was my father's, my grandfather's, my great-grandfather's, and now a villain has unjustly wrung me out and took possession on't.

DAMPIT. Has he such feats? Thy best course is to bring thy *ejectione firmae*,[3] and in seven year thou mayst shove him out by the law.

120 LANC. Alas, an't please your worship, I have small friends and less money.

DAMPIT. Hoyday! This gear[4] will fadge[5] well! Hast no money? Why, then, my advice is thou must set fire a' th' house, and so get him out.

LAMP. That will break strife indeed!

LANC. I thank your worship for your hot counsel, sir. [*Aside*] Altering but my voice a little, you see he knew me not. You may

---

[1] Foolishness.   [2] Counsel.   [3] i.e. *ejectionem firmam*, a writ of ejection.
[4] Business.   [5] Succeed.

observe by this that a drunkard's memory holds longer in the
voice than in the person. But, gentlemen, shall I show you a
30   sight? Behold the little dive-dapper [1] of damnation, Gulf the
usurer, for his time worse than tother.

Enter [W.] Hoard *with* Gulf

LAMP. What's he comes with him?

LANC. Why, Hoard, that married lately the widow Medlar.

LAMP. Oh, I cry you mercy, sir.

W. HOARD. Now, gentlemen visitants, how does Master
Dampit?

LANC. Faith, here he lies, e'en drawing in, sir, good canary as
fast as he can, sir. A very weak creature, truly. He is almost past
memory.

40   W. HOARD. Fie, Master Dampit, you lie lazing abed here, and I
come to invite you to my wedding dinner. Up, up, up!

DAMPIT. Who's this? Master Hoard? Who has thou married, in
the name of foolery?

W. HOARD. A rich widow.

DAMPIT. A Dutch widow!

W. HOARD. A rich widow, one widow Medlar.

DAMPIT. Medlar! She keeps open house. [2]

W. HOARD. She did, I can tell you, in her tother husband's days,
open house for all comers. Horse and man was welcome, and
50   room enough for 'em all.

DAMPIT. There's too much for thee then. Thou mayst let out
some to thy neighbours.

GULF. What, hung alive in chains? Oh, spectacle! Bedstaffs of
steel? *O monstrum horrendum, informe, ingens cui lumen
ademptum!* [3] O Dampit, Dampit, here's a just judgment shown
upon usury, extortion, and trampling villainy.

LANC. [*Aside*] This [is] ex'llent, thief rails upon the thief!

GULF. Is this the end of cut-throat usury, brothel, and blasphemy? Now mayst thou see what race a usurer runs.

60   DAMPIT. Why, thou rogue of universality, do not I know thee?
Thy sound is like the cuckoo, the Welsh ambassador. [4] Thou
cowardly slave, that offers to fight with a sick man when his
weapon's down! Rail upon me in my naked bed? [5] Why, thou

---

[1] Didapper or dabchick, a small diving waterfowl.   [2] See note at II, i, 35,
for the innuendo.   [3] 'O horrible monster, misshapen, huge, from whom
sight is taken away!' (Virgil, *Aeneid*, III, 658). The allusion is to the blinded
Polyphemus.   [4] A sarcastic allusion to the cuckoo as the messenger of
love, in contemporary Welsh and English poetry.   [5] i.e. naked (unarmed)
in my bed.

great Lucifer's little vicar, I am not so weak but I know a knave
at first sight. Thou inconscionable rascal, thou that goest upon
Middlesex juries and will make haste to give up thy verdict
because thou wilt not lose thy dinner, are you answered?

GULF. An't were not for shame— *Draws his dagger*

DAMPIT. Thou wouldst be hang'd then.

170 LAMP. Nay, you must exercise patience, Master Gulf, always in
a sick man's chamber.

LANC. [*To* Dampit] He'll quarrel with none, I warrant you, but
those that are bedrid.

DAMPIT. Let him come, gentlemen, I am arm'd. Reach my close-
stool [1] hither.

LANC. Here will be a sweet fray anon. I'll leave you, gentlemen.

LAMP. Nay, we'll along with you. Master Gulf.

GULF. Hang him, usuring rascal.

LANC. Push! Set your strength to his, your wit to his.

180 AUDREY. Pray, gentlemen, depart, His hour's come upon him.—
Sleep in my bosom, sleep.

LANC. Nay, we have enough of him, i' faith. Keep him for the
house.
Now make your best;
For thrice his wealth, I would not have his breast.

GULF. A little thing would make me beat him, now he's asleep.

LANC. Mass, then 'twill be a pitiful day when he wakes. I would
be loath to see that day.

GULF. You overrule me, gentlemen, i' faith. *Exeunt.*

ACT V [SCENE 1]

[Lucre's *house*]

Enter Lucre *and* Witgood

WIT. Nay, uncle, let me prevail with you so much.
I' faith, go, now he has invited you.

LUCRE. I shall have great joy there when he has borne away the
widow!

WIT. Why, la, I thought where I should find you presently.
Uncle, a' my troth, 'tis nothing so.

LUCRE. What's nothing so, sir? Is not he married to the widow?

---

[1] Cabinet containing a chamber-pot.

wit. No, by my troth, is he not, uncle.

lucre. How!

10 wit. Will you have the truth on't? He is married to a whore, i'
faith.

lucre. I should laugh at that.

wit. Uncle, let me perish in your favour if you find it not so, and
that 'tis I that have married the honest woman.

lucre. Ha! I'd walk ten mile afoot to see that,[1] i' faith.

wit. And see't you shall, or I'll ne'er see you again.

lucre. A quean, i' faith? Ha, ha, ha!

Exeunt.

[ACT V SCENE 2]

[W. Hoard's *house*]

Enter [W.] Hoard, *tasting wine, the* Host *following in a livery
cloak*

w. hoard. Pup, pup, pup, pup. I like not this wine. Is there
never a better tierce[2] in the house?

host. Yes, sir, there are as good tierce in the house as any are
in England.

w. hoard. Desire your mistress, you knave, to taste 'em all
over; she has better skill.

host. Has she so? [*Aside*] The better for her and the worse for
you.   *Exit.*

[*Enter* Servant]

w. hoard. Arthur, is the cupboard of plate set out?

10 arthur. All's in order, sir.   [*Exit.*]

w. hoard. I am in love with my liveries every time I think on
'em. They make a gallant show, by my troth.—Niece!

[*Enter* Niece]

niece. Do you call, sir?

w. hoard. Prithee, show a little diligence and overlook the
knaves a little. They'll filch and steal today, and send whole
pasties[3] home to their wives. And thou be'st a good niece, do
not see me purloin'd.

---

[1] i.e. W. Hoard's discomfiture.   [2] A cask of wine.   [3] Pies.

NIECE. Fear it not, sir, I have cause. [*Aside*] Though the feast be prepared for you, yet it serves fit for my wedding dinner too.
[*Exit.*]

Enter two Gentlemen

20 W. HOARD. Master Lamprey, and Master Spitchcock too! The most welcome gentlemen alive! Your fathers and mine were all free o' th' fishmongers.[1]

LAMP. They were indeed, sir. You see bold guests, sir, soon entreated.

W. HOARD. And that's best, sir.

[*Enter* Servant]

How now, sirrah?

SERV. There's a coach come to th' door, sir.   [*Exit.*]

W. HOARD. My Lady Foxstone, a' my life!—Mistress Jane Hoard! Wife!—Mass, 'tis her ladyship indeed.

[*Enter* Lady Foxstone]

30 Madam, you are welcome to an unfurnish'd house, dearth of cheer, scarcity of attendance.

LADY. You are pleas'd to make the worst, sir.

W. HOARD. Wife!

[*Enter* Courtesan]

LADY. Is this your bride?

W. HOARD. Yes, madam.—Salute my Lady Foxstone.

COURT. Please you, madam, a while to taste the air in the garden?

LADY. 'Twill please us well.

Exeunt [Lady Foxstone *and* Courtesan].

W. HOARD. Who would not wed? The most delicious life!
40 No joys are like the comforts of a wife.

LAMP. So we bachelors think, that are not troubled with them.

Enter Servant

SERV. Your worship's brother, with another ancient gentleman, are newly alighted, sir.   [*Exit.*]

W. HOARD. Master Onesiphorus Hoard! Why, now our company begins to come in.

[*Enter* Onesiphorus Hoard, Limber, *and* Kix]

My dear and kind brother, welcome, i' faith.

---

[1] i.e. freemen of the Fishmongers' Company. The surnames of Walkadine Hoard's friends give point to the joke.

o. HOARD. You see we are men at an hour, brother.

w. HOARD. Ay, I'll say that for you, brother; you keep as good
an hour to come to a feast as any gentleman in the shire.—What,
old Master Limber and Master Kix! Do we meet, i' faith, jolly
gentlemen?

LIMBER. We hope you lack guests, sir.

w. HOARD. Oh, welcome, welcome! We lack still such guests as
your worships.

o. HOARD. Ah, sirrah brother, have you catch'd up widow
Medlar?

w. HOARD. From 'em all, brother, and, I may tell you, I had
mighty enemies, those that stuck sore. Old Lucre is a sore fox,
I can tell you, brother.

o. HOARD. Where is she? I'll go seek her out. I long to have a
smack at her lips.

w. HOARD. And most wishfully, brother. See where she comes.

[*Enter* Courtesan]

Give her a smack now we may hear it all the house over.

COURT. O Heaven, I am betray'd! I know that face.[1]

Both turn back

w. HOARD. Ha, ha, ha! Why, how now? Are you both asham'd?
Come, gentlemen, we'll look another way.

o. HOARD. Nay, brother, hark you. Come, y'are dispos'd to be
merry.

w. HOARD. Why do we meet else, man?

o. HOARD. That's another matter. I was ne'er so 'fraid in my
life but that you had been in earnest.

w. HOARD. How mean you, brother?

o. HOARD. You said she was your wife.

w. HOARD. Did I so? By my troth, and so she is.

o. HOARD. By your troth, brother?

w. HOARD. What reason have I to dissemble with my friends,
brother? If marriage can make her mine, she is mine. Why?

o. HOARD. Troth, I am not well of a sudden. I must crave pardon, brother. I came to see you, but I cannot stay dinner, i'
faith.

w. HOARD. I hope you will not serve me so, brother.

LIMBER. By your leave, Master Hoard.

w. HOARD. What now? What now? Pray, gentlemen, you were
wont to show yourselves wise men.

---

[1] Onesiphorus Hoard and his friends saw the Courtesan in Leicestershire
(I, i).

LIMBER. But you have shown your folly too much here.

W. HOARD. How!

KIX. Fie, fie! A man of your repute and name!
You'll feast your friends, but cloy 'em first with shame.

W. HOARD. This grows too deep. Pray, let us reach the sense.

90 LIMBER. In your old age dote on a courtesan!

W. HOARD. Ha!

KIX. Marry a strumpet!

W. HOARD. Gentlemen!

O. HOARD. And Witgood's quean!

W. HOARD. Oh! Nor lands nor living?

O. HOARD. Living?

W. HOARD. [*To* Courtesan] Speak!

COURT.   Alas, you know at first, sir.
I told you I had nothing.[1]

W. HOARD. Out, out! I am cheated, infinitely cozen'd!

100 LIMBER. Nay, Master Hoard.

W. HOARD. A Dutch widow, a Dutch widow, a Dutch widow!

Enter Witgood *and* Lucre

LUCRE. Why, nephew, shall I trace thee still a liar?
Wilt make me mad? Is not yon thing the widow?

WIT. Why, la, you are so hard a' belief, uncle.
By my troth, she's a whore.

LUCRE.   Then thou'rt a knave.

WIT. *Negatur argumentum,*[2] uncle.

LUCRE. *Probo tibi,*[3] nephew. He that knows a woman to be a
quean must needs be a knave. Thou say'st thou know'st her to
be one. *Ergo*, if she be a quean, thou'rt a knave.

110 WIT. *Negatur sequela majoris,*[4] uncle. He that knows a woman to
be a quean must needs be a knave, I deny that.

W. HOARD. Lucre and Witgood, y'are both villains! Get you out
of my house!

LUCRE. Why, didst not invite me to thy wedding dinner?

WIT. And are not you and I sworn perpetual friends, before
witness, sir, and were both drunk upon't?

W. HOARD. Daintily abused! Y'ave put a junt[5] upon me.

LUCRE. Ha, ha, ha!

W. HOARD. A common strumpet!

120 WIT. Nay, now
You wrong her, sir. If I were she, I'd have

---

[1] See III, ii, 94.   [2] The argument is denied.   [3] I am proving it to you.
[4] Freely, 'The conclusion doesn't follow'.   [5] Trick.

The law on you for that. I durst depose for her
She ne'er had common use nor common thought.
COURT. Despise me, publish me, I am your wife.
What shame can I have now but you'll have part?
If in disgrace you share, I sought not you.
You pursued me, nay, forc'd me.
Had I friends would follow it,
Less than your action has been prov'd a rape.
O. HOARD. Brother,—
COURT. Nor did I ever boast of lands unto you,
Money, or goods. I took a plainer course,
And told you true I'd nothing.
If error were committed, 'twas by you,
Thank your own folly. Nor has my sin been
So odious but worse has been forgiven.
Nor am I so deform'd but I may challenge
The utmost power of any old man's love.
She that tastes not sin before,[1] twenty to one but she'll taste it
after. Most of you old men are content to marry young virgins
and take that which follows; where, marrying one of us, you
both save a sinner and are quit from a cuckold for ever.
And more, in brief, let this your best thoughts win,
She that knows sin, knows best how to hate sin.
W. HOARD. Curs'd be all malice! Black are the fruits of spite
And poison first their owners. Oh, my friends,
I must embrace shame to be rid of shame.
Conceal'd disgrace prevents a public name.
Ah, Witgood, ah, Theodorus,—
WIT. Alas, sir, I was prick'd in conscience to see her well be-
stow'd, and where could I bestow her better than upon your
pitiful worship? Excepting but myself, I dare swear she's a
virgin; and now by marrying your niece I have banish'd myself
for ever from her. She's mine aunt now, by my faith, and there's
no meddling with mine aunt, you know, a sin against my nuncle.
COURT. Lo, gentlemen, before you all
In true reclaimed form I fall.   [Kneels]
Henceforth for ever I defy[2]
The glances of a sinful eye,
Waving of fans, which some suppose
Tricks of fancy,[3] treading of toes,
Wringing of fingers, biting the lip,

[1] i.e. before marriage.   [2] Renounce.   [3] Love.

The wanton gait, th'alluring trip,
All secret friends and private meetings,
Close-borne letters and bawds' greetings,
Feigning excuse to women's labours
When we are sent for to th' next neighbours,
Taking false physic and ne'er start
To be let blood, though sign be at heart,[1]
170 Removing chambers, shifting beds,
To welcome friends in husbands' steads,
Them to enjoy and you to marry,
They first serv'd while you must tarry,
They to spend and you to gather,
They to get and you to father.
These and thousand thousand more,
New reclaim'd, I now abhor.
LUCRE. Ah, here's a lesson, rioter, for you!
WIT. I must confess my follies. I'll down too,
180 And here for ever I disclaim
The cause of youth's undoing: Game,
Chiefly dice, those true outlanders[2]
That shake out beggars, thieves, and panders;
Soul-wasting surfeits, sinful riots,
Queans' evils,[3] doctors' diets,
'Pothecaries' drugs, surgeons' glisters,[4]
Stabbing of arms[5] for a common mistress,
Riband[6] favours, ribald speeches,
Dear perfum'd jackets, penniless breeches,
190 Dutch flapdragons,[7] healths in urine,
Drabs that keep a man too sure in,
I do defy you all.
Lend me each honest hand, for here I rise
A reclaim'd man, loathing the general vice.
W. HOARD. So, so, all friends. The wedding dinner cools.
Who seem most crafty prove oftimes most fools.   [*Exeunt.*]

FINIS

---

[1] When the astrological signs were inauspicious.   [2] Aliens.
[3] i.e. the evils which are associated with queans or strumpets, syphilis; also a punning allusion to 'King's evil', scrofula.   [4] Enemas.   [5] Blood or urine was sometimes mixed with wine to drink the healths of mistresses.
[6] Ribboned.   [7] Raisins immersed in burning brandy.

THE WITCH OF EDMONTON

WILLIAM ROWLEY
(*c.* 1585–1626)

A character actor with various companies for many years. Collaborated with several other dramatists; with Middleton he wrote *A Fair Quarrel*, *The Spanish Gipsy*, etc. Wrote independently several undistinguished plays, including *All's Lost by Lust* and *A Shoemaker a Gentleman*.

THOMAS DEKKER
(*c.* 1572–1632)

Born in London; associated with producer Philip Henslowe; wrote plays, including *Old Fortunatus*, *The Shoemakers' Holiday*, *The Honest Whore* (two parts); collaborated in *Satiromastix*, *The Roaring Girl*, *The Witch of Edmonton*, etc.; pageants; prose pamphlets, *The Wonderful Year*, *The Gull's Hornbook*, etc.; involved in the War of the Theatres, 1599–1601; imprisoned for debt, 1613–19.

JOHN FORD
(baptized 17th April 1586–*c.* 1639)

Born at Ilsington in Devon. Middle Temple. Few early plays survive, most of them apparently written in collaboration. Best independent plays are tragedies, written *c.* 1624–*c.* 1634, *'Tis Pity She's a Whore*, *The Broken Heart*, and *The Chronicle History of Perkin Warbeck*.

THE WITCH OF EDMONTON (1621)

A lively interest in witchcraft had pervaded England for fifty years or more before the trial and execution of Elizabeth Sawyer in April 1621—in popular mythology, books like King James's *Daemonology* (1597), pamphlets, ballads, and other plays. A moralistic essay by Henry Goodcole, *The Wonderfull Discoverie of Elizabeth Sawyer a Witch, late of Edmonton* .... followed immediately, providing a major theme and several episodes for this play, performed before the end of the year. The quarto edition was not, however, published until 1658.

The wish of the three authors named on the title-page to capitalize quickly on a local *cause célèbre* probably accounts for small lapses in detail and a failure to integrate the two plots closely.[1] The individual contributions of the playwrights can be identified in general terms, but it is occasionally evident that more than one collaborator shared in the scenes in which the plots cross one another. The gentle, tolerant tone that Thomas Dekker reveals in plays like *The Shoemakers' Holiday* and *The Honest Whore* suggests his responsibility for the Mother Sawyer plot and the 'yeoman' scenes involving the Carter family. *The Witch of Edmonton* was probably the first play to which John Ford contributed, but distinctive verse and characterization identify him as the principal force behind the Thorney story, with some softening touches of Dekker. The lively and unsubtle humour of the somewhat irrelevant Cuddy Banks episodes is the mark of William Rowley, who may have acted the role.

Although Thomas Dekker was the primary author of the Mother Sawyer story, he may not have explicitly believed in witchcraft; through an unusually intelligent justice of the peace, he both echoed and ridiculed popular beliefs in the subject, creating a remarkably sympathetic picture of the deformed and irascible old woman who had witchcraft thrust upon her.

> Some call me witch,
> And being ignorant of myself, they go
> About to teach me how to be one. (II, i, 8–10)

---

[1] In Act V Winnifride's pregnancy, alluded to repeatedly in Act I, has been forgotten, although in the concluding scene there are many opportunities for reference to Frank's child providing future consolation to Winnifride and Old Thorney.

She was the almost inevitable focus for the *post hoc propter hoc* logic of the superstitious villagers, who were unable to understand why pigs suddenly died or people became apparently insane. For example, reading between the lines of Goodcole's account suggests that mad Anne Ratcliffe may have been an epileptic, not bewitched.

Twentieth-century readers or viewers of *The Witch of Edmonton* may sympathize deeply with Mother Sawyer, as a representative of all sufferers of irrational persecution; Frank Thorney's universal shortcomings may also provoke twinges of conscience. He offered a series of virtuous vows, made many attempts at self-justification, and avoided accepting responsibility for his actions as long as possible. Like Giovanni in Ford's *'Tis Pity She's a Whore*, he could argue speciously that his destiny drove him.

Frank's marital involvements incorporate several ironies. The furtiveness of his marriage to Winnifride was prompted by his anxiety to assure himself of his father's estate, an inheritance which he belatedly learned was largely mythical. Winnifride created a related irony; she repulsed her melodramatic seducer, Sir Arthur, because she believed Frank's vow of faithfulness.

The relationships of the principal characters with the devil's mephistophelean agent, the black dog, illustrate how the play combines a repressive morality with a degree of tolerance which looks forward, however tentatively, to the twentieth century.

Mother Sawyer's commitment to the black dog was prompted by a very negative force: revenge on the community which had unjustly condemned her. Like a minor Faustus, she solemnized the perverse bargain with a blood oath. In the end she had to pay unrepentantly the ultimate price both for her temerity in conniving with the devil and for her violation of the Christian code of turning the other cheek. (When the dog appeared in white form he represented the repudiation of his black role in her life and a triumph over her.) Despite all this, there is a sympathy for her.

Significantly, the black dog never materialized to Frank Thorney. In Act III, in invisible form, the dog crystallized an impulse already in Frank's subconscious: to rid himself of his encumbering second wife. Later, in the bedchamber, the dog, still invisible, seemed to be teasing Frank, taking pleasure in the revelation of his crime. Thus, distinct from the Mother Sawyer situation, the dog was to Frank no more than an accessory after the fact. Frank was the master of his fate, and sincerely repented his foolhardiness, leaving one convinced that his soul was safe.

Cuddy Banks's association with the dog was on yet a third level, that of fun, typical of Rowley. Cuddy was an innocent, with nothing malicious in his simple mind. He sought the dog's aid only to help him woo Katherine (whose conquest by Cuddy was rather unlikely). Cuddy's pursuit of the supernatural brought him to no greater harm than a ducking.

There is then much variety of tone in *The Witch of Edmonton*, and although both plots have a predictable, moralizing conclusion, the final effect is unsentimental. The play has still a considerable tragic impact, through the timeless persecution of Mother Sawyer, the lesson in the naïve, self-indulgent career of Frank Thorney, and the sad fate of Susan Carter. *The Witch of Edmonton* has been produced twice in London in modern times, at the Old Vic in 1936 and the Mermaid in 1962.

THE WITCH OF EDMONTON

by William Rowley, Thomas Dekker, and John Ford
[1621]

Actors' Names

Sir Arthur Clarington
Old Thorney, *a gentleman*
Old Carter, *a rich yeoman*
Old Banks, *a countryman*
W. Mago,[1]
W. Hamluc,[1] } *two countrymen*
Three other countrymen
Warbeck,
Somerton, } *suitors to Carter's daughters*
Frank, *Thorney's son*
Young Cuddy Banks, *the clown*
Four morris dancers
Old Ratcliffe
Sawgut, *an old fiddler*
Poldavis,[1] *a barber's boy*
Justice
Constable, officers, serving-men
Dog, *a familiar* [2]
A spirit

Women

Mother Sawyer, *the witch*
Anne, *Ratcliffe's wife*
Susan,
Katherine, } *Carter's daughters*
Winnifride, *Sir Arthur's maid*
[Jane, *a servant in Carter's house*]

[The scene: in and near Edmonton; London]

---

[1] Perhaps an accidental survival of the names of three minor actors who performed in a revival of the play *c.* 1635. Only William Mago is known as an actor.　　[2] A spirit, usually invisible, which served a human being for diabolical purposes, capable of taking varying forms. See below, II, i, 99 ff.

The whole argument is this distich:

Forc'd marriage, murder; murder, blood requires;
Reproach, revenge; revenge, Hell's help desires.

Prologue

The town of Edmonton hath lent the stage
A devil [1] and a witch, both in an age.
To make comparisons it were uncivil
Between so even a pair, a witch and devil;
But as the year doth with his plenty bring
As well a latter as a former spring,
So has this witch enjoy'd the first, and reason
Presumes she may partake the other season.
In acts deserving name the proverb says,
'Once good, and ever.' Why not so in plays?
Why not in this, since, gentlemen, we flatter
No expectation? Here is mirth and matter.
                                    Mr Bird. [2]

[1] An allusion to *The Merry Devil of Edmonton* (produced *c.* 1600), a very
popular anonymous romantic comedy with few parallels to this play.
[2] Theophilus Bird (d. 1663), probably the speaker of these lines and a
performer in the play; he acted with Queen Henrietta's company and the
King's men *c.* 1625–*c.* 1642.

ACT I SCENE 1

[Sir Arthur's *house*]

Enter Frank Thorney, [*and*] Winnifride (*with child*)[1]

FRANK. Come, wench; why, here's a business soon dispatch'd.
　Thy heart I know is now at ease; thou need'st not
　Fear what the tattling gossips in their cups
　Can speak against thy fame; thy child shall know
　Who to call dad now.

WIN. 　　　　　　　You have discharg'd
　The true part of an honest man. I cannot
　Request a fuller satisfaction
　Than you have freely granted; yet methinks
　'Tis an hard case, being lawful man and wife,
　We should not live together.

FRANK. 　　　　　　　　Had I fail'd
　In promise of my truth to thee, we must
　Have then been ever sund'red; now the longest
　Of our forbearing either's company
　Is only but to gain a little time
　For our continuing thrift, that so hereafter
　The heir that shall be born may not have cause
　To curse his hour of birth, which made him feel
　The misery of beggary and want,
　Two devils that are occasions to enforce
　A shameful end. My plots aim but to keep
　My father's love.

WIN. 　　　　　And that will be as difficult
　To be preserv'd, when he shall understand
　How you are married, as it will be now,
　Should you confess it to him.

FRANK. 　　　　　　　　　Fathers are
　Won by degrees, not bluntly, as our masters
　Or wronged friends are; and besides, I'll use
　Such dutiful and ready means that ere
　He can have notice of what's past, th'inheritance
　To which I am born heir shall be assur'd.
　That done, why, let him know it; if he like it not,

[1] Pregnant.

81

Yet he shall have no power in him left
To cross the thriving of it.

WIN.   You who had
The conquest of my maiden love may easily
Conquer the fears of my distrust. And whither
Must I be hurried?

FRANK.   Prithee do not use
A word so much unsuitable to the constant
Affections of thy husband. Thou shalt live
Near Waltham Abbey [1] with thy uncle Selman.
I have acquainted him with all at large.[2]
40 He'll use thee kindly; thou shalt want no pleasures,
Nor any other fit supplies whatever,
Thou canst in heart desire.

WIN.   All these are nothing
Without your company.

FRANK.   Which thou shalt have
Once every month at least.

WIN.   Once every month!
Is this to have an husband?

FRANK.   Perhaps oft'ner;
That's as occasion serves.

WIN.   Ay, ay; in case
No other beauty tempt your eye, whom you
Like better, I may chance to be rememb'red,
And see you now and then. Faith, I did hope
50 You'ld not have us'd me so; 'tis but my fortune.
And yet, if not for my sake, have some pity
Upon the child I go with, that's your own,
And, 'less you'll be a cruel-hearted father,
You cannot but remember that.
Heaven knows how—

FRANK.   To quit which fear at once,
As by the ceremony late perform'd,
I plighted thee a faith as free from challenge
As any double thought. Once more, in hearing
Of Heaven and thee, I vow that never henceforth
60 Disgrace, reproof, lawless affections, threats,
Or what can be suggested 'gainst our marriage
Shall cause me falsify that bridal oath
That binds me thine. And, Winnifride, whenever

---

[1] A town five miles north-east of Edmonton.   [2] Fully.

The wanton heat of youth, by subtle baits
Of beauty or what woman's art can practise,
Draw[s] me from only loving thee, let Heaven
Inflict upon my life some fearful ruin.
I hope thou dost believe me.

WIN.   Swear no more.
I am confirm'd, and will resolve to do
What you think most behoveful for us.

FRANK.   Thus then:
Make thyself ready; at the furthest house
Upon the green, without the town, your uncle
Expects you. For a little time, farewell.

WIN.   Sweet,
We shall meet again as soon as thou canst possibly?

FRANK. We shall. One kiss. Away!   [*Exit* Winnifride.]

                Enter Sir Arthur Clarington

SIR ART.   Frank Thorney.

FRANK.   Here, sir.

SIR ART. Alone? Then must I tell thee in plain terms
Thou hast wrong'd thy master's house basely and lewdly.

FRANK. Your house, sir?

SIR ART.   Yes sir. If the nimble devil
That wanton'd in your blood rebell'd against
All rules of honest duty, you might, sir,
Have found out some more fitting place than here
To have built a stews [1] in. All the country whispers
How shamefully thou hast undone a maid,
Approv'd for modest life, for civil carriage,
Till thy prevailing perjuries entic'd her
To forfeit shame. Will you be honest yet,
Make her amends and marry her?

FRANK.   So, sir,
I might bring both myself and her to beggary,
And that would be shame worse than the other.

SIR ART. You should have thought on this before, and then
Your reason would have oversway'd the passion
Of your unruly lust. But that you may
Be left without excuse, to salve the infamy
Of my disgraced house, and 'cause you are
A gentleman, and both of you my servants,
I'll make the maid a portion.

---

[1] Brothel.

FRANK.   So you promis'd me
Before, in case I married her. I know
Sir Arthur Clarington deserves the credit
Report hath lent him, and presume you are
100 A debtor to your promise; but upon
What certainty shall I resolve? [1] Excuse me
For being somewhat rude.
SIR ART.   'Tis but reason.
Well, Frank, what think'st thou of two hundred pounds
And a continual friend?
FRANK.   Though my poor fortunes
Might happily prefer me to a choice
Of a far greater portion, yet to right
A wronged maid and to preserve your favour,
I am content to accept your proffer.
SIR ART.   Art thou?
FRANK. Sir, we shall every day have need to employ
The use of what you please to give.
110 SIR ART.   Thou shalt have't.
FRANK. Then I claim your promise. We are man and wife.
SIR ART. Already?
FRANK.   And more than so. I have promis'd her
Free entertainment in her uncle's house
Near Waltham Abbey, where she may securely
Sojourn, till time and my endeavours work
My father's love and liking.
SIR ART.   Honest Frank!
FRANK. I hope, sir, you will think I cannot keep her
Without a daily charge.
SIR ART.   As for the money,
'Tis all thine own; and though I cannot make thee
120 A present payment, yet thou shalt be sure
I will not fail thee.
FRANK.   But our occasions—
SIR ART.   Nay, nay,
Talk not of your occasions. Trust my bounty;
It shall not sleep. Hast married her, i' faith, Frank?
'Tis well, 'tis passing well. [*Aside*] Then, Winnifride,
Once more thou art an honest woman.—Frank,
Thou hast a jewel. Love her; she'll deserve [2] it.
And when to Waltham?

---

[1] Assure myself.   [2] Requite.

FRANK.   She is making ready;
  Her uncle stays for her.
SIR ART.   Most provident speed.
  Frank, I will be [thy] friend, and such a friend.
  Thou'lt bring her thither?
FRANK.   Sir, I cannot. Newly
  My father sent me word I should come to him.
SIR ART. Marry, and do. I know thou hast a wit
  To handle him.
FRANK.   I have a suit t'ye.
SIR ART.   What is't?
  Anything, Frank; command it.
FRANK.   That you'll please,
  By letters, to assure my father that
  I am not married.
SIR ART.   How!
FRANK.   Someone or other
  Hath certainly inform'd him that I purpos'd
  To marry Winnifride; on which he threat'ned
  To disinherit me. To prevent it,
  Lowly I crave your letters, which he seeing
  Will credit; and I hope ere I return,
  On such conditions as I'll frame, his lands
  Shall be assur'd.
SIR ART.   But what is that to quit[1]
  My knowledge of the marriage?
FRANK.   Why, you were not
  A witness to it.
SIR ART.   I conceive; and then,
  His land confirmed, thou wilt acquaint him throughly[2]
  With all that's past.
FRANK.   I mean no less.
SIR ART.   Provided
  I never was made privy to it.
FRANK.   Alas, sir,
  Am I a talker?
SIR ART.   Draw thyself the letter;
  I'll put my hand to it. I commend thy policy.
  Th'art witty, witty, Frank. Nay, nay, 'tis fit;
  Dispatch it.
FRANK.   I shall write effectually.   *Exit.*

---

[1] Relinquish.   [2] Fully.

SIR ART. Go thy way, cuckoo. Have I caught the young man?
  One trouble then is freed. He that will feast
  At others' cost must be a bold-fac'd guest.
            Enter Winnifride, *in a riding suit*
WIN. I have heard the news. All now is safe;
  The worst is past.
SIR ART.   Thy lip, wench. I must bid
  Farewell, for fashion's sake; but I will visit thee
  Suddenly, girl. This was cleanly carried;
  Ha, was 't not, Win?
160 WIN.   Then were my happiness
  That I in my heart repent I did not bring him
  The dower of a virginity. Sir, forgive me,
  I have been much to blame. Had not my lewdness [1]
  Given way to your immoderate waste of virtue,
  You had not with such eagerness pursu'd
  The error of your goodness.
SIR ART.   Dear, dear Win,
  I hug this art of thine; it shows how cleanly
  Thou canst beguile in case occasion serve
  To practise; it becomes thee. Now we share
170 Free scope enough, without control or fear,
  To interchange our pleasures; we will surfeit
  In our embraces, wench. Come, tell me, when
  Wilt thou appoint a meeting?
WIN.   What to do?
SIR ART. Good, good! To con the lesson of our loves,
  Our secret game.
WIN.   Oh, blush to speak it further!
  As y'are a noble gentleman, forget
  A sin so monstrous; 'tis not gently done
  To open a cur'd wound. I know you speak
  For trial; troth, you need not.
SIR ART.   I for trial?
  Not I, by this good sunshine!
180 WIN.   Can you name
  That syllable of good, and yet not tremble
  To think to what a foul and black intent
  You use it for an oath? Let me resolve you:
  If you appear in any visitation
  That brings not with it pity for the wrongs

---

[1] Supplied by Dyce; Q has 'laundress'.

Done to abused Thorney, my kind husband;
If you infect mine ear with any breath
That is not throughly perfum'd with sighs
For former deeds of lust, may I be curs'd
90 Even in my prayers, when I vouchsafe
To see or hear you! I will change my life,
From a loose whore to a repentant wife.

SIR ART. Wilt thou turn monster now? Art not asham'd
After so many months to be honest at last?
Away, away! Fie on't!

WIN.   My resolution
Is built upon a rock. This very day
Young Thorney vow'd, with oaths not to be doubted,
That never any change of love should cancel
The bonds in which we are to either bound
100 Of lasting truth. And shall I then for my part
Unfile [1] the sacred oath set on record
In Heaven's book? Sir Arthur, do not study
To add to your lascivious lust the sin
Of sacrilege, for if you but endeavour
By any unchaste word to tempt my constancy,
You strive as much as in you lies to ruin
A temple hallowed to the purity
Of holy marriage. I have said enough;
You may believe me.

SIR ART.   Get you to your nunnery;
110 There freeze in your old cloister. This is fine!

WIN. Good angels guide me. Sir, you'll give me leave
To weep and pray for your conversion?

SIR ART.   Yes!
Away to Waltham. Pox on your honesty.
Had you no other trick to fool me? Well,
You may want money yet.

WIN.   None that I'll send for
To you, for hire of a damnation.
When I am gone, think on my just complaint.
I was your devil; oh, be you my saint!   *Exit* Winnifride.

SIR ART. Go, go thy ways, as changeable a baggage
120 As ever cozen'd knight! I'm glad I'm rid of her.
Honest? Marry, hang her! Thorney is my debtor;
I thought to have paid him too, but fools have fortune.
                                            Exit Sir Arthur.

---

[1] Delete.

[ACT I] SCENE 2

[Carter's *house*]

Enter Old Thorney *and* Old Carter

THOR. You offer, Mr[1] Carter, like a gentleman; I cannot find
fault with it, 'tis so fair.

CAR. No gentleman I, Mr Thorney. Spare the mastership; call
me by my name, John Carter. 'Master' is a title my father nor
his before him were acquainted with, honest Hertfordshire
yeomen. Such an one am I; my word and my deed shall be
proved one at all times. I mean to give you no security for the
marriage money.

THOR. How, no security? Although it need not so long as you
10 live, yet who is he has surety of his life one hour? Men, the
proverb says, are mortal; else, for my part I distrust you not,
were the sum double.

CAR. Double, treble, more or less, I tell you, Mr Thorney, I'll
give no security. Bonds and bills are but terriers to catch fools
and keep lazy knaves busy; my security shall be present payment. And we here about Edmonton hold present payment as
sure as an alderman's bond in London, Mr Thorney.

THOR. I cry you mercy, sir, I understood you not.

CAR. I like young Frank well; so does my Susan too. The girl has
20 a fancy to him, which makes me ready in my purse. There be
other suitors within, that make much noise to little purpose.
If Frank love Sue, Sue shall have none but Frank. 'Tis a
mannerly girl, Mr Thorney, though but an homely man's
daughter. There have worse faces look'd out of black bags, man.

THOR. You speak your mind freely and honestly. I marvel my
son comes not; I am sure he will be here some time today.

CAR. Today or tomorrow, when he comes he shall be welcome to
bread, beer, and beef—yeoman's fare. We have no kickshaws;
full dishes, whole bellyfuls. Should I diet three days at one of
30 the slender city suppers, you might send me to Barber-Surgeons' Hall the fourth day, to hang up for an anatomy![2] Here
come they that—

Enter Warbeck *with* Susan, Somerton *with* Katherine.

How now, girls? Every day play-day with you? Valentine's Day
too, all by couples? Thus will young folks do when we are laid

---

[1] Then pronounced 'master'.   [2] Skeleton. An oblique allusion to the
long tradition of annual lectures in dissection given at Barber-Surgeons'
Hall, Monkwell St., using cadavers and skeletons.

in our graves, Mr Thorney; here's all the care they take.
And how do you find the wenches, gentlemen? Have they any
mind to a loose gown [1] and a strait [2] shoe? Win 'em and wear
'em. They shall choose for themselves by my consent.

WAR. You speak like a kind father. [*The lovers move apart, as
two couples*] Sue, thou hearest the liberty that's granted thee.
What sayest thou? Wilt thou be mine?

SUSAN. Your what, sir? I dare swear
Never your wife.

WAR.   Canst thou be so unkind,
Considering how dearly I affect [3] thee,
Nay, dote on thy perfections?

SUSAN.   You are studied,
Too scholarlike in words. I understand not;
I am too coarse for such a gallant's love
As you are.

WAR.   By the honour of gentility,—

SUSAN. Good sir, no swearing. 'Yea' and 'nay' with us
Prevails above all oaths you can invent.

WAR. By this white hand of thine,—

SUSAN.   Take a false oath?
Fie, fie! Flatter the wise; fools not regard it,
And one of these am I.

WAR.   Dost thou despise me?

CAR. Let 'em talk on, Mr Thorney; I know Sue's mind. The fly
may buzz about the candle; he shall but singe his wings when
all's done. Frank, Frank is he has her heart.

SOM. But shall I live in hope, Kate?

KATH. Better so than be a desperate man.

SOM. Perhaps thou think'st it is thy portion
I level at. Wert thou as poor in fortunes
As thou art rich in goodness, I would rather
Be suitor for the dower of thy virtues
Than twice thy father's whole estate, and prithee
Be thou resolved so.

KATH.   Mr Somerton,
It is an easy labour to deceive
A maid that will believe men's subtle promises;
Yet I conceive of you as worthily
As I presume you do deserve.

---

[1] i.e., stylish. By about 1620 the loose gown, falling freely from a gathering
at the throat and worn with bodice and under-skirt, had largely supplanted
the farthingale.   [2] Tight.   [3] Love.

SOM.   Which is
As worthily in loving thee sincerely
70   As thou art worthy to be so belov'd.
KATH. I shall find time to try you.
SOM.   Do, Kate, do;
And when I fail, may all my joys forsake me.
CAR. Warbeck and Sue are at it still. I laugh to myself, Mr
Thorney, to see how earnestly he beats the bush, while the bird
is flown into another's bosom. A very [1] unthrift, Mr Thorney,
one of the country roaring lads. We have such as well as the city,
and as arrant rakehells as they are, though not so nimble at their
prizes of wit. Sue knows the rascal to an hair's breadth and will
fit [2] him accordingly.
80   THOR. What is the other gentleman?
CAR. One Somerton, the honester man of the two by five pounds
in every stone [3] weight; a civil fellow. He has a fine, convenient
estate of land in West Ham, by [4] Essex. Mr Ranges, that dwells
by Enfield, sent him hither. He likes Kate well; I may tell you,
I think she likes him as well. If they agree, I'll not hinder the
match for my part. But that Warbeck is such another—I use
him kindly for Mr Somerton's sake, for he came hither first as a
companion of his. Honest men, Mr Thorney, may fall into
knaves' company now and then.
WAR. Three hundred a year jointure, [5] Sue.
90   SUSAN.   Where lies it?
By sea [6] or by land? I think by sea.
WAR. Do I look like a captain?
SUSAN.   Not a whit, sir.
Should all that use the seas be reckon'd captains,
There's not a ship should have a scullion in her
To keep her clean.
WAR.   Do you scorn me, Mistress Susan?
Am I a subject to be jeer'd at?
SUSAN.   Neither
Am I a property for you to use
As stale [7] to your fond, wanton, loose discourse.
Pray, sir, be civil.
WAR.   Wilt be angry, wasp?
CAR. God-a-mercy, Sue. [To Old Thorney] She'll firk [8] him, on
100 my life, if he fumble with her.

---

[1] Veritable.   [2] Punish.   [3] A unit of fourteen pounds.   [4] Near.
[5] He offers her the joint ownership of an estate of this value, with widow's
rights.   [6] i.e. in ships, thus less secure than property.   [7] Tool.   [8] Beat.

Enter Frank

Mr Francis Thorney, you are welcome indeed. Your father
expected your coming. How does the right worshipful knight,
Sir Arthur Clarington, your master?

FRANK. In health this morning. [*To his father*] Sir, my duty.

THOR.   Now
You come as I could wish.

WAR. [*Aside*]   Frank Thorney, ha!

SUSAN. [*To Warbeck*] You must excuse me.

FRANK.   Virtuous Mistress Susan.
Kind Mistress Katherine. *Salutes*[1] *them* Gentlemen to both
Good time o' th' day.

SOM.   The like to you.

WAR. [*To Somerton*]   'Tis he.
10 A word, friend. On my life, this is the man
Stands fair in crossing Susan's love to me.

SOM. [*To Warbeck*] I think no less. Be wise and take no notice
                                                              on't.
He that can win her, best deserves her.

WAR. [*To Somerton*]   Marry
A serving-man? Mew!

SOM. [*To Warbeck*]   Prithee, friend, no more.

CAR. Gentlemen all, there's within a slight dinner ready, if you
please to taste of it. Mr Thorney, Mr Francis, Mr Somerton—
Why, girls? What,[2] huswives?[3] Will you spend all your fore-
noon in tittle-tattles? Away! It's well, i' faith. Will you go in,
gentlemen?

20 THOR. We'll follow presently; my son and I
Have a few words of business.

CAR.   At your pleasure. *Exeunt the rest.*

THOR. I think you guess the reason, Frank, for which
I sent for you.

FRANK.   Yes, sir.

THOR.   I need not tell you
With what a labyrinth of dangers daily
The best part of my whole estate's encumb'red,
Nor have I any clew[4] to wind it out
But what occasion proffers me; wherein
If you should falter, I shall have the shame
And you the loss. On these two points rely

[1] Greets.   [2] Like 'why', a casual exclamation of impatience.   [3] Minxes.
[4] An allusion to the thread, provided by Ariadne, that enabled Theseus to
escape from the labyrinth of the Minotaur.

130   Our happiness or ruin. If you marry
       With wealthy Carter's daughter, there's a portion
       Will free my land; all which I will instate[1]
       Upon the marriage to you. Otherwise
       I must be of necessity enforc'd
       To make a present sale of all; and yet,
       For aught I know, live in as poor distress,
       Or worse, than now I do. You hear the sum.
       I told you thus before; have you considered on't?

FRANK. I have, sir, and however I could wish
140   To enjoy the benefit of single freedom
       (For that I find no disposition in me
       To undergo the burden of that care
       That marriage brings with it), yet to secure
       And settle the continuance of your credit,
       I humbly yield to be directed by you
       In all commands.

THOR.   You have already us'd
       Such thriving protestations to the maid
       That she is wholly yours. And—speak the truth—
       You love her, do you not?

FRANK.   'Twere pity, sir,
       I should deceive her.

150 THOR.   Better y'had been unborn!
       But is your love so steady that you mean,
       Nay, more, desire to make her your wife?

FRANK.   Else, sir,
       It were a wrong not to be righted.

THOR.   True,
       It were. And you will marry her?

FRANK.   Heaven prosper it,
       I do intend it.

THOR.   Oh, thou art a villain,
       A devil like a man! Wherein have I
       Offended all the powers so much to be
       Father to such a graceless, godless son?

FRANK. To me, sir, this? [*Aside*] O my cleft heart!

THOR.   To thee,
160   Son of my curse. Speak truth and blush, thou monster:
       Hast thou not married Winnifride, a maid
       Was fellow-servant with thee?

---

[1] Endow.

FRANK. [*Aside*]   Some swift spirit
  Has blown this news abroad; I must outface it.
THOR. D'you study for excuse? Why, all the country
  Is full on't!
FRANK.   With your licence, 'tis not charitable,
  I am sure it is not fatherly, so much
  To be o'ersway'd with credulous conceit
  Of mere impossibilities; but fathers
  Are privileg'd to think and talk at pleasure.
70 THOR. Why, canst thou yet deny thou hast no wife?
  FRANK. What do you take me for, an atheist?
  One that nor hopes the blessedness of life
  Hereafter, neither fears the vengeance due
  To such as make the marriage-bed an inn,
  Which travellers day and night,
  After a toilsome lodging, leave at pleasure?
  Am I become so insensible of losing
  The glory of creation's work, my soul?
  Oh, I have liv'd too long!
THOR.   Thou hast, dissembler!
80 Darest thou persever yet, and pull down wrath
  As hot as flames of Hell to strike thee quick
  Into the grave of horror? I believe thee not.
  Get from my sight.
FRANK.   Sir, though mine innocence
  Needs not a stronger witness than the clearness
  Of an unperish'd conscience, yet for that [1]
  I was inform'd how mainly [2] you had been
  Possess'd of this untruth, to quit all scruple,
  Please you peruse this letter; 'tis to you.
THOR. From whom?
FRANK.   Sir Arthur Clarington, my master. [*Thorney reads*]
THOR. Well, sir?
90 FRANK. [*Aside*]   On every side I am distracted,
  Am waded deeper into mischief
  Than virtue can avoid. But on I must;
  Fate leads me, I will follow.—There you read
  What may confirm you.
THOR.   Yes, and wonder at it.
  Forgive me, Frank. Credulity abus'd me.
  My tears express my joy, and I am sorry
  I injur'd innocence.

                    [1] Because.   [2] Forcefully.

FRANK.   Alas, I knew
Your rage and grief proceeded from your love
To me; so I conceiv'd it.

THOR.   My good son,
200   I'll bear with many faults in thee hereafter;
Bear thou with mine.

FRANK.   The peace is soon concluded.

Enter Old Carter [*and* Susan]

CAR. Why, Mr Thorney, d'ye mean to talk out your dinner? The
company attends your coming. What must it be, 'Mr Frank' or
'Son Frank'? I am plain Dunstable.[1]

THOR. Son, brother, if your daughter like to have it so.

FRANK. I dare be confident she's not alter'd
From what I left her at our parting last.
Are you, fair maid?

SUSAN.   You took too sure possession
Of an engaged heart.

FRANK.   Which now I challenge.[2]

210   CAR. Marry, and much good may it do thee, son. Take her to
thee. Get me a brace of boys at a burden,[3] Frank; the nursing
shall not stand thee in a pennyworth of milk. Reach her
home and spare not. When's the day?

THOR. Tomorrow, if you please. To use ceremony
Of charge [4] and custom were to little purpose;
Their loves are married fast enough already.

CAR. A good motion. We'll e'en have an household dinner, and
let the fiddlers go scrape.[5] Let the bride and bridegroom dance
at night together; no matter for the guests. Tomorrow, Sue,
220   tomorrow! Shall's to dinner now?

THOR. We are on all sides pleas'd, I hope.

SUSAN. Pray Heaven I may deserve the blessing sent me.
Now my heart is settled.

FRANK.   So is mine.

CAR. Your marriage-money shall be receiv'd before your wedding shoes can be pull'd on. Blessing on you both.

FRANK. [*Aside*] No man can hide his shame from Heaven that
views him;
In vain he flees whose destiny pursues him.   *Exeunt omnes.*

---

[1] Straightforward, like a person from Dunstable (proverbial).   [2] Claim.
[3] One birth.   [4] Expense.   [5] Be dismissed.

ACT II SCENE 1

[*A field belonging to* Old Banks]

Enter [Mother] Elizabeth Sawyer, *gathering sticks*

MOTHER.[1] And why on me? Why should the envious world
  Throw all their scandalous malice upon me?
  'Cause I am poor, deform'd, and ignorant,
  And like a bow buckl'd and bent together
  By some more strong in mischiefs than myself?
  Must I for that be made a common sink
  For all the filth and rubbish of men's tongues
  To fall and run into? Some call me witch,
  And being ignorant of myself, they go
  About to teach me how to be one; urging
  That my bad tongue, by their bad usage made so,
  Forespeaks [2] their cattle, doth bewitch their corn,
  Themselves, their servants, and their babes at nurse.
  This they enforce upon me, and in part
  Make me to credit it.

Enter Old Banks

                        And here comes one
  Of my chief adversaries.
BANKS. Out, out upon thee, witch!
MOTHER. Dost call me witch?
BANKS. I do, witch, I do, and worse I would, knew I a name more
  hateful. What makest thou upon my ground?
MOTHER. Gather a few rotten sticks to warm me.
BANKS. Down with them when I bid thee, quickly! I'll make thy
  bones rattle in thy skin else.
MOTHER. You won't, churl, cutthroat, miser. There they be.
  [*Drops her sticks*] Would they stuck 'cross thy throat, thy
  bowels, thy maw, thy midriff!
BANKS. Say'st thou me so? Hag, out of my ground!
                                              [*Belabours her*]
MOTHER. Dost strike me, slave, curmudgeon? Now thy bones
  [have] aches, thy joints cramps, and convulsions stretch and
  crack thy sinews!
BANKS. Cursing, thou hag? Take that, and that!
                                        [*Beats her, and*] *exit.*

---

[1] Q speech prefix throughout is *Sawy.*   [2] Casts a spell on.

MOTHER. Strike, do, and wither'd may that hand and arm,
Whose blows have lam'd me, drop from the rotten trunk!
Abuse me? Beat me? Call me hag and witch?
What is the name, where, and by what art learn'd,
What spells, what charms, or invocations,
May the thing call'd 'familiar' be purchas'd?

Enter Young [Cuddy] Banks *and three or four more*

CUDDY.[1] A new head for the tabor,[2] and silver tipping for the
pipe. Remember that, and forget not five leash[3] of new bells.

1. Double bells![4] Crooked Lane![5] ye shall have 'em straight in.
40　　Crooked Lane! Double bells all, if it be possible.

CUDDY. Double bells? Double coxcombs! Trebles![6] Buy me
trebles, all trebles, for our purpose is to be in the altitudes.[7]

2. All trebles? Not a mean?[8]

CUDDY. Not one. The morris is so cast we'll have neither mean
nor bass in our company, fellow Rowland.

3. What, nor a counter?[9]

CUDDY. By no means, no hunting counter;[10] leave that to Envile[11]
Chase men. All trebles, all in the altitudes. Now for the dis-
posing of parts in the morris, little or no labour will serve.

50　　2. If you that be minded to follow your leader know me (an
ancient honour belonging to our house) for a fore-horse [12]
[i' th'] team and fore-gallant [13] in a morris, my father's stable is
not unfurnish'd.

3. So much for the fore-horse; but how for a good hobby-horse?[14]

CUDDY. For a hobby-horse? Let me see an almanac.[15] Mid-
summer moon, let me see ye. 'When the moon's in the full,
then's wit in the wane.' No more. Use your best skill; your
morris will suffer an eclipse.

1. An eclipse?

60　　CUDDY. A strange one.

2. Strange?

---

[1] Q gives 'Y. Bank.' for Cuddy's speech prefixes in the remainder of this
scene. 　[2] A small drum. 　[3] Set of three. 　[4] Perhaps a pair of hand
bells in harmony. 　[5] Off King William Street, London; possibly an
oblique, punning allusion to the nearby Black Bell inn. 　[6] The smallest
bells in a peal. 　[7] Heights. 　[8] The middle part of a harmony, between
tenor and bass. 　[9] Counter-tenor. 　[10] Following the trail of game in
the wrong direction. 　[11] Modern Enfield, three miles north of Edmonton.
[12] Leader. 　[13] Principal performer. 　[14] During the long tradition of
English morris dancing, the hobby-horse, a man or sometimes a woman
(III, i, 9) wearing a model of a caparisoned horse, became one of the
major figures in the dance. 'The hobby-horse is forgot' (see lines 63-5)
was a popular catch-phrase, as in Shakespeare's *Love's Labour's Lost*, III,
i, 30, apparently from a lost ballad. It should be understood that Cuddy is
anxious to be the hobby-horse. 　[15] A calendar containing astrological
information pertaining to lucky days, etc.

CUDDY. Yes, and most sudden. Remember the fore-gallant, and forget the hobby-horse. The whole body of your morris will be dark'ned. There be of us—but 'tis no matter. Forget the hobby-horse.

1. Cuddy Banks, have you forgot since he pac'd it from Envile Chase to Edmonton? Cuddy, honest Cuddy, cast thy stuff.[1]

CUDDY. Suffer may ye all! It shall be known I can take mine ease as well as another man. Seek your hobby-horse where you can get him.

1. Cuddy, honest Cuddy, we confess, and are sorry for our neglect.

2. The old horse shall have a new bridle.

3. The caparisons [2] new painted.

4. The tail repair'd.

1. The snaffle [3] and the bosses [4] new saffron'd [5] o'er. Kind,—

2. Honest,—

3. Loving, ingenious,—

4. Affable Cuddy.

CUDDY. To show I am not flint, but affable, as you say, very well stuff'd, a kind of warm dough or puff-paste,[6] I relent, I connive,[7] most affable Jack. Let the hobby-horse provide a strong back, he shall not want a belly when I am in 'em.[8] But, 'uds me,[9] Mother Sawyer!

1. The old witch of Edmonton! If our mirth be not cross'd,—

2. Bless us, Cuddy, and let her curse her tother eye out. What dost now?

CUDDY. Ungirt, unbless'd,[10] says the proverb. But my girdle shall serve a riding knot, and a fig for all the witches in Christendom! What wouldst thou?

1. The devil cannot abide to be cross'd.

2. And scorns to come at any man's whistle.

3. Away—

4. With the witch!

OMNES. Away with the witch of Edmonton!

Exeunt in strange posture.[11]

MOTHER. Still vex'd? Still tortur'd? That curmudgeon Banks

---

[1] 'Don't take offence'.   [2] Trappings put over a saddle or harness. [3] The bit of a bridle, without curb.   [4] Metal knobs on either side of a bridle bit.   [5] Coloured with saffron, i.e. orange.   [6] Fine pastry. [7] Take no notice.   [8] i.e. him.   [9] 'God save me'.   [10] 'One is not ready until both girded (belted) and blessed.' Cuddy implies that he takes some risk in removing his belt to threaten Mother Sawyer with a running or hanging noose.   [11] Probably in imitation of Mother Sawyer's gait. Goodcole reported that she was 'crooked and deformed, even bending together'.

Is ground of all my scandal. I am shunn'd
And hated like a sickness, made a scorn
To all degrees and sexes. I have heard old beldams
100   Talk of familiars in the shape of mice,
Rats, ferrets, weasels, and I wot not what,
That have appear'd and suck'd, some say, their blood.
But by what means they came acquainted with them
I'm now ignorant. Would some power, good or bad,
Instruct me which way I might be reveng'd
Upon this churl, I'd go out of myself,
And give this fury leave to dwell within
This ruin'd cottage ready to fall with age,
Abjure all goodness, be at hate with prayer,
110   And study curses, imprecations,
Blasphemous speeches, oaths, detested oaths,
Or anything that's ill, so I might work
Revenge upon this miser, this black cur
That barks and bites and sucks the very blood
Of me and of my credit. 'Tis all one
To be a witch as to be counted one.
Vengeance, shame, ruin light upon that canker!

Enter Dog

DOG. Ho! Have I found thee cursing? Now thou art
    Mine own.
MOTHER.   Thine? What art thou?
DOG.   He thou hast so often
120   Importun'd to appear to thee, the devil.
MOTHER. Bless me! The devil?
DOG. Come, do not fear; I love thee much too well
    To hurt or fright thee. If I seem terrible,
    It is to such as hate me. I have found
    Thy love unfeign'd, have seen and pitied
    Thy open wrongs, and come, out of my love,
    To give thee just revenge against thy foes.
MOTHER. May I believe thee?
DOG.   To confirm't, command me
    Do any mischief unto man or beast,
130   And I'll effect it, on condition
    That, uncompell'd, thou make a deed of gift
    Of soul and body to me.
MOTHER.   Out, alas!
    My soul and body?

DOG.   And that instantly,
  And seal it with thy blood. If thou deniest,
  I'll tear thy body in a thousand pieces.
MOTHER. I know not where to seek relief. But shall I,
  After such covenants seal'd, see full revenge
  On all that wrong me?
DOG.   Ha, ha, silly woman!
  The devil is no liar to such as he loves.
40 Didst ever know or hear the devil a liar
  To such as he affects?
MOTHER. When I am thine, at least so much of me
  As I can call mine own,—
DOG.   Equivocations?
  Art mine or no? Speak, or I'll tear—
MOTHER.   All thine!
DOG. Seal't with thy blood.

      [She] sucks her arm. Thunder and lightning

                    See, now I dare call thee mine.
  For proof, command me. Instantly I'll run
  To any mischief; goodness can I none.
MOTHER. And I desire as little. There's an old churl,
  One Banks—
DOG.   That wrong'd thee; he lam'd thee, call'd thee witch.
50 MOTHER. The same! First upon him I'ld be reveng'd.
DOG. Thou shalt. Do but name how.
MOTHER.   Go, touch his life.
DOG. I cannot.
MOTHER.   Hast thou not vow'd? Go, kill the slave!
DOG. I wonnot.
MOTHER.   I'll cancel then my gift.
DOG.   Ha, ha!
MOTHER. Dost laugh? Why wilt not kill him?
DOG.   Fool, because I cannot.
  Though we have power, know it is circumscrib'd
  And tied in limits. Though he be curs'd to thee,
  Yet of himself he is loving to the world,
  And charitable to the poor. Now men
  That, as he, love goodness, though in smallest measure,
60 Live without compass of our reach. His cattle
  And corn I'll kill and mildew, but his life,
  Until I take him, as I late found thee,
  Cursing and swearing, I have no power to touch.

MOTHER. Work on his corn and cattle then.
DOG.   I shall.
  The witch of Edmonton shall see his fall,
  If she at least put credit in my power,
  And in mine only, make orisons to me,
  And none but me.
MOTHER.   Say how and in what manner.
DOG. I'll tell thee. When thou wishest ill,
170 Corn, man or beast would spoil or kill,
  Turn thy back against the sun
  And mumble this short orison:
  'If thou to death or shame pursue 'em,
  Sanctibicetur nomen tuum.' [1]
MOTHER. 'If thou to death or shame pursue 'em,
  Sanctibecetur nomen tuum.'
DOG. Perfect. Farewell. Our first-made promises
  We'll put in execution against Banks.   *Exit.*
MOTHER. *Contaminetur nomen tuum.* [2] I'm an expert scholar,
180 Speak Latin, or I know not well what language,
  As well as the best of 'em. But who comes here?

Enter Young [Cuddy] Banks

  The son of my worst foe! 'To death pursue 'em,
  Et sanctabecetur nomen tuum.'
CUDDY. [*Aside*] What's that she mumbles? The devil's pater-
  noster? Would it were else.—Mother Sawyer, good morrow.
MOTHER. Ill morrow to thee and all the world that flout
  A poor old woman. [*Aside*] 'To death pursue 'em,
  And *sanctabacetur nomen tuum.*'
CUDDY. Nay, good Gammer Sawyer, whate'er it pleases
  My father to call you, I know you are—
190 MOTHER.   A witch.
CUDDY. A witch? Would you were else, i' faith!
MOTHER.   Your father
  Knows I am by this. [3]
CUDDY.   I would he did.
MOTHER. And so in time may you.
CUDDY. I would I might else. But witch or no witch, you are a
  motherly woman, and though my father be a kind of God-bless-
  us, as they say, I have an earnest suit to you, and if you'll be so

---

[1] Hallowed be thy name. The correct form of the verb is *sanctificetur*; the word is used six times in the play, with six different spellings, possibly to avoid an accusation of blasphemy.   [2] Cursed be thy name.
[3] i.e. by this time.

kind to ka me one good turn, I'll be so courteous as to kob[1]
you another.

MOTHER. What's that? To spurn, beat me, and call me witch, as
your kind father doth?

CUDDY. My father? I am asham'd to own him. If he has hurt the
head of thy credit, there's money to buy thee a plaster, and a
small courtesy I would require at thy hands.

MOTHER. You seem a good young man,—[*Aside*] and I must
dissemble,
The better to accomplish my revenge.—
But for this silver, what wouldst have me do?
Bewitch thee?

CUDDY. No, by no means. I am bewitch'd already. I would have
thee so good as to unwitch me, or witch another with me for
company.

MOTHER. I understand thee not. Be plain, my son.

CUDDY. As a pikestaff, mother. You know Kate Carter?

MOTHER. The wealthy yeoman's daughter. What of her?

CUDDY. That same party has bewitch'd me.

MOTHER. Bewitch'd thee?

CUDDY. Bewitch'd me, *hisce auribus!*[2] I saw a little devil fly out
of her eye like a burbolt,[3] which sticks at this hour up to the
feathers in my heart. Now my request is, to send one of thy
what-d'ye-call-'ems either to pluck that out or stick another
as fast in hers. Do, and here's my hand; I am thine for three
lives.

MOTHER. [*Aside*] We shall have sport.—Thou art in love with
her?

CUDDY. Up to the very hilts, mother.

MOTHER. And thou'ldst have me make her love thee too?

CUDDY. [*Aside*] I think she'll prove a witch in earnest!—
Yes, I could find in my heart to strike her three quarters deep
in love with me too.

MOTHER. But dost thou think that I can do't, and I alone?

CUDDY. Truly, Mother Witch, I do verily believe so, and when I
see it done, I shall be half persuaded so too.

MOTHER. It's enough. What art can do, be sure of.
Turn to the west, and whatsoe'er thou hearest
Or seest, stand silent, and be not afraid.   *She stamps*

Enter the Dog; *he fawns and leaps upon her*

CUDDY. Afraid, Mother Witch? [*Aside*] Turn my face to the

---

[1] Variant of 'ka me, ka thee', 'one good turn deserves another'.
[2] 'By these very ears!'   [3] i.e. bird-bolt, a blunt-headed arrow.

west? I said I should always have a backfriend [1] of her, and now
it's out. And [2] her little devil should be hungry, come sneaking
behind me like a cowardly catchpole,[3] and clamp his talents [4]
on my haunches! 'Tis woundy [5] cold sure; I dudder [6] and shake
240   like an aspen leaf, every joint of me.

MOTHER. 'To scandal and disgrace pursue 'em,
    Et sanctabicetur nomen tuum.'   *Exit* Dog.
    How now, my son, how is't?

CUDDY. Scarce in a clean life, Mother Witch. But did your
    goblin and you spout Latin together?

MOTHER. A kind of charm I work by. Didst thou hear me?

CUDDY. I heard I-know-not-the-devil-what mumble in a scurvy
    base tone, like a drum that had taken cold in the head the last
    muster. Very comfortable words. What were they, and who
250   taught them you?

MOTHER. A great learned man.

CUDDY. Learned man? Learned devil it was as soon! But what,
    what comfortable news about the party?

MOTHER. Who? Kate Carter? I'll tell thee. Thou know'st the
    stile at the west end of thy father's pease-field? Be there
    tomorrow night after sunset, and the first live thing thou seest
    be sure to follow, and that shall bring thee to thy love.

CUDDY. In the pease-field? Has she a mind to codlings [7] already?
    The first living thing I meet, you say, shall bring me to her?

260 MOTHER. To a sight of her I mean. She will seem wantonly coy
    and flee thee, but follow her close and boldly. Do but embrace
    her in thy arms once, and she is thine own.

CUDDY. At the stile at the west end of my father's pease-land,
    the first live thing I see, follow and embrace her, and she shall
    be thine. Nay, and I come to embracing once, she shall be mine!
    I'll go near to make [8] at eaglet [9] else.   *Exit.*

MOTHER. A ball well bandied! Now the set's [10] half won.
    The father's wrong I'll wreak upon the son.   *Exit.*

---

[1] Secret enemy.   [2] Suppose.   [3] Minor officer of the law.   [4] Claws.
[5] Extremely.   [6] Shiver.   [7] Usually a hard or unripe apple. The context
suggests peas, a meaning not confirmed elsewhere. Perhaps the inappropriate word was included here for the sake of the pun on 'cuddlings'.
[8] Win.   [9] Perhaps an obscure card game.   [10] A unit of 6–8 games, as
in tennis.

[ACT II] SCENE 2

[Carter's *house*]

Enter Carter, Warbeck, Somerton

CAR. How now, gentlemen? Cloudy? I know, Mr Warbeck, you are in a fog about my daughter's marriage.

WAR. And can you blame me, sir?

CAR. Nor you me justly. Wedding and hanging are tied up both in a proverb,[1] and destiny is the juggler that unties the knot. My hope is you are reserved to a richer fortune than my poor daughter.

WAR. However, your promise—

CAR. Is a kind of debt, I confess it.

WAR. Which honest men should pay.

CAR. Yet some gentlemen break in that point now and then, by your leave, sir.

SOM. I confess thou hast had a little wrong in the wench, but patience is the only salve to cure it. Since Thorney has won the wench, he has most reason to wear [2] her.

WAR. Love in this kind admits no reason to wear her.

CAR. Then love's a fool, and what wise man will take exception?

SOM. Come, frolic [3] Ned, were every man master of his own fortune, fate might pick straws,[4] and destiny go a-woolgathering.

WAR. You hold yours in a string though. 'Tis well, but if there be any equity, look thou to meet the like usage ere long.

SOM. In my love to her sister Katherine? Indeed, they are a pair of arrows drawn out of one quiver, and should fly at an even length, if she do run after her sister.

WAR. Look for the same mercy at my hands as I have received at thine.

SOM. She'll keep a surer compass; I have too strong a confidence to mistrust her.

WAR. And that confidence is a wind that has blown many a married man ashore at Cuckold's Haven [5] I can tell you. I wish yours more prosperous though.

---

[1] 'Hanging and wiving go by destiny' (Dekker, *The Shoemakers' Holiday*, IV, iii, 69–70).   [2] Possess.   [3] Merry.   [4] Fuss over detail.
[5] Perhaps an allusion to Security's landfall here, in Jonson, Chapman, and Marston's *Eastward Ho* (1605), IV, i; however, there are many contemporary references to this place on the Thames, near Rotherhithe, associated in legend with the miller to whom King John granted the surrounding land after the miller had discovered the monarch dallying with his wife.

CAR. Whate'er you wish, I'll master my promise to him.

WAR. Yes, as you did to me!

CAR. No more of that, if you love me. But for the more assurance, the next offer'd occasion shall consummate the marriage, and that once seal'd,—

Enter Young [Frank] Thorney *and* Susan

SOM. Leave the manage of the rest to my care. But see, the bridegroom and bride comes, the new pair of Sheffield knives
40   fitted both to one sheath.

WAR. The sheath might have been better fitted if somebody had their due, but—

SOM.[1] No harsh language, if thou lovest me. Frank Thorney has done—

WAR. No more than I or thou or any man, things so standing, would have attempted.

SOM. Good morrow, Mr Bridegroom.

WAR. Come, give thee joy. Mayst thou live long and happy in thy fair choice.

50   FRANK. I thank ye, gentlemen. Kind Mr Warbeck, I find you loving.

WAR. Thorney, that creature—[*Aside*] Much good do thee with
                                                            her—
Virtue and beauty hold fair mixture in her;
She's rich, no doubt, in both. Yet were she fairer,
Thou art right worthy of her. Love her, Thorney.
'Tis nobleness in thee; in her but duty.
The match is fair and equal; the success
I leave to censure. [2] Farewell, Mrs [3] Bride.
Till now elected, thy old scorn deride.   *Exit.*

60   SOM. Good Mr Thorney,—

CAR. Nay, you shall not part till you see the barrels run atilt,[4]
gentlemen.   *Exit* [, *with* Somerton].

SUSAN. Why change you your face, sweetheart?

FRANK. Who, I? For nothing.

SUSAN. Dear, say not so. A spirit of your constancy cannot endure this change for nothing. I have observ'd strange variations in you.

FRANK. In me?

SUSAN. In you, sir. Awake, you seem to dream, and in your
70   sleep you utter sudden and distracted accents, like one at enmity with peace. Dear loving husband, if I may dare to chal-

---

[1] Q has *Car.*   [2] Judgment.   [3] i.e. Mistress.   [4] Almost empty.

lenge[1] any interest in you, give me the reason fully. You may
trust my breast as safely as your own.

FRANK. With what? You half amaze me. Prithee,—

SUSAN. Come, you shall not,
Indeed you shall not shut me from partaking
The least dislike that grieves you. I am all yours.

FRANK. And I all thine.

SUSAN.   You are not, if you keep
The least grief from me. But I find the cause:
It grew from me.

FRANK.   From you?

SUSAN.   From some distaste
In me or my behaviour. You are not kind
In the concealment. 'Las, sir, I am young,
Silly, and plain; more, strange to those contents
A wife should offer. Say but in what I fail,
I'll study satisfaction.

FRANK.   Come, in nothing.

SUSAN. I know I do. Knew I as well in what,
You should not long be sullen. Prithee, love,
If I have been immodest or too bold,
Speak't in a frown; if peevishly too nice,[2]
Show't in a smile. Thy liking is the glass
By which I'll habit[3] my behaviour.

FRANK. Wherefore dost weep now?

SUSAN.   You, sweet, have the power
To make me passionate as an April day:
Now smile, then weep; now pale, then crimson red;
You are the powerful moon of my blood's sea,
To make it ebb or flow into my face
As your looks change.

FRANK.   Change thy conceit, I prithee.
Thou art all perfection; Diana[4] herself
Swells in thy thoughts and moderates[5] thy beauty.
Within thy left eye amorous Cupid sits,
Feathering love shafts, whose golden heads he dipp'd
In thy chaste breast; in the other lies
Blushing Adonis,[6] scarf'd in modesties.
And still as wanton Cupid blows love-fires,
Adonis quenches out unchaste desires;
And from these two I briefly do imply

---

[1] Claim.   [2] Fastidious.   [3] Clothe.   [4] Protectress of chastity.
[5] Presides over.   [6] A handsome youth, from Greek mythology.

A perfect emblem of thy modesty.
Then prithee, dear, maintain no more dispute,
For where thou speak'st it's fit all tongues be mute.
110 SUSAN. Come, come, those golden strings of flattery
Shall not tie up my speech, sir; I must know
The ground of your disturbance.
FRANK.   Then look here,
For here, here is the fen in which this hydra
Of discontent grows rank.
SUSAN.   Heaven shield it! Where?
FRANK. In mine own bosom. Here the cause has root.
The poison'd leeches twist about my heart,
And will, I hope, confound [1] me.
SUSAN.   You speak riddles.
FRANK. Take't plainly then: 'Twas told me by a woman
Known and approv'd in palmistry
I should have two wives.
120 SUSAN.   Two wives? Sir, I take it
Exceeding likely! But let not conceit [2]
Hurt you. You are afraid to bury me?
FRANK. No, no, my Winnifride.
SUSAN.   How say you? Winnifride? You forget me.
FRANK. No, I forget myself, Susan.
SUSAN.   In what?
FRANK. Talking of wives, I pretend [3] Winnifride,
A maid that at my mother's waited on me,
Before thyself.
SUSAN.   I hope, sir, she may live
To take my place. But why should all this move you?
FRANK. [Aside] The poor girl!—She has't before thee,
And that's the fiend torments me.
130 SUSAN.   Yet why should this
Raise mutiny within you? Such presages
Prove often false; or say it should be true?
FRANK. That I should have another wife?
SUSAN.   Yes, many;
If they be good, the better.
FRANK.   Never any
Equal to thee in goodness.
SUSAN.   Sir, I could wish
I were much better for you; yet if I knew your fate
Ordain'd you for another I could wish

---

[1] Destroy.   [2] A fanciful notion.   [3] Claim.

(So well I love you and your hopeful pleasure)
Me in my grave, and my poor virtues added
To my successor.

FRANK.   Prithee, prithee, talk not
Of death or graves; thou art so rare a goodness
As Death would rather put itself to death
Than murder thee. But we, as all things else,
Are mutable and changing.

SUSAN.   Yet you still move
In your first sphere of discontent. Sweet, chase
Those clouds of sorrow and shine clearly on me.

FRANK. At my return I will.

SUSAN.   Return? Ah me!
Will you then leave me?

FRANK.   For a time I must.
But how?[1] As birds their young, or loving bees
Their hives, to fetch home richer dainties.

SUSAN. Leave me? Now has my fear met its effect. You shall not!
Cost it my life, you shall not.

FRANK.   Why? Your reason?

SUSAN. Like to the lapwing[2] have you all this while
With your false love deluded me, pretending
Counterfeit senses for your discontent,
And now at last it is by chance stole from you.

FRANK. What? What by chance?

SUSAN.   Your preappointed meeting
Of single combat with young Warbeck.

FRANK.   Ha!

SUSAN. Even so. Dissemble not; 'tis too apparent.
Then in his look I read it. Deny it not;
I see't apparent. Cost it my undoing,
And unto that[3] my life, I will not leave you.

FRANK. Not until when?

SUSAN.   Till he and you be friends.
Was this your cunning? And then flam me off[4]
With an old witch, two wives, and Winnifride?
Y'are not so kind indeed as I imagin'd.

FRANK. [Aside] And you more fond by far than I expected;
It is a virtue that attends thy kind.—
But of our business within. And by this kiss,
I'll anger thee no more; troth, chuck, I will not.

[1] i.e., in what manner.   [2] Proverbially deceptive (in leading searchers away from its nest).   [3] Even.   [4] Deceive me.

SUSAN. You shall have no just cause.
FRANK.   Dear Sue, I shall not. *Exeunt.*

ACT III SCENE 1

[*A field,* Old Banks's *farm*]

Enter Cuddy Banks *and morris-dancers*

1. Nay, Cuddy, prithee do not leave us now; if we part all this night, we shall not meet before day.
2. I prithee, Banks, let's keep together now.

CUDDY.[1] If you were wise, a word would serve; but, as you are, I must be forc'd to tell you again. I have a little private business, an hour's work; it may prove but an half hour's, as luck may serve, and then I take horse and along with you. Have we e'er a witch in the morris?

1. No, no; no woman's part but Maid Marian[2] and the hobby-horse.

CUDDY. I'll have a witch; I love a witch.

1. Faith, witches themselves are so common nowadays that the counterfeit will not be regarded. They say we have three or four in Edmonton besides Mother Sawyer.
2. I would she would dance her part with us.
3. So would not I, for if she comes, the devil and all comes along with her.

CUDDY. Well, I'll have a witch. I have lov'd a witch ever since I play'd at cherry-pit.[3] Leave me, and get my horse dress'd. Give him oats, but water him not till I come. Whither do we foot it first?

2. To Sir Arthur Clarington's first, then whither thou wilt.

CUDDY. Well, I am content; but we must up to Carter's, the rich yeoman. I must be seen on hobby-horse there.

1. Oh, I smell him now. I'll lay my ears Banks is in love, and that's the reason he would walk melancholy by himself.

CUDDY. Ha! Who was that said I was in love?

---

[1] In the remainder of the Q text Cuddy is identified in speech prefixes as 'Clown'.   [2] Mawd [i.e. mad] Marian, the partner of the fool in the morris dances; in the sixteenth century she took over the name of Robin Hood's companion.   [3] A children's game involving throwing cherry stones into a hole.

1. Not I.
2. Nor I.

CUDDY. Go to! No more of that. When I understand what you
speak, I know what you say, believe that.

1. Well, 'twas I, I'll not deny it. I meant no hurt in't. I have seen
you walk up to Carter's of Chessum.[1] Banks, were not you
there last Shrovetide?[2]

CUDDY. Yes, I was ten days together there the last Shrovetide.

2. How could that be, when there are but seven days in the week?

CUDDY. Prithee, peace! I reckon *stila nova*,[3] as a traveller; thou
understandest as a freshwater farmer that never sawest a week
beyond sea. Ask any soldier that ever received his pay but in the
Low Countries, and he'll tell thee there are eight days in the
week[4] there hard by. How dost thou think they rise in high
Germany, Italy, and those remoter places?

3. Ay, but simply there are but seven days in the week yet.

CUDDY. No, simply as thou understandest. Prithee, look but in
the lover's almanac, when he has been but three days absent;
'Oh,' says he, 'I have not seen my love these seven years.'
There's a long cut! When he comes to her again and embraces
her, 'Oh,' says he, 'now methinks I am in Heaven.' And that's
a pretty step! He that can get up to Heaven in ten days need
not repent his journey. You may ride a hundred days in a
caroche[5] and be further off than when you set forth. But I
pray you, good morris-mates, now leave me. I will be with you
by midnight.

1. Well, since he will be alone, we'll back again and trouble him
no more.

OMNES. But remember, Banks.

CUDDY. The hobby-horse shall be rememb'red. But hark you,
get Poldavis,[6] the barber's boy, for the witch, because he can
show his art better than another.   *Exeunt [morris-dancers]*.
Well, now to my walk. I am near the place where I should meet
I know not what. Say I meet a thief, I must follow him, if to
the gallows; say I meet a horse, or hare, or hound, still I must
follow. Some slow-pac'd beast, I hope. Yet love is full of light-
ness in the heaviest lovers. Ha! My guide is come.

[Enter the Dog]

[1] Modern Chesham, twenty-five miles west of Edmonton,   [2] A period
of merriment immediately preceding Ash Wednesday.   [3] The Gregorian
calendar was adopted in France and Italy in 1582, but not in England until
1751.   [4] An implication of hardship.   [5] Coach.   [6] Although listed
among the *dramatis personae*, he is referred to only at this point in the play.

A water dog! I am thy first man, sculler; I go with thee. Ply no
other but myself. Away with the boat; land me but at
Katherine's Dock,[1] my sweet Katherine's Dock, and I'll be a
fare to thee. That way? Nay, which way thou wilt; thou
know'st the way better than I. Fine, gentle cur it is, and well
70   brought up, I warrant him. We go a-ducking, spaniel; thou shalt
fetch me the ducks, pretty, kind rascal.

Enter Spirit, *in shape of* Katherine, *vizarded,[2] and takes it off*

SPIRIT. [*Aside*] Thus throw I off mine own essential horror,
And take the shape of a sweet, lovely maid
Whom this fool dotes on. We can meet his folly,
But from his virtues must be runaways.
We'll sport with him, but when we reckoning call,
We know where to receive; th' witch pays for all. Dog *barks*.

CUDDY. Ay, is that the watchword? She's come. Well, if ever we
be married, it shall be at Barking Church,[3] in memory of thee.
80   Now come behind, kind cur.
And have I met thee, sweet Kate?
I will teach thee to walk so late.
Oh, see, we meet in metre. What? Dost thou trip from me? Oh,
that I were upon my hobby-horse; I would mount after thee so
nimble! 'Stay, nymph, stay, nymph,' sing'd Apollo;
'Tarry and kiss me, sweet nymph, stay;
Tarry and kiss me, sweet.'
We will to Chessum Street, and then to the house stands in the
highway. Nay, by your leave, I must embrace you.

Exeunt Spirit *and* Banks[, *pursuing*].

90   [CUDDY *within*] Oh, help, help! I am drown'd, I am drown'd!

Enter [Cuddy,] *wet*

DOG. Ha, ha, ha, ha!

CUDDY. This was an ill night to go a-wooing in! I find it now in
Pond's Almanac.[4] Thinking to land at Katherine's Dock, I
was almost at Gravesend. I'll never go to a wench in the dog
days [5] again; yet 'tis cool enough. Had you never a paw in this
dog-trick? A mangie take that black hide of yours! I'll throw
you in at Limehouse,[6] in some tanner's pit or other.

---

[1] In east London.   [2] Masked, to appear in its ordinary, diabolical state.
The Spirit removes this mask in order to look like Katherine, its present
human form.   [3] In Great Tower Street, London; referred to here for the
sake of the pun.   [4] An early seventeenth-century collection of progno-
stications , etc., issued, apparently annually, by Edward Pond.
[5] The hottest period of the year, when Sirius, the dog-star, rises (July–early
August).   [6] East London, near Wapping, long notable for tanning; lime
is used to remove hair from hides.

DOG. Ha, ha, ha, ha!

CUDDY. How now? Who's that laughs at me? Hist to him!

Dog barks

O   Peace, peace! Thou didst but thy kind [1] neither. 'Twas my own
     fault.

DOG. Take heed how thou trustest the devil another time.

CUDDY. How now? Who's that speaks? I hope you have not
your reading tongue about you.

DOG. Yes, I can speak.

CUDDY. The devil you can! You have read Aesop's *Fables*
then; I have play'd one of your parts then: the dog that catch'd
at the shadow in the water.[2] Pray you, let me catechize you a
little. What might one call your name, dog?

O DOG. My dame calls me Tom.

CUDDY. 'Tis well; and she may call me Ass, so there's a whole
one betwixt us: Tom-Ass. She said I should follow you indeed.
Well, Tom, give me thy fist; we are friends. You shall be mine
ingle.[3] I love you, but, I pray you, let's have no more of these
ducking devices.

DOG. Not, if you love me. Dogs love where they are beloved.
Cherish me and I'll do anything for thee.

CUDDY. Well, you shall have jowls and livers; I have butchers to
my friends that shall bestow 'em, and I will keep crusts and bones

O   for you, if you'll be a kind dog, Tom.

DOG. Anything. I'll help thee to thy love.

CUDDY. Wilt thou? That promise shall cost me a brown loaf,
though I steal it out of my father's cupboard. You'll eat stolen
goods, Tom, will you not?

DOG. Oh, best of all! The sweetest bits those.

CUDDY. You shall not starve, ningle [4] Tom; believe that. If you
love fish,[5] I'll help you to maids [6] and soles; I'm acquainted with
a fishmonger.

DOG. Maids and soles? Oh, sweet bits! Banqueting stuff those.

O CUDDY. One thing I would request you, ningle, as you have
play'd the knavish cur with me a little, that you would mingle
amongst our morris-dancers in the morning. You can dance?

DOG. Yes, yes, anything. I'll be there, but unseen to any but
thyself. Get thee gone before. Fear not my presence. I have
work tonight. I serve more masters, more dames than one.

---

[1] Nature.   [2] A dog carrying a piece of meat saw its reflection in a
stream and attacked, losing the meat.   [3] Favourite.   [4] i.e. mine ingle.
[5] Slang term for prostitutes, as 'fishmonger' was for procurer (Shakespeare,
Hamlet, II, ii, 73–6).   [6] Skate.

CUDDY. [*Aside*] He can serve Mammon and the devil too.

DOG. It shall concern thee and thy love's purchase.
There's a gallant rival[1] loves the maid,
And likely is to have her. Mark what a mischief
140 Before the morris ends shall light on him.

CUDDY. Oh, sweet ningle, thy neuf[2] once again. Friends must
part for a time. Farewell, with this remembrance; shalt have
bread too when we meet again. If ever there were an honest
devil, 'twill be the devil of Edmonton,[3] I see. Farewell,
Tom. I prithee dog me as soon as thou canst.

Exit [Cuddy] Banks.

DOG. I'll not miss[4] thee, and be merry with thee.
Those that are joys denied must take delight
In sins and mischiefs; 'tis the devil's right.　　　*Exit* Dog.

[ACT III SCENE 2]

[*A road near Edmonton*]

Enter Young [Frank] Thorney [*and*] Winnifride, *as a boy*

FRANK. Prithee, no more; those tears give nourishment
To weeds and briars in me, which shortly will
O'ergrow and top my head. My shame will sit
And cover all that can be seen of me.

WIN. I have not shown this cheek in company;
Pardon me now. Thus singled[5] with yourself,
It calls a thousand sorrows round about,
Some going before, and some on either side,
But infinite behind, all chain'd together.
10 Your second adulterous marriage leads;
That's the sad eclipse; the effects must follow,
As plagues of shame, spite, scorn, and obloquy.

FRANK. Why? Hast thou not left one hour's patience
To add to all the rest? One hour bears us
Beyond the reach of all these enemies.
Are we not now set forward in the flight,

---

[1] Somerton.　　　[2] Fist.　　　[3] In *The Merry Devil of Edmonton* Peter Fabell
manipulates the plot in an amusing, unmalicious way.　　　[4] Fail to take
advantage of.　　　[5] Alone.

Provided with the dowry of my sin[1]
To keep us in some other nation?
While we together are, we are at home
In any place.
WIN.   'Tis foul, ill-gotten coin,
Far worse than usury or extortion.
FRANK. Let my father then make the restitution,
Who forc'd me take the bribe. It is his gift
And patrimony to me; so I receive it.
He would not bless, nor look a father on me,
Until I satisfied his angry will.
When I was sold, I sold myself again—
Some knaves have done't in lands, and I in body—
For money, and I have the hire. But, sweet, no more;
'Tis hazard of discovery, our discourse;
And then prevention takes off all our hopes.
For only but to take her leave of me
My wife is coming.
WIN.   Who coming? Your wife?
FRANK. No, no; thou art here. The woman—I knew
Not how to call her now, but after this day
She shall be quite forgot and have no name
In my remembrance. See, see; she's come.

                    Enter Susan

[*To* Winnifride]   Go lead
The horses to the hill's top; there I'll meet thee.
SUSAN. Nay, with your favour let him stay a little.
I would part with him too, because he is
Your sole companion; and I'll begin with him,
Reserving you the last.
FRANK.   Ay, with all my heart. [*Moves to leave*]
SUSAN. You may hear, if it please you, sir.
FRANK.   No, 'tis not fit.
Some rudiments,[2] I conceive, they must be
To overlook my slippery footings; and so—
SUSAN. No indeed, sir.
FRANK.   Tush, I know it must be so,
And 'tis necessary. On, but be brief. [*Stands aside*]
WIN. What charge soe'er you lay upon me, mistress,
I shall support it faithfully, being honest,

[1] The dowry offered by Susan's father (I, ii, 1–16). 'Sin' alludes to Frank's
bigamy.   [2] Imperfect beginnings.

To my best strength.

50   SUSAN.   Believe't shall be no other.
I know you were commended to my husband
By a noble knight.

WIN.   Oh, gods! Oh, mine eyes!

SUSAN. How now? What ail'st thou, lad?

WIN. Something hit mine eye—it makes it water still—
Even as you said, 'Commended to my husband.'
Some dor[1] I think it was. I was, forsooth,
Commended to him by Sir Arthur Clarington.

SUSAN. Whose servant once my Thorney was himself.
That title, methinks, should make you almost fellows,
60   Or at the least much more than a servant;
And I am sure he will respect you so.
Your love to him then needs no spur from me,
And what for my sake you will ever do,
'Tis fit it should be bought with something more
Than fair entreats. Look, here's a jewel for thee,
A pretty, wanton label for thine ear;
And I would have it hang there, still to whisper
These words to thee, 'Thou hast my jewel with thee.'
It is but earnest of a larger bounty
70   When thou return'st with praises of thy service,
Which I am confident thou wilt deserve.
Why, thou art many now besides thyself;
Thou mayst be servant, friend, and wife to him;
A good wife is then all. A friend can play
The wife and servant's part, and shift[2] enough;
No less the servant can the friend and wife.
'Tis all but sweet society, good counsel,
Interchang'd loves, yes, and counsel-keeping.

FRANK. Not done yet?

80   SUSAN. Even now, sir.

WIN. Mistress, believe my vow. Your severe eye,
Were it present to command; your bounteous hand,
Were it then by to buy or bribe my service,
Shall not make me more dear or near unto him
Than I shall voluntary. I'll be all your charge,
Servant, friend, wife to him.

SUSAN.   Wilt thou?
Now blessings go with thee for't; courtesies

---

[1] Beetle.   [2] Get on well.

Shall meet thee coming home.

WIN.   Pray you, say plainly, mistress,
  Are you jealous of him? If you be,
  I'll look to him that way too.

SUSAN.   Say'st thou so?
  I would thou hadst a woman's bosom now;
  We have weak thoughts within us. Alas,
  There's nothing so strong in us as suspicion;
  But I dare not, nay, I will not think
  So hardly of my Thorney.

WIN.   Believe it, mistress,
  I'll be no pander to him, and if I find
  Any loose lubric [1] scapes in him, I'll watch him,
  And at my return protest I'll show you all.
  He shall hardly offend without my knowledge.

SUSAN. Thine own diligence is that I press,
  And not the curious eye over his faults.
  Farewell. If I should never see thee more,
  Take it [2] for ever.

FRANK.   Prithee take that along with thee,
                 Gives his sword [*to* Winnifride]
  And haste thee to the hill's top; I'll be there instantly.
                        Exit Winnifride.

SUSAN. No haste, I prithee; slowly as thou canst.
  Pray let him obey me now; 'tis happily [3]
  His last service to me. My power is e'en
  A-going out of sight.

FRANK.   Why would you delay?
  We have no other business now but to part.

SUSAN. And will not that, sweetheart, ask [4] a long time?
  Methinks it is the hardest piece of work
  That e'er I took in hand.

FRANK.   Fie, fie! Why, look,
  I'll make it plain and easy to you: Farewell. *Kisses* [*her*]

SUSAN. Ah, 'las, I am not half perfect in it yet.
  I must have it read over an hundred times.
  Pray you, take some pains; I confess my dullness. [5]

FRANK. [*Aside*] What a thorn this rose grows on! Parting were
                                sweet,
  But what a trouble 'twill be to obtain it.—
  Come, again and again, farewell. *Kisses* [*her*]. Yet wilt return?

[1] Lascivious.   [2] i.e. my farewell.   [3] Haply, perhaps.   [4] Demand.
[5] Stupidity.

120   All questions of my journey, my stay, employment,
       And revisitation, fully I have answer'd all.
       There's nothing now behind, but nothing.
SUSAN.   And
       That 'nothing' is more hard than anything,
       Than all the everythings. This request—
FRANK.   What is it?
SUSAN. That I may bring you through one pasture more,
       Up to yon knot of trees. Amongst those shadows
       I'll vanish from you; they shall teach me how.
FRANK. Why, 'tis granted. Come, walk then.
SUSAN.   Nay, not too fast.
       They say slow things have best perfection;
130   The gentle shower wets to fertility,
       The churlish storm may mischief with his bounty.
       The baser beasts take strength even from the womb,
       But the lord lion's whelp is feeble long.   *Exeunt.*

[ACT III SCENE 3]

[*A road near Edmonton*]

Enter Dog[1]

DOG. Now for an early mischief and a sudden.
      The[2] mind's about it now; one touch from me
      Soon sets the body forward.

               Enter Young [Frank] Thorney *and* Susan

FRANK. Your request is out; yet will you leave me?
SUSAN. What? So churlishly? You'll make me stay for ever
       Rather than part with such a sound from you.
FRANK. Why, you almost anger me. Pray you, begone.
       You have no company, and 'tis very early;
       Some hurt may betide you homewards.
SUSAN.   Tush, I fear none.
10   To leave you is the greatest hurt I can suffer.
       Besides, I expect your father and mine own
       To meet me back, or overtake me with you.

       [1] Invisible except to the audience.   [2] Frank's.

They began to stir when I came after you;
  I know they'll not be long.
FRANK. [*Aside*] So, I shall have more trouble. Dog *rubs him.*
  Thank you for that.[1] Then I'll ease all at once. 'Tis done now;
  what I ne'er thought on.—You shall not go back.
SUSAN. Why, shall I go along with thee? Sweet music!
FRANK. No, to a better place.
SUSAN.   Any place I;
  I'm there at home where thou pleasest to have me.
FRANK. At home? I'll leave you in your last lodging.
  I must kill you.
SUSAN.   Oh, fine! You'ld fright me from you.
FRANK. You see I had no purpose; I'm unarm'd.
  'Tis this minute's decree, and it must be.
  Look, this will serve your turn.   [*Draws a knife*]
SUSAN.   I'll not turn from it
  If you be in earnest, sir. Yet you may tell me
  Wherefore you'll kill me.
FRANK.   Because you are a whore.
SUSAN. There's one deep wound already. A whore?
  'Twas ever further from me than the thought
  Of this black hour. A whore?
FRANK.   Yes. I'll prove it,
  And you shall confess it. You are my whore,
  No wife of mine. The word admits no second.
  I was before wedded to another, have her still.
  I do not lay the sin unto your charge;
  'Tis all mine own. Your marriage was my theft,
  For I espous'd your dowry, and I have it.
  I did not purpose to have added murder;
  The devil did not prompt me. Till this minute
  You might have safe returned; now you cannot;
  You have dogg'd your own death.   *Stabs her*
SUSAN.   And I deserve it.
  I'm glad my fate was so intelligent.[2]
  'Twas some good spirit's motion. Die? Oh, 'twas time.
  How many years might I have slept in sin,
  Sin of my most hatred too, adultery?
FRANK. Nay, sure 'twas likely that the most was past,
  For I meant never to return to you
  After this parting.

---

[1] He thanks Susan (aside) for the reminder of imminent interruption.
[2] Quick to understand.

SUSAN.   Why, then, I thank you more.
   You have done lovingly, leaving yourself,
   That you would thus bestow me on another.
50 Thou art my husband, Death, and I embrace thee
   With all the love I have. Forget the stain
   Of my unwitting sin, and then I come
   A crystal virgin to thee. My soul's purity
   Shall with bold wings ascend the doors of Mercy,
   For Innocence is ever her companion.
FRANK. Not yet mortal? I would not linger you,
   Or leave you a tongue to blab.   [*Stabs her again*]
SUSAN. Now Heaven reward you ne'er the worse for me.
   I did not think that Death had been so sweet,
60 Nor I so apt to love him. I could ne'er die better
   Had I stay'd forty years for preparation,
   For I'm in charity with all the world.
   Let me for once be thine example, Heaven;
   Do to this man as I him free forgive,
   And may he better die and better live.   *Moritur*
FRANK. 'Tis done, and I am in. Once past our height,
   We scorn the deep'st abyss. This follows now
   To hele her wounds [1] by dressing [2] of the weapon.
   Arms, thighs, hands, any place; we must not fail
                                        Wounds himself
70 Light scratches, giving such deep ones. The best I can
   To bind myself to this tree. Now's the storm,
   Which if blown o'er, many fair days may follow.
                         Dog ties him[, and exits].
   So, so, I'm fast; I did not think I could
   Have done so well behind me. How prosperous
   And effectual mischief sometimes is! Help, Help!
   Murder, murder, murder!

                  Enter Carter *and* Old Thorney

CAR. Ha! Whom tolls the bell for?
FRANK.   Oh, oh!
THOR.   Ah me,
   The cause appears too soon! My child, my son!
CAR. Susan, girl, child! Not speak to thy father? Hah!
80 FRANK. Oh, lend me some assistance to o'ertake
   This hapless woman.

---

[1] To disguise the source of her wounds.   [2] Metaphorically cleansing the
weapon by covering it with his own blood.

THOR.   Let's o'ertake the murderers.
  Speak whilst thou canst; anon may be too late.
  I fear thou hast death's mark upon thee too.
FRANK. I know them both; yet such an oath is pass'd
  As pulls damnation up if it be broke.
  I dare not name 'em. Think what forc'd men do.
THOR. Keep oath with murderers? That were a conscience
  To hold the devil in.
FRANK.   Nay, sir, I can describe 'em,
  Shall show them as familiar as their names.
  The taller of the two at this time wears
  His satin doublet white, but crimson lin'd,
  Hose of black satin, cloak of scarlet,—
THOR.   Warbeck,
  Warbeck, Warbeck! Do you list to this, sir?
CAR. Yes, yes, I listen you; here's nothing to be heard.
FRANK. Th'other's cloak branch'd[1] velvet, black, velvet lin'd his
  suit.
THOR. I have 'em already. Somerton, Somerton!
  Binal[2] revenge all this. Come, sir, the first work
  Is to pursue the murderers, when we have
  Remov'd these mangled bodies hence.
CAR. Sir, take that carcass there, and give me this.
  I'll not own her now; she's none of mine.
  Bob me off[3] with a dumb show? No I'll have life.
  This is my son[4] too, and while there's life in him
  'Tis half mine; take you half that silence for't.[5]
  When I speak, I look to be spoken to.
  Forgetful slut!
THOR.   Alas, what grief may do now!
  Look, sir, I'll take this load of sorrow with me.
                    [*Exit, bearing* Susan.]
CAR. Ay, do, and I'll have this. How do you, sir?
FRANK. Oh, very ill, sir.
CAR. Yes, I think so; but 'tis well you can speak yet.
  There's no music but in sound; sound it must be.
  I have not wept these twenty years before,
  And that I guess was ere that girl was born.
  Yet now methinks, if I but knew the way,
  My heart's so full I could weep night and day.   *Exeunt.*

---

[1] Embroidered.   [2] Twofold.   [3] Deceive me.   [4] i.e. son-in-law.
[5] 'I'll exchange half of the body of my silent daughter for my half of your
son.'

[ACT III SCENE 4]

[*Near* Sir Arthur Clarington's *house*]

Enter Sir Arthur Clarington, Warbeck, Somerton

SIR ART. Come, gentlemen, we must all help to grace
The nimble-footed youth of Edmonton
That are so kind
To call us up today with an high morris.
WAR. I could wish it for the best it were the worst now.
Absurdity's in my opinion ever the best dancer in a morris.
SOM. I could rather sleep than see 'em.
SIR ART. Not well, sir?
SOM. Faith, not ever thus leaden; yet I know no cause for't.
10 WAR. Now am I beyond mine own condition highly dispos'd to
mirth.
SIR ART. Well, you may have yet a morris to help both,
To strike you in a dump, and make him merry.

Enter Fiddler *and* morris, *all but* Banks

FID. Come, will you set yourselves in morris ray?[1] The forebell,
second bell, tenor, and great bell;[2] Maid Marian[3] for the same
bell. But where's the weathercock now, the hobby-horse?
1. Is not Banks come yet? What a spite 'tis!
SIR ART. When set you forward, gentlemen?
1. We stay but for the hobby-horse, sir; all our footmen are
20 ready.
SOM. 'Tis marvel your horse should be behind your foot.
2. Yes, sir. He goes further about; we can come in at the wicket,[4]
but the broad gate must be opened for him.

Enter [Cuddy] Banks [*as*] Hobby-horse, *and* Dog[5]

SIR ART. Oh, we stay'd for you, sir.
CUDDY. Only my horse wanted a shoe, sir; but we shall make you
amends ere we part.
SIR ART. Ay, well said. Make 'em drink ere they begin.

Enter Servants with beer

CUDDY. A bowl, I prithee, and a little for my horse; he'll mount
the better. Nay, give me. I must drink to him; he'll not pledge[6]

---

[1] Array.   [2] Morris dancers customarily wore tiny bells attached to their
costumes (II, i, 37–42); rarely they also carried handbells played in harmony.
[3] The role was sometimes taken by a man.   [4] A small gate for pedestrians.
[5] Invisible, as in III, iii.   [6] Drink a reciprocal health.

else. Here, hobby. *Holds him the bowl.* I pray you. No? Not drink? You see, gentlemen, we can but bring our horse to the water; he may choose whether he'll drink or no.

SOM. A good moral made plain by history.

1. Strike up, Father Sawgut, strike up.

FID. E'en when you will, children. Now in the name of the best foot forward,—[*Begins to play, but no sound is produced*] How now? Not a word in thy guts? I think, children, my instrument has caught cold on the sudden.

CUDDY. [*Aside*] My ningle's knavery, black Tom's doing!

OMNES. Why, what mean you, Father Sawgut?

CUDDY. Why, what would you have him do? You hear his fiddle is speechless.

FID. I'll lay mine ear to my instrument that my poor fiddle is bewitch'd. I play'd 'The Flowers in May' e'en now, as sweet as a violet; now 'twill not go against the hair. You see I can make no more music than a beetle of a cow turd.

CUDDY. Let me see, Father Sawgut. [*Takes his fiddle*] Say once you had a brave hobby-horse that you were beholding to. I'll play and dance too. [*Aside*] Ningle, away with it.

Dog *plays the morris*,[1] *which ended, enter a* Constable *and officers.*

OMNES. Ay, marry, sir.

CON. Away with jollity, 'tis too sad an hour.
    Sir Arthur Clarington, your own assistance,
    In the king's name, I charge,[2] for apprehension
    Of these two murderers, Warbeck and Somerton.

SIR ART. Ha! Flat murderers?

SOM. Ha, ha, ha! This has awakened my melancholy.

WAR. And struck my mirth down flat. Murderers?

CON. The accusation is flat against you, gentlemen.
    Sir, you may be satisfied with this. [*Shows* Sir Arthur *a warrant*]
    [*To* Warbeck, *and* Somerton] I hope you'll quietly obey my
                                                                    power.

'Twill make your cause the fairer.

AMBO.[3] Oh, with all our hearts, sir.

CUDDY. There's my rival taken up for hangman's meat. Tom told me he was about a piece of villainy. Mates and morris-men, you see here's no longer piping, no longer dancing. This news of murder has slain the morris. You that go the footway, fare ye well. I am for a gallop. [*Aside*] Come, ningle.

                                        Exeunt [Banks *and* Dog].

[1] Presumably Cuddy seems to hold the instrument whilst the dog (invisible to the actors) plays a tune.   [2] Command.   [3] Both.

FID. *Strikes his fiddle.* Ay? Nay, and my fiddle be come to him-
self again I care not. I think the devil has been abroad amongst
70   us today; I'll keep thee out of thy fit now if I can.   *Exit.*
SIR ART. These things are full of horror, full of pity;
But if this time be constant to the proof,
The guilt of both these gentlemen I dare take
Upon mine own danger; yet howsoever, sir,
Your power must be obey'd.   Oh, most willingly, sir.
WAR.
'Tis a most sweet affliction. I could not meet
A joy in the best shape with better will.
Come, fear not, sir. Nor judge nor evidence
Can bind him o'er who's freed by conscience.
80   SOM. Mine stands so upright to the middle zone
It takes no shadow to't; it goes alone.   *Exeunt.*

ACT IV SCENE 1

[*Near* Old Banks's *house*]

Enter Old Banks *and two or three countrymen*

BANKS. My horse this morning runs most piteously of the
glanders,[1] whose nose yesternight was as clean as any man's
here now coming from the barber's; and this, I'll take my
death upon't, is long[2] of this jadish witch, Mother Sawyer.
1. I took my wife and a serving-man in our town of Edmonton,
thrashing in my barn together such corn as country wenches
carry to market; and, examining my polecat[3] why she did so,
she swore in her conscience she was bewitch'd. And what witch
have we about us but Mother Sawyer?
10   2. Rid the town of her, else all our wives will do nothing else but
dance about other country maypoles.
3. Our cattle fall, our wives fall, our daughters fall, and maid-
servants fall; and we ourselves shall not be able to stand if this
beast be suffered to graze amongst us.

Enter W. Hamluc, *with thatch and a link*[4]

HAM. Burn the witch, the witch, the witch, the witch!

---

[1] A contagious disease of horses, marked by swellings under the jaw and
discharge of mucous matter from the nostrils.   [2] Because.   [3] Harlot.
[4] Torch.

OMNES. What hast got there?

HAM. A handful of thatch pluck'd off a hovel of hers; and they say when 'tis burning, if she be a witch she'll come running in.[1]

BANKS. Fire it, fire it. I'll stand between thee and home for any danger.

As that burns, enter the witch [, Mother Sawyer]

MOTHER. Disease, plagues, the curse of an old woman follow and fall upon you!

OMNES. Are you come, you old trot?

BANKS. You hot whore, must we fetch you with fire in your tail?

1. This thatch is as good as a jury to prove she is a witch.

OMNES. Out, witch! Beat her, kick her, set fire on her!

MOTHER. Shall I be murdered by a bed of serpents? Help, help!

Enter Sir Arthur Clarington *and a* Justice

OMNES. Hang her, beat her, kill her!

JUST. How now? Forbear this violence!

MOTHER. A crew of villains, a knot of bloody hangmen set to torment me, I know not why.

JUST. Alas, neighbour Banks, are you a ringleader in mischief? Fie, to abuse an aged woman!

BANKS. Woman? A she-hellcat, a witch! To prove her one, we no sooner set fire on the thatch of her house, but in she came running, as if the devil had sent her in a barrel of gunpowder; which trick as surely proves her a witch as the pox in a snuffling nose is a sign a man is a whoremaster.

JUST. Come, come! Firing her thatch? Ridiculous!
Take heed, sirs, what you do; unless your proofs
Come better arm'd, instead of turning her
Into a witch, you'll prove yourselves stark fools.

OMNES. Fools?

JUST. Arrant fools.

BANKS. Pray, Mr Justice What-do-you-call-'em, hear me but in one thing: This grumbling devil owes me, I know, no good will ever since I fell out with her.

MOTHER. And breakedst my back with beating me.

BANKS. I'll break it worse.

MOTHER. Wilt thou?

JUST. You must not threaten her; 'tis against law. Go on.

BANKS. So, sir, ever since, having a dun cow tied up in my backside,[2] let me go thither or but cast mine eye at her, and if I

[1] Recorded by Goodcole as an actual part of the testing of Mother Sawyer for witchcraft.   [2] Back yard.

should be hang'd, I cannot choose, though it be ten times in an
hour, but run to the cow and, taking up her tail, kiss—saving
your worship's reverence—my cow behind, that the whole town
of Edmonton has been ready to bepiss themselves with laughing
me to scorn.

JUST. And this is long of her?

60 BANKS. Who the devil else? For is any man such an ass to be
such a baby, if he were not bewitch'd?

SIR ART. Nay, if she be a witch, and the harms she does end in
such sports, she may scape burning.

JUST. Go, go. Pray, vex her not. She is a subject,
And you must not be judges of the law
To strike her as you please.

OMNES. No, no, we'll find cudgel enough to strike her.

BANKS. Ay, no lips to kiss but my cow's ————?[1]

Exeunt [Banks *and* countrymen].

MOTHER. Rots and foul maladies eat up thee and thine!

70 JUST. Here's none now, Mother Sawyer, but this gentleman,
Myself, and you. Let us to some mild questions;
Have you mild answers? Tell us honestly,
And with a free confession—we'll do our best
To wean you from it—are you a witch or no?

MOTHER. I am none!

JUST.   Be not so furious.

MOTHER.   I am none!
None but base curs so bark at me. I am none;
Or would I were. If every poor old woman
Be trod on thus by slaves, revil'd, kick'd, beaten,
As I am daily, she to be reveng'd
Had need turn witch.

80 SIR ART.   And you, to be reveng'd,
Have sold your soul to th' devil.

MOTHER.   Keep thine own from him.

JUST. You are too saucy and too bitter.

MOTHER.   Saucy?
By what commission can he send my soul
On the devil's errand more than I can his?
Is he a landlord of my soul, to thrust it
When he list out of door?

JUST.   Know whom you speak to.

MOTHER. A man. Perhaps no man. Men in gay clothes,

[1] *Sic* Q.

Whose backs are laden with titles and honours,
Are within far more crooked than I am,
And if I be a witch, more witchlike.
SIR ART. Y'are a base hellhound!
   And now, sir, let me tell you, far and near
   She's bruited for a woman that maintains
   A spirit that sucks her.
MOTHER.   I defy thee!
SIR ART.   Go, go.
   I can, if need be, bring an hundred voices,
   E'en here in Edmonton, that shall loud proclaim
   Thee for a secret and pernicious witch.
MOTHER. Ha ha!
JUST. Do you laugh? Why laugh you?
MOTHER.   At my name,
   The brave name this knight gives me: 'Witch'.
JUST. Is the name of witch so pleasing to thine ear?
SIR ART. Pray, sir, give way, and let her tongue gallop on.
MOTHER. A witch? Who is not?
   Hold not that universal name in scorn then.
   What are your painted things in princes' courts,
   Upon whose eyelids lust sits, blowing fires
   To burn men's souls in sensual, hot desires,
   Upon whose naked paps a lecher's thought
   Acts sin in fouler shapes than can be wrought?
JUST. But those work not as you do.
MOTHER.   No, but far worse.
   These by enchantments can whole lordships[1] change
   To trunks of rich attire, turn ploughs and teams
   To Flanders mares and coaches, and huge trains
   Of servitors to a French butterfly.
   Have you not city witches who can turn
   Their husbands' wares, whole standing shops of wares,
   To sumptuous tables, gardens of stol'n sin,
   In one year wasting what scarce twenty win?
   Are not these witches?
JUST.   Yes, yes, but the law
   Casts not an eye on these.
MOTHER.   Why then on me,
   Or any lean old beldam? Reverence once
   Had wont to wait on age; now an old woman,

[1] Estates.

Ill-favour'd grown with years, if she be poor,
Must be call'd bawd or witch. Such so abus'd
Are the coarse witches; t'other are the fine,
Spun for the devil's own wearing.

SIR ART.   And so is thine.

MOTHER. She on whose tongue a whirlwind sits to blow
A man out of himself, from his soft pillow,
To lean his head on rocks and fighting waves,
130   Is not that scold a witch? The man of law
Whose honeyed hopes the credulous client draws—
As bees to tinkling basins—to swarm to him
From his own hive. to work the wax in his—
He is no witch, not he!

SIR ART.   But these men-witches
Are not in trading with Hell's merchandise,
Like such as you are, that for a word, a look,
Denial of a coal of fire, kill men,
Children, and cattle.

MOTHER.   Tell them, sir, that do so.
Am I accus'd for such an one?

SIR ART.   Yes; 'twill be sworn.

140   MOTHER. Dare any swear I ever tempted maiden,
With golden hooks flung at her chastity,
To come and lose her honour, and being lost
To pay not a denier [1] for't? Some slaves have done it.
Men-witches can, without the fangs of law
Drawing once one drop of blood, put counterfeit pieces
Away for true gold.

SIR ART.   By one thing she speaks
I know now she's a witch, and dare no longer
Hold conference with the fury.

JUST.   Let's then away.
Old woman, mend thy life; get home and pray.
                              Exeunt [Justice *and* Sir Arthur].

MOTHER. For his confusion!

Enter Dog

150   My dear Tom-boy, welcome!
I am torn in pieces by a pack of curs
Clapp'd all upon me, and for want of thee.
Comfort me; thou shalt have the teat anon.

DOG. Bow wow! I'll have it now.

---

[1] A French coin of little value.

MOTHER.   I am dried up
  With cursing and with madness, and have yet
  No blood to moisten these sweet lips of thine.
  Stand on thy hind legs up. Kiss me, my Tommy,
  And rub away some wrinkles on my brow
  By making my old ribs to shrug for joy
60 Of thy fine tricks. What hast thou done? Let's tickle.[1]
  Hast thou struck the horse lame as I bid thee?
DOG.   Yes,
  And nipp'd the sucking child.
MOTHER.   Ho, ho, my dainty,
  My little pearl! No lady loves her hound,
  Monkey, or parakeet, as I do thee.
DOG. The maid has been churning butter nine hours, but it shall
  not come.
MOTHER. Let 'em eat cheese and choke.
DOG.   I had rare sport
  Among the clowns i' th' morris.
MOTHER.   I could dance
  Out of my skin to hear thee. But, my curl-pate,
70 That jade, that foul-tongu'd whore, Nan Ratcliffe,
  Who for a little soap lick'd by my sow,[2]
  Struck and almost had lam'd it; did not I charge thee
  To pinch that quean to th' heart?
DOG.   Bow, wow, wow! Look here else.

Enter Anne Ratcliffe *mad*

ANNE. See, see, see! The man i' th' moon has built a new windmill, and what running there's from all quarters of the city to
  learn the art of grinding!
MOTHER. Ho, ho, ho! I thank thee, my sweet mongrel.
ANNE. Hoyda! A pox of the devil's false hopper! All the golden
  meal runs into the rich knaves' purses, and the poor have noth-
80 ing but bran. Hey derry down! Are not you Mother Sawyer?
MOTHER. No, I am a lawyer.
ANNE. Art thou? I prithee let me scratch thy face, for thy pen
  has flay'd off a great many men's skins. You'll have brave
  doings in the vacation,[3] for knaves and fools are at variance
  in every village. I'll sue Mother Sawyer, and her own sow shall
  give in evidence against her.

---

[1] Give ourselves pleasure.   [2] 'Who, because my sow licked a little of
her soap, . . .' (A detail from Goodcole).   [3] Between terms, when
lawyers returned to the country.

MOTHER. [*To* Dog] Touch her.

ANNE. Oh, my ribs are made of a pan'd hose,[1] and they break.
There's a Lancashire hornpipe in my throat. Hark how it
190 tickles it, with doodle, doodle, doodle, doodle. Welcome,
sergeants. Welcome, devil. Hands, hands, hold hands, and
dance around, around, around!

Enter Old Banks, *his son* [Cuddy] *the Clown,*
Old Ratcliffe, *country fellows*

RAT. She's here; alas, my poor wife is here.

BANKS. Catch her fast and have her into some close chamber, do,
for she's as many wives are, stark mad.

CUDDY. The witch, Mother Sawyer, the witch, the devil!

RAT. O my dear wife! Help, sirs!

[*Several*] *carry her off*

BANKS. You see your work, Mother Bumby.[2]

MOTHER. My work? Should she and all you here run mad, is the
200 work mine?

CUDDY. No, on my conscience, she would not hurt a devil of two
years old.

[*Re-*]*enter* Old Ratcliffe *and the rest*

How now? What's become of her?

RAT. Nothing. She's become nothing but the miserable trunk of
a wretched woman. We were in her hands as reeds in a mighty
tempest. Spite of our strengths, away she brake, and nothing
in her mouth being heard but, 'The devil, the witch, the witch,
the devil!' She beat out her own brains, and so died.

CUDDY. It's any man's case, be he never so wise, to die when his
210 brains go a-woolgathering.

BANKS. Masters, be rul'd by me; let's all to a justice. Hag, thou
hast done this, and thou shalt answer it.

MOTHER. Banks, I defy thee.

BANKS. Get a warrant first to examine her; then ship her to
Newgate.[3] Here's enough, if all her other villainies were
pardon'd, to burn her for a witch. You have a spirit, they say,
comes to you in the likeness of a dog. We shall see your cur at
one time or other. If we do, unless it be the devil himself, he
shall go howling to the gaol in one chain and thou in another.

220 MOTHER. Be hang'd thou in a third, and do thy worst!

---

[1] Hose made by sewing together strips of cloth in varied colours.
[2] An inappropriate reference to the harmless fortune-teller in Lyly's comedy
Mother Bombie (1590).   [3] The historical Mother Sawyer was incarcerated
in this London prison.

CUDDY. How, father? You send the poor dumb thing howling to the gaol? He that makes him [1] howl makes me roar.

BANKS. Why, foolish boy, dost thou know him?

CUDDY. No matter if I do or not. He's bailable, I am sure, by law. But if the dog's word will not be taken, mine shall.

BANKS. Thou bail for a dog?

CUDDY. Yes, or a bitch either, being my friend. I'll lie by the heels [2] myself before puppison shall. His dog days are not come yet, I hope.

BANKS. What manner of dog is it? Didst ever see him?

CUDDY. See him? Yes, and given him a bone to gnaw twenty times. The dog is no court foisting [3] hound that fills his belly full by base wagging his tail. Neither is it a citizen's water spaniel, enticing his master to go a-ducking twice or thrice a week, whilst his wife makes ducks and drakes at home. This is no Paris Garden [4] bandog neither, that keeps a bow, wow, wowing to have butchers bring their curs thither, and when all comes to all, they run away like sheep. Neither is this the black dog of Newgate.[5]

BANKS. No, goodman son-fool, but the dog of Hellgate.

CUDDY. I say, goodman father-fool, it's a lie.

OMNES. He's bewitch'd.

CUDDY. A gross lie, as big as myself. The devil in Saint Dunstan's [6] will as soon drink with this poor cur as with any Temple Bar laundress [7] that washes and wrings lawyers.

DOG. Bow, wow, wow, wow!

OMNES. Oh, the dog's here, the dog's here!

BANKS. It was the voice of a dog.

CUDDY. The voice of a dog? If that voice were a dog's, what voice had my mother? So am I a dog: Bow, wow, wow! It was I that bark'd so, father, to make coxcombs of these clowns.

BANKS. However, we'll be coxcomb'd no longer. Away therefore to th' justice for a warrant, and then Gammer Gurton,[8] have at your needle of witchcraft!

---

[1] i.e. the dog.   [2] Be put in irons or the stocks.   [3] Cheating.
[4] A popular London arena where bulls or bears were baited by fierce dogs.
[5] The title of a poem and essay by Luke Hutton (1600) and a lost play (1602). In Hutton's work a rapacious prison officer is described metaphorically as a black dog.   [6] A tavern called Saint Dunstan and the Devil was opposite Saint Dunstan's Church, Fleet Street. The inn sign showed the saint pulling the devil by the nose with a pair of tongs.   [7] Possibly a recognizable woman who did the laundry of bachelor lawyers. John Ford was a member of the Middle Temple for many years.   [8] The central figure in *Gammer Gurton's Needle* (c. 1560); Banks's allusion is almost irrelevant in that Gammer Gurton has no association with witchcraft, although she is irascible.

MOTHER. And prick thine own eyes out! Go, peevish fools.
　　　　　Exeunt [Old Banks, Ratcliffe, *and country fellows*].
CUDDY. Ningle, you had like to have spoil'd all with your bow-
　　ings. I was glad to put 'em off with one of my dog-tricks on a
　　sudden. I am bewitch'd, little cost-me-naught, to love thee. A
　　pox! That morris makes me spit in thy mouth.[1] I dare not stay.
260　Farewell, ningle, you whoreson dog's nose; farewell, witch.
　　　　　　　　　　　　　　　　　　　　　　　　　　　Exit.
DOG. Bow, wow, wow, wow!
MOTHER. Mind him not; he's not worth thy worrying. Run at a
　　fairer game, that foul-mouth'd knight, scurvy Sir Arthur; fly at
　　him, my Tommy, and pluck out's throat.
DOG. No, there['s] a dog already biting 's conscience.
MOTHER. That's a sure bloodhound. Come, let's home and play;
　　Our black work ended, we'll make holiday.　　　　*Exeunt.*

[ACT IV] SCENE 2

[Old Carter's *house*]

Enter Katherine; *a bed thrust forth, on it* Frank *in a slumber*

KATH. Brother, brother![2] So sound asleep? That's well.
FRANK. No, not I, sister.[3] He that's wounded here
　　As I am—all my other hurts are bitings
　　Of a poor flea—but he that here once bleeds
　　Is maim'd incurably.
KATH.　　　　　　My good sweet brother,
　　For now my sister must grow up in you,
　　Though her loss strikes you through, and that I feel
　　The blow as deep, I pray thee be not cruel
　　To kill me too, by seeing you cast away
10　In your own helpless sorrow. Good love, sit up,
　　And if you can give physic to yourself
　　I shall be well.
FRANK.　　　　I'll do my best.
KATH.　　　　　　　　　I thank you.
　　What do you look about for?

---

[1] 'Do you a good turn.'　　[2] i.e. brother-in-law.　　[3] i.e. sister-in-law.

FRANK.   Nothing, nothing;
   But I was thinking, sister,—
KATH.   Dear heart, what?
FRANK. Who but a fool would thus be bound to a bed
   Having this room to walk in?
KATH.   Why do you talk so?
   Would you were fast asleep!
FRANK.   No, no, I'm not idle;[1]
   But here's my meaning: Being robb'd as I am,
   Why should my soul, which married was to hers,
   Live in divorce, and not fly after her?
   Why should not I walk hand in hand with death
   To find my love out?
KATH.   That were well indeed,
   Your time being come. When death is sent to call you,
   No doubt you shall meet her.
FRANK.   Why should not I
   Go without calling?
KATH.   Yes, brother, so you might,
   Were there no place to go to when y'are gone
   But only this.
FRANK.   Troth, sister, thou say'st true;
   For when a man has been an hundred years
   Hard travelling o'er the tottering bridge of age,
   He's not the thousand part upon his way.
   All life is but a wand'ring to find home;
   When we are gone, we are there. Happy were man
   Could here his voyage end; he should not then
   Answer how well or ill he steer'd his soul
   By Heaven's or by Hell's compass, how he put in
   (Losing bless'd goodness' shore) at such a sin,
   Nor how life's dear provision he has spent,
   Nor how far he in's navigation went
   Beyond commission.[2] This were a fine reign,
   To do ill and not hear of it again.
   Yet then were man more wretched than a beast,
   For, sister, our dead pay[3] is sure the best.
KATH. 'Tis so, the best or worst. And I wish Heaven
   To pay, and so I know it will, that traitor,
   That devil Somerton (who stood in mine eye
   Once as an angel) home to his deservings.
   What villain but himself, once loving me,

[1] Light-headed.   [2] Authority.   [3] Retribution.

With Warbeck's soul would pawn his own to Hell
To be reveng'd on my poor sister?

FRANK.   Slaves!

50   A pair of merciless slaves! Speak no more of them.

KATH. I think this talking hurts you.

FRANK.   Does me no good, I'm sure.
I pay for't everywhere.

KATH.   I have done then.
Eat, if you cannot sleep. You have these two days
Not tasted any food. [*Calls off-stage*] Jane, is it ready?

FRANK. What's ready? What's ready?

KATH. I have made ready a roasted chicken for you.

                    [*Enter* Jane]
Sweet, wilt thou eat?

FRANK. A pretty stomach on a sudden, yes.
There's one in the house can play upon a lute;
Good girl, let's hear him too.

60   KATH.   You shall, dear brother. [*Exit* Jane.]
Would I were a musician, you should hear   *Lute plays*
How I would feast your ear. Stay, mend your pillow,
And raise you higher.

FRANK.   I am up too high,
Am I not, sister, now?

KATH.   No, no, 'tis well.
Fall to, fall to. A knife! Here's never a knife.
Brother, I'll look out yours.

        Enter Dog, *shrugging as it were for joy, and dances*

FRANK.   Sister, oh, sister,
I am ill upon a sudden and can eat nothing.

KATH. In very deed you shall. The want of food
Makes you so faint. Ha! [*Finds the bloody knife and returns it
to his pocket*]   Here's none in your pocket.
I'll go fetch a knife.   *Exit.*

70   FRANK.   Will you? 'Tis well.
All's well.

*She gone, he searches first one, then the other pocket. Knife
found.* Dog *runs off. He lies on one side. The spirit of* Susan, *his
second wife, comes to the bedside. He stares at it, and turning to
the other side, it's there too. In the meantime* Winnifride *as a
page comes in, stands at his bed's feet sadly. He, frighted, sits
upright. The spirit [of* Susan] *vanishes.*

            What art thou?

WIN.   A lost creature.

FRANK. So am I too. Win? Ah, my she-page!

WIN. For your sake I put on a shape that's false;
Yet do I wear a heart true to you as your own.

FRANK. Would mine and thine were fellows in one house.
Kneel by me here. On this side now? How dar'st
Thou come to mock me on both sides of my bed?

WIN. When?

FRANK.   But just now. Outface me, stare upon me
With strange postures, turn my soul wild by
A face in which were drawn a thousand ghosts
Leap'd newly from their graves to pluck
Me into a winding sheet?

WIN.   Believe it,
I came no nearer to you than yon place
At your bed's feet; and of the house had leave,
Calling myself your horse-boy, in to come
And visit my sick master.

FRANK.   Then 'twas my fancy,
Some windmill in my brains for want of sleep.

WIN. Would I might never sleep, so you could rest.
But you have pluck'd a thunder on your head,
Whose noise cannot cease suddenly. Why should you
Dance at the wedding of a second wife,
When scarce the music which you heard at mine
Had ta'en a farewell of you? Oh, this was ill!
And they who thus can give both hands away
In th'end shall want their best limbs.

FRANK.   Winnifride,
The chamber door fast?

WIN.   Yes.

FRANK.   Sit thee then down,
And when th'ast heard me speak, melt into tears.
Yet I, to save those eyes of thine from weeping,
Being to write a story of us two,
Instead of ink, dipp'd my sad pen in blood.
When of thee I took leave I went abroad
Only for pillage, as a freebooter,
What gold soe'er I got, to make it thine.
To please a father, I have Heaven displeas'd.
Striving to cast two wedding rings in one,
Through my bad workmanship I now have none.
I have lost her and thee.

WIN.   I know she's dead,
But you have me still.
FRANK.   Nay, her this hand
Murdered; and so I lose thee too.
WIN.   Oh me!
110 FRANK. Be quiet, for thou my evidence art,
Jury, and judge. Sit quiet, and I'll tell all.

As they whisper, enter at one end o' th' stage Old Carter *and*
Katherine, Dog *at th' other, pawing softly at* Frank

KATH. I have run madding up and down to find you,
Being laden with the heaviest news that ever
Poor daughter carried.
CAR.   Why, is the boy dead?
KATH.   Dead, sir?
Oh, father, we are cozen'd. You are told
The murderer sings in prison, and he laughs here.
This villain kill'd my sister! See else, see,
A bloody knife in's pocket.
CAR.   Bless me! Patience!
FRANK. [*Noticing* Katherine *and* Old Carter] The knife, the
120 knife, the knife!
KATH. What knife?   *Exit* Dog.
FRANK.   To cut my chicken up, my chicken.
Be you my carver, father.
CAR.   That I will.
KATH. [*Aside*] How the devil steels our brows after doing ill!
FRANK. My stomach and my sight are taken from me;
All is not well within me.
CAR. I believe thee, boy. I that have seen so many moons clap
their horns on other men's foreheads to strike them sick,[1] yet
mine to scape and be well; I that never cast away a fee upon
urinals,[2] but am as sound as an honest man's conscience when
130 he's dying, I should cry out as thou dost, 'All is not well
within me,' felt I but the bag of thy imposthumes.[3] Ah, poor
villain! Ah, my wounded rascal! All my grief is, I have now
small hope of thee.
FRANK. Do the surgeons say my wounds are dangerous then?
CAR. Yes, yes, and there's no way with thee but one.
FRANK. Would he were here to open them!
CAR. I'll go fetch him. I'll make an holiday to see thee as I wish.
                              Exit to fetch officers.

[1] The implication is not specifically of cuckoldry, but of madness.
[2] Vessels for the medical examination of urine.   [3] Abscesses.

FRANK. A wondrous kind old man.

WIN. [*To* Frank] Your sin's the blacker so to abuse his goodness.
Master, how do you?

FRANK.   Pretty well now, boy.
I have such odd qualms come cross my stomach.
I'll fall to. Boy, cut me.

WIN. [*Aside*]   You have cut me, I'm sure.
A leg or wing, sir?

FRANK.   No, no, no!—[*Aside*] A wing?
Would I had wings but to soar up yon tower;
But here's a clog that hinders me.—What's that?

[*Enter* Susan's] *father with her in a coffin*

CAR. That? What? Oh, now I see her. 'Tis a young wench, my
daughter, sirrah, sick to the death; and hearing thee to be an
excellent rascal for letting blood, she looks out at a casement and
cries, 'Help, help! Stay that man; him I must have or none!'

FRANK. For pity's sake, remove her! See, she stares
With one broad open eye still in my face.

CAR. Thou puttest both hers out, like a villain as thou art; yet
see, she is willing to lend thee one again to find out the murderer,
and that's thyself.

FRANK. Old man, thou liest.

CAR.   So shalt thou, i' th' gaol.
Run for officers.

KATH.   O thou merciless slave!
She was, though yet above ground, in her grave
To me, but thou hast torn it up again.
Mine eyes, too much drown'd, now must feel more rain.

CAR. Fetch officers.   *Exit* Katherine.

FRANK. For whom?

CAR. For thee, sirrah, sirrah! Some knives have foolish posies [1]
upon them, but thine has a villainous one. [*Seizes knife from
Frank's pocket*] Look! Oh, it is enamell'd with the heart-blood
of thy hated wife, my beloved daughter! What say'st thou to this
evidence? Is't not sharp? Does't not strike home? Thou canst
not answer honestly and without a trembling heart to this one
point, this terrible bloody point.

WIN. I beseech you, sir, strike him no more; you see he's dead
already.

CAR. Oh, sir, you held his horses. You are as arrant a rogue as
he! Up go you too.

---

[1] Short inscriptions in verse.

FRANK. As y'are a man, throw not upon that woman
Your loads of tyranny, for she's innocent.
CAR. How? How? A woman? Is't grown to a fashion for women
in all countries to wear the breeches?
WIN. I am not as my disguise speaks me, sir,
His page, but his first, only wife, his lawful wife.
CAR. How? How? More fire i' th' bedstraw? [1]
180 WIN. The wrongs which singly fell on your daughter
On me are multiplied; she lost a life,
But I an husband, and my self must lose,
If you call him to a bar for what he has done.
CAR. He has done it then?
WIN. Yes, 'tis confess'd to me.
FRANK.   Dost thou betray me?
WIN. Oh, pardon me, dear heart! I am mad to lose thee,
And know not what I speak; but if thou didst,
I must arraign this father for two sins:
Adultery and murder.

Enter Katherine

KATH.   Sir, they are come.
190 CAR. Arraign me for what thou wilt, all Middlesex knows me
better for an honest man than the middle of a marketplace [2]
knows thee for an honest woman. Rise, sirrah, and don your
tacklings; [3] rig yourself for the gallows, or I'll carry thee thither
on my back. Your trull shall to th' gaol go with you. There be as
fine Newgate birds as she, that can draw him in. Pox on's
wounds!
FRANK. I have serv'd thee, and my wages now are paid;
Yet my worst punishment shall, I hope, be stay'd.   *Exeunt.*

ACT V SCENE 1

[*Near* Mother Sawyer's *house*]

Enter Mother Sawyer *alone*

MOTHER. Still wrong'd by every slave, and not a dog
Bark in his dame's defence? I am call'd witch,

[1] Concealed mischief.   [2] The location of the pillory.
[3] Accroutrements.

Yet am myself bewitched from doing harm.
Have I given up myself to thy black lust
Thus to be scorn'd? Not see me in three days?
I'm lost without my Tomalin. Prithee, come;
Revenge to me is sweeter far than life.
Thou art my raven, on whose coal-black wings
Revenge comes flying to me. O my best love!
I am on fire, even in the midst of ice,
Raking my blood up till my shrunk knees feel
Thy curl'd head leaning on them. Come then, my darling;
If in the air thou hover'st, fall upon me
In some dark cloud; and, as I oft have seen
Dragons and serpents in the elements,
Appear thou now so to me. Art thou i' th' sea?
Muster up all the monsters from the deep,
And be the ugliest of them, so that my bulch [1]
Show but his swarth cheek to me, let earth cleave
And break from Hell, I care not. Could I run
Like a swift powder mine beneath the world,
Up would I blow it all, to find out thee,
Though I lay ruin'd in it. Not yet come?
I must then fall to my old prayer:
Sanctibiceter nomen tuum.
Not yet come? Worrying of wolves,
Biting of mad dogs, the manges and the—

Enter Dog [*, now white*]

DOG. How now? Whom art thou cursing?
MOTHER. Thee. Ha! No, 'tis my black cur I am cursing
  For not attending on me.
DOG.   I am that cur.
MOTHER. Thou liest! Hence! Come not nigh me.
DOG.   Bow, wow!
MOTHER. Why dost thou thus appear to me in white,
  As if thou wert the ghost of my dear love?
DOG. I am dogged. List not to tell thee; yet to torment thee, my
  whiteness puts thee in mind of thy winding sheet.
MOTHER. Am I near death?
DOG. Yes, if the dog of Hell be near thee. When the devil comes
  to thee as a lamb, have at thy throat.
MOTHER. Off, cur!
DOG. He has the back of a sheep, but the belly of an otter,

---

[1] Bull calf, a term of endearment.

devours by sea and land. Why am I in white? Didst thou not pray to me?

MOTHER. Yes, thou dissembling hellhound. Why now in white more than at other times?

DOG. Be blasted with the news. Whiteness is day's footboy, a forerunner to light, which shows thy old rivell'd face. Villains are stripp'd naked; the witch must be beaten out of her cockpit.

MOTHER. Must she? She shall not. Thou art a lying spirit.
50   Why to mine eyes art thou a flag of truce?
I am at peace with none; 'tis the black colour
Or none, which I fight under. I do not like
Thy puritan paleness; glowing furnaces
Are far more hot than they which flame outright.
If thou my old dog art, go and bite such
As I shall set thee on.

DOG.   I will not.

MOTHER. I'll sell myself to twenty thousand fiends
To have thee torn in pieces then.

DOG. Thou canst not; thou art so ripe to fall into Hell
60   That no more of my kennel will so much
As bark at him that hangs thee.

MOTHER.   I shall run mad!

DOG. Do so. Thy time is come to curse and rave and die;
The glass of thy sins is full, and it must run out at gallows.

MOTHER. It cannot, ugly cur; I'll confess nothing.
And not confessing, who dare come and swear
I have bewitched them? I'll not confess one mouthful.

DOG. Choose, and be hang'd or burn'd.

MOTHER. Spite of the devil and thee, I'll muzzle up
My tongue from telling tales.

DOG.   Spite of thee
And the devil, thou'lt be condemn'd.

70 MOTHER.   Yes, when?

DOG. And ere the executioner catch thee
Full in's claws, thou'lt confess all.

MOTHER.   Out, dog!

DOG. Out, witch! Thy trial is at hand.
Our prey being had, the devil does laughing stand.

                         The Dog *stands aloof*

        Enter Old Banks, Ratcliffe, *and countrymen*

BANKS. She's here; attach her. Witch, you must go with us.

MOTHER. Whither? To Hell?

BANKS. No, no, no, old crone. Your mittimus[1] shall be made
thither, but your own jailors shall receive you. Away with her!

MOTHER. My Tommy! My sweet Tom-boy! O thou dog!
Dost thou now fly to thy kennel and forsake me?
Plagues and consumptions—   *Exeunt[, except* Dog].

DOG. Ha, ha, ha, ha!
Let not the world, witches, or devils condemn;
They follow us, and then we follow them.

[*Enter*] Young [Cuddy] Banks *to the* Dog

CUDDY. I would fain meet with mine ingle once more. He has had
a claw amongst 'um. My rival that lov'd my wench is like to be
hang'd like an innocent.[2] A kind cur where he takes, but where
he takes not, a dogged rascal. I know the villain loves me.
No,—[Dog *barks*. Art thou there? That's Tom's voice, but
'tis not he. [Dog *becomes visible to him*] This is a dog of another
hair, this. Bark and not speak to me? Not Tom then. There's
as much difference betwixt Tom and this as betwixt white and
black.

DOG. Hast thou forgot me?

CUDDY. That's Tom again. Prithee, ningle, speak. Is thy name
Tom?

DOG. Whilst I serv'd my old Dame Sawyer, 'twas. I'm gone from
her now.

CUDDY. Gone? Away with the witch then too; she'll never thrive
if thou leav'st her. She knows no more how to kill a cow, or a
horse, or a sow without thee than she does to kill a goose.

DOG. No, she has done killing now, but must be kill'd for what
she has done. She's shortly to be hang'd.

CUDDY. Is she? In my conscience, if she be, 'tis thou hast brought
her to the gallows, Tom.

DOG. Right. I serv'd her to that purpose; 'twas part of my wages.

CUDDY. This was no honest servant's part, by your leave, Tom.
This remember, I pray you, between you and I; I entertain'd you
ever as a dog, not as a devil.

DOG. True, and so I us'd thee doggedly, not devilishly.
I have deluded thee for sport to laugh at.
The wench thou seek'st after thou never spakest with,
But a spirit in her form, habit, and likeness. Ha, ha!

CUDDY. I do not then wonder at the change of your garments, if
you can enter into shapes of women too.

Warrant.   [2] Half-wit.

DOG. Any shape, to blind such silly eyes as thine; but chiefly
   those coarse creatures, dog, or cat, hare, ferret, frog, toad.
CUDDY. Louse or flea?
DOG. Any poor vermin.
120 CUDDY. It seems you devils have poor, thin souls, that you can
   bestow yourselves in such small bodies. But pray you, Tom,
   one question at parting—I think I shall never see you more—
   where do you borrow those bodies that are none of your own?
   The garment-shape you may hire at broker's.
DOG. Why wouldst thou know that? Fool, it avails thee not.
CUDDY. Only for my mind's sake, Tom, and to tell some of my
   friends.
DOG. I'll thus much tell thee: Thou never art so distant
   From an evil spirit but that thy oaths,
130 Curses, and blasphemies pull him to thine elbow.
   Thou never tell'st a lie but that a devil
   Is within hearing it. Thy evil purposes
   Are ever haunted, but when they come to act,
   As thy tongue slandering, bearing false witness,
   Thy hand stabbing, stealing, cozening, cheating,
   He's then within thee. Thou play'st; he bets upon thy part.
   Although thou lose, yet he will gain by thee.
CUDDY. Ay? Then he comes in the shape of a rook.
DOG. The old cadaver of some self-strangled wretch
140 We sometimes borrow, and appear humane.
   The carcass of some disease-slain strumpet
   We varnish fresh, and wear as her first beauty.
   Didst never hear? If not, it has been done.
   An hot, luxurious lecher in his twines,[1]
   When he has thought to clip his dalliance,
   There has provided been for his embrace
   A fine, hot, flaming devil in her place.
CUDDY. Yes, I am partly a witness to this, but I never could
   embrace her. I thank thee for that, Tom. Well, again I thank
150 thee, Tom, for all this counsel, without a fee too. There's few
   lawyers of thy mind now. Certainly, Tom, I begin to pity thee.
DOG. Pity me? For what?
CUDDY. Were it not possible for thee to become an honest dog
   yet? 'Tis a base life that you lead, Tom, to serve witches, to kill
   innocent children, to kill harmless cattle, to stroy corn and
   fruit, etc. 'Twere better yet to be a butcher, and kill for yourself.

---

[1] Embraces.

DOG. Why? These are all my delights, my pleasures, fool.

CUDDY. Or, Tom, if you could give your mind to ducking, I
know you can swim, fetch, and carry; some shopkeeper in
London would take great delight in you, and be a tender master
over you. Or if you have a mind to the game, either at bull or
bear, I think I could prefer [1] you to Moll Cutpurse.[2]

DOG. Ha, ha! I should kill all the game—bulls, bears, dogs
and all; not a cub to be left.

CUDDY. You could do, Tom, but you must play fair; you should
be stav'd [3] off else. Or if your stomach did better like to serve in
some nobleman's, knight's, or gentleman's kitchen, if you
could brook [4] the wheel and turn the spit—your labour could
not be much—when they have roast meat—that's but once or
twice in the week at most—here you might lick your own toes
very well. Or if you could translate yourself into a lady's
arming puppy, there you might lick sweet lips and do many
pretty offices. But to creep under an old witch's coats, and suck
like a great puppy—fie upon't! I have heard beastly things of
you, Tom.

DOG. Ha, ha! The worst thou heard'st of me, the better 'tis.
Shall I serve thee, fool, at the selfsame rate?

CUDDY. No, I'll see thee hang'd; thou shalt be damn'd first.
I know thy qualities too well. I'll give no suck to such whelps;
therefore, henceforth I defy thee. Out, and avaunt!

DOG. Nor will I serve for such a silly soul.
I am for greatness now, corrupted greatness.
There I'll shug [5] in and get a noble countenance; [6]
Serve some Briarean [7] footcloth-strider [8]
That has an hundred hands to catch at bribes,
But not a finger's nail of charity.
Such, like the dragon's tail, shall pull down hundreds,
To drop and sink with him. I'll stretch myself
And draw this bulk small as a silver wire,
Enter at the least pore tobacco fume
Can make a breach for. Hence, silly fool;
I scorn to prey on such an atom [9] soul.

---

[1] Recommend.   [2] Mary Frith (c. 1589–c. 1659), a notorious woman-
about-town who smoked, wore male clothing, was a pickpocket, trickster,
whore, bawd, etc. She was referred to in several other plays, especially
Middleton and Dekker, *The Roaring Girl* (c. 1610).   [3] Beaten.
[4] Tolerate.   [5] Wriggle.   [6] Patronage.   [7] Alluding to Briareus, a
mythological giant with a hundred arms and fifty heads.
[8] One who mounts a horse with a richly ornamented cloth on its back.
[9] Insignificant.

CUDDY. Come out, come out, you cur. I will beat thee out of the bounds of Edmonton, and tomorrow we go in procession, and after thou shalt never come in again. If thou goest to London, I'll make thee go about by Tyburn,[1] stealing in by Thieving Lane.[2] If thou canst rub thy shoulder against a lawyer's gown as thou passest by Westminster Hall, do; if not, to the stairs amongst the bandogs,[3] take water,[4] and the devil go with thee!

Exeunt Young [Cuddy] Banks, [*and*] Dog, *barking*.

[ACT V SCENE 2]

[*A street in London*]

Enter Justice, Sir Arthur, Warbeck, [Somerton,] Carter, Kate

JUST. Sir Arthur, though the bench hath mildly censur'd your errors, yet you have indeed been the instrument that wrought all their misfortunes. I would wish you paid down your fine speedily and willingly.

SIR ART. I'll need no urging to it.

CAR. If you should, 'twere a shame to you; for, if I should speak my conscience, you are worthier to be hang'd of the two, all things considered; and now make what you can of it. But I am glad these gentlemen are freed.

WAR. We knew our innocence.

10 SOM.   And therefore fear'd it not.

KATH. But I am glad that I have you safe.   *Noise within*

JUST. How now? What noise is that?

CAR. Young Frank is going the wrong way. Alas, poor youth, now I begin to pity him.   [*Exeunt.*]

---

[1] Site of the Middlesex gallows, near Marble Arch, London.   [2] Now Great George St, Westminster.   [3] Mastiffs.   [4] Embark (on the Thames).

[ACT V SCENE 3]

[*A street in London*]

Enter Young [Frank] Thorney *and halberts.*[1] *Enter, as to see the*
execution, Old Carter, Old Thorney, Katherine, Winnifride,
weeping

THOR. Here let our sorrows wait him; to press nearer
The place of his sad death, some apprehensions
May tempt our grief too much, at height already.
Daughter,[2] be comforted.

WIN.   Comfort and I
Are too far separated to be join'd
But in eternity. I share too much
Of him that's going thither.

CAR. Poor woman, 'twas not thy fault. I grieve to see
Thee weep for him that hath my pity too.

WIN. My fault was lust, my punishment was shame;
Yet I am happy that my soul is free
Both from consent, foreknowledge, and intent
Of any murder but of mine own honour,
Restor'd again by a fair satisfaction,
And since not to be wounded.

THOR.   Daughter, grieve not
For what necessity forceth. Rather, resolve
To conquer it with patience. Alas, she faints.

WIN. My griefs are strong upon me; my weakness scarce
Can bear them.

WITHIN. Away with her! Hang her, witch!

Enter [Mother] Sawyer *to execution,*[3] *officers with halberts,*
country people

CAR. The witch, that instrument of mischief! Did not she witch
the devil into my son-in-law, when he kill'd my poor daughter?
Do you hear, Mother Sawyer?

MOTHER. What would you have? Cannot a poor old woman
Have your leave to die without vexation?

CAR. Did not you bewitch Frank to kill his wife?
He could never have done't without the devil.

MOTHER. Who doubts it? But is every devil mine?

---

[1] Officers carrying battle-axes.   [2] i.e. daughter-in-law.   [3] Mother
Sawyer was tried at the Old Bailey, London, on 14th April 1621, and
hanged at Tyburn on 19th April.

Would I had one now whom I might command
30 To tear you all in pieces! Tom would have done't
Before he left me.

CAR. Thou didst bewitch Anne Ratcliffe to kill herself.

MOTHER. Churl, thou liest! I never did her hurt.
Would you were all as near your ends as I am,
That gave evidence against me for it!

COUN.[1] I'll be sworn, Mr Carter, she bewitched Gammer Wash-
bowl's sow to cast her pigs a day before she would have farried.
Yet they were sent up to London and sold for as good Westminster dog pigs at Bartholomew Fair[2] as ever great-bellied
40 ale-wife longed for.

MOTHER. These dogs will mad me. I was well resolv'd
To die in my repentance, though 'tis true
I would live longer if I might. Yet since
I cannot, pray torment me not. My conscience
Is settled as it shall be. All take heed
How they believe the devil; at last he'll cheat you.

CAR. Th'adst best confess all truly.

MOTHER.   Yet again?
Have I scarce breath enough to say my prayers,
And would you force me to spend that in bawling?
50 Bear witness, I repent all former evil;
There is no damned conjurer like the devil.

OMNES. Away with her, away!   [*She is led off*]

Enter Frank [Thorney] *to execution, officers,* Justice,
Sir Arthur, Warbeck, Somerton

THOR. Here's the sad object which I yet must meet
With hope of comfort, if a repentant end
Make him more happy than misfortune would
Suffer him here to be.

FRANK.   Good sirs, turn from me.
You will revive affliction almost kill'd
With my continual sorrow.

THOR.   O Frank, Frank!
Would I had sunk in mine own wants, or died
60 But one bare minute ere thy fault was acted.

FRANK. To look upon your sorrows executes me
Before my execution.

---

[1] i.e. countryman.   [2] An annual carnival and fair, held in September,
in Smithfield, London. The following phrase may allude to Ursula, the
seller of ale and pork in Jonson's *Bartholomew Fair* (1614), II, ii, 48 ff.

WIN.   Let me pray you, sir,—
FRANK. Thou much wrong'd woman, I must sigh for thee,
  As he that's only loath to leave the world
  For that he leaves thee in it unprovided,
  Unfriended; and for me to beg a pity
  From any man to thee when I am gone
  Is more than I can hope, nor, to say truth,
  Have I deserv'd it. But there is a payment
  Belongs to goodness from the great exchequer
  Above; it will not fail thee, Winnifride;
  Be that thy comfort.
THOR.   Let it be thine too,
  Untimely lost young man.
FRANK.   He is not lost
  Who bears his peace within him. Had I spun
  My web of life out at full length and dream'd
  Away my many years in lusts, in surfeits,
  Murders of reputations, gallant sins
  Commended or approv'd, then though I had
  Died easily, as great and rich men do,
  Upon my own bed, not compell'd by justice,
  You might have mourn'd for me indeed; my miseries
  Had been as everlasting as remediless.
  But now the law hath not arraign'd, condemn'd
  With greater rigour my unhappy fact [1]
  Than I myself have every little sin
  My memory can reckon from my childhood.
  A court hath been kept here, where I am found
  Guilty; the difference is, my impartial judge
  Is much more gracious than my faults
  Are monstrous to be nam'd. Yet they are monstrous.
THOR. Here's comfort in this penitence.
WIN.   It speaks
  How truly you are reconcil'd, and quickens
  My dying comfort, that was near expiring
  With my last breath. Now this repentance makes thee
  As white as innocence; and my first sin with thee,
  Since which I knew none like it, by my sorrow
  Is clearly cancell'd. Might our souls together
  Climb to the height of their eternity
  And there enjoy what earth denied us, happiness.

[1] Deed.

But since I must survive and be the monument
Of thy lov'd memory, I will preserve it
With a religious care, and pay thy ashes
A widow's duty, calling that end best
Which, though it stain the name, makes the soul blest.

FRANK. Give me thy hand, poor woman; do not weep.
Farewell. Thou dost forgive me?

WIN.   'Tis my part
To use that language.

FRANK.   Oh, that my example
Might teach the world hereafter what a curse
Hangs on their heads who rather choose to marry
110 A goodly portion than a dower of virtues.
Are you there, gentlemen? There is not one
Amongst you whom I have not wrong'd. [*To* Carter] You most;
[I] robb'd you of a daughter, but she is
In Heaven, and I must suffer for it willingly.

CAR. Ay, ay, she's in Heaven, and I am glad to see thee so well
prepared to follow her. I forgive thee with all my heart. If thou
hadst not had ill counsel thou would'st not have done as thou
didst; the more shame for them.

SOM. Spare your excuse to me; I do conceive
120 What you would speak. I would you could as easily
Make satisfaction to the law as to my wrongs.
I am sorry for you.

WAR.   And so am I,
And heartily forgive you.

KATH.   I will pray for you
For her sake who, I am sure, did love you dearly.

SIR ART. Let us part friendly too. I am asham'd
Of my part in thy wrongs.

FRANK.   You are all merciful,
And send me to my grave in peace. Sir Arthur,
Heavens send you a new heart. [*To* Thorney] Lastly, to you, sir;
And though I have deserv'd not to be call'd
130 Your son, yet give me leave upon my knees
To beg a blessing.

THOR.   Take it; let me wet
Thy cheeks with the last tears my griefs have left me.
O Frank, Frank, Frank!

FRANK.   Let me beseech you, gentlemen,
To comfort my old father; keep him with ye,
Love this distressed widow, and as often

As you remember what a graceless man
I was, remember likewise that these are
Both free, both worthy of a better fate
Than such a son or husband as I have been.
140 All help me with your prayers. On, on. 'Tis just
That law should purge the guilt of blood and lust.

Exit [,*with guards*].

CAR. Go thy ways. I did not think to have shed one tear for thee,
but thou hast made me water my plants spite of my heart.
Mr Thorney, cheer up, man; whilst I can stand by you, you
shall not want help to keep you from falling. We have lost our
children, both on's the wrong way, but we cannot help it. Better
or worse, 'tis now as 'tis.

THOR. I thank you, sir. You are more kind than I
Have cause to hope or look for.

150 CAR. Mr Somerton, is Kate yours or no?

SOM. We are agreed.

KATH. And but my faith is pass'd, I should fear to be married;
husbands are so cruelly unkind. Excuse me that I am thus
troubled.

SOM. Thou shalt have no cause.

JUST. Take comfort, Mistress Winnifride. Sir Arthur,
For his abuse to you and to your husband,
Is by the bench enjoin'd to pay you down
A thousand marks.[1]

SIR ART.   Which I will soon discharge.

160 WIN. Sir, 'tis too great a sum to be employ'd
Upon my funeral.

CAR. Come, come! If luck had serv'd, Sir Arthur, and every man
had his due, somebody might have totter'd ere this, without
paying fines, like it as you list. Come to me, Winnifride; shalt
be welcome. Make much of her, Kate, I charge you. I do not
think but she's a good wench, and hath had wrong as well as we.
So let's every man home to Edmonton with heavy hearts, yet as
merry as we can, though not as we would.

JUST. Join friends in sorrow; make of all the best.
170 Harms past may be lamented, not redress'd.   *Exeunt.*

---

[1] A mark represented two-thirds of a pound; hence about £666.

Epilogue

WIN. I am a widow still and must not sort [1]
A second choice without a good report,
Which though some widows find, and few deserve,
Yet I dare not presume, but will not swerve
From modest hopes. All noble tongues are free;
The gentle may speak one kind word for me.   Phen.[2]

FINIS

[1] Select.   [2] Ezekiel Fenn, a London actor *c.* 1620–*c.* 1639.

A JOVIAL CREW

RICHARD BROME

(c. 1590–c. 1652)

Little is known about his personal life. Began his career as servant and protégé of Ben Jonson. Playwright c. 1629–42; 15 comedies, notably *The Late Lancashire Witches* (with Thomas Heywood, 1634), *The Sparagus Garden* (1635), *The Antipodes* (1638), and *A Jovial Crew* (1641).

A JOVIAL CREW (1641)

Nostalgia pervades this play. On the surface it is romantic and sentimental, 'built upon fairy ground', but underneath it incorporates much criticism of the Caroline era, then disintegrating, and the Puritan era, just beginning.

Many scenes of the play are dominated by Squire Oldrents, the benevolent landlord and master, but he clearly typified a way of life rapidly passing, just as Fielding's Squire Allworthy a century later represented a similar mode of life disappearing. The sentimental theme is represented by Oldrents's unrealistic fretting about his daughters becoming beggars, even though he possessed an income of £4,000 a year, and was surrounded by devoted servants, happy tenants, and a crew of jovial beggars.

> Are you not th'only rich man lives unenvied?
> Have you not all the praises of the rich,
> And prayers of the poor? (I, i, 67–69)

An indication of the romantic nature of the Oldrents plot is provided by Meriel and Rachel, with their lovers, Vincent and Hilliard. The text does not allow one to identify which of the men is in love with which of the girls. The men address both girls at once or *vice versa*, and there is no interchange that reveals an affection between a particular man and girl. A producer must decide early how to pair them off, for there is no textual evidence to aid in this decision even in the denouement, when the two couples enter hand in hand. (By contrast, it is never possible to confuse the allegiances among the young couples in *The Witch of Edmonton*.)

The tone of the Oldrents situation is repeated in the subplot, a conventional story of a girl who ran away with an unprepossessing man in order to avoid marriage to an even less appealing suitor, chosen by her uncle. In spite of Amie's vicissitudes every reader can predict that she will ultimately find happiness—as she does, in the arms of Springlove, a man surrounded by romantic mystery.

A Jovial Crew is a part of its troubled times in the over-stress on merriment and happiness. Hearty, Oldrents, his daughters and their lovers strove, almost desperately, for gaiety. Only the beggars

151

demonstrated a spontaneous *joie de vivre*, but one immediately suspects that Brome's picture of their lives was purposely one-sided.

The four episodes in or near the beggar camp are superficially romantic. The beggars opted out, to use a familiar twentieth-century phrase, having rejected or been rejected by the competitive world of law, commerce, literature, the court, etc. They chose the casual freedom of the road, the shelter of a hedge, or a bed of straw in a barn, occasionally facetiously alluding to the life that they had abandoned. The beggar wedding, for example, with its pseudo-earnest concern for property and inheritance, parodies the kind of marriage against which Amie and Oldrents's daughters protested.

Yet, for all the joviality in the beggar camp, it is evident that Brome was carefully selective in detail, pointedly ignoring inevitable problems like illness, hardship and death. There is almost no reference to the reprehensible customs of the hordes of beggars which infested and intimidated rural seventeenth-century England.

Overtones of hard realism may be heard behind the gay façade of each plot or situation in the play. The realities of a vagrant life appear in the disillusionment of the young gentry after a night in 'the pigs' palace of pleasure' among 'the six-legged blood-hounds' hidden in the straw. Later, Vincent, Hilliard, Meriel and Rachel attempted ineptly to beg money of passersby; the young men were threatened with being 'well whipp'd and set to work', and the ladies were accosted by the amorous Oliver.

In the interwoven stories concerning the Oldrents family and Amie and her successive fiancés there are many contrasts to the surface charm of the predictable plots, contrasts that remind a reader of the distress and confusion of the early 1640's. As Springlove catalogued Oldrents's assets for the year the steward referred repeatedly to his master's exceptional prosperity; despite Oldrents's habitual generosity, Springlove must list

> some old debts, and almost desperate ones,
> As well from country cavaliers as courtiers.
>
> (I, i, 128–9)

Brome was doing nothing new in alluding to financial irresponsibility among the urban gentry, but he was evidently critical of the efforts of 'country cavaliers' to ape the customs of the city.

The dialogue of *A Jovial Crew* includes a few sly anti-Puritan allusions, but, more important, the tone of the play conveys an antipathy to the Puritan way of life. The humorous scenes make carefree gaiety, irresponsibility, the pleasures of food, drink, dancing and play-acting very attractive. In Act IV the beggar-poet devised a Utopia (for the masque which was never performed) with representatives of several social and professional groups; a wrangle immediately began, put down, significantly, by a soldier with a cudgel. Ultimately, however, all were overcome by the beggar, an action symbolizing a truly egalitarian commonwealth. (Realist that Brome was, he referred elsewhere in the play to a social and administrative hierarchy among the beggars.)

An extra, though properly speaking irrelevant, dimension is added to the anti-Puritan theme in the play by the dedication and commendatory verses appended eleven years after the first performance in 1641. (The theatres were closed in 1642.) Richard Brome alluded in the dedication to his distressed circumstances, and the verses by friends include several references to the difficulties experienced by anyone connected with the theatre.

Richard Brome's dramatic artistry deserves more extensive analysis than is possible here. He achieved an atmosphere of authenticity in the beggar scenes by his use of jargon, borrowed from several publications which included glossaries of vagabond cant. He was evidently familiar with books like *The Bellman of London* (1608) and *English Villanies* (1638), both by Thomas Dekker, and with a notable volume by Thomas Harman, *A Caveat or Warening for Commen Cursetors Vulgarely Called Vagabones* (1567). Apart from the language of the canting crew, Brome's naturalness of dialogue, often purposely old-fashioned or formal, as appropriate to the speakers, contributes to the plausibility of the play. Figures of speech are rare in his fluid, effortless verse that smoothly links with the prose.

Individuality of dialogue and the amusing use of catch phrases contribute to the great variety of characterization in this play, which includes people from many levels of society and ways of life. Several—Squire Oldrents, Hearty, Justice Clack, Randal—clearly derive from the tradition of Jonsonian humours, but they are carefully individualized.

It is notable too how clearly the servants and other secondary characters are delineated—the outspoken Randal, the girl-watching Oliver, the morose Talboy. Indeed, one suspects that Brome felt too great an affection for his minor characters. In IV, i the long dialogue between Oliver and Oldrents's loyal servants, although amusing ('He is no snail, I assure you'), is extended much further than necessary to make the point about Oldrents's generous spirit.

Richard Brome was, for his time, an unusually original playwright who had great talent in organizing diverse materials. *A Jovial Crew* reveals a variety of influences, some of them incidental, others probably unconscious. As one might expect, Brome drew suggestions from several Jonson plays, such as *Bartholomew Fair* (echoes of Justice Overdo and Bartholomew Cokes) and the masque *The Gipsies Metamorphosed* (Justice Jug). He was also indebted to Middleton and Rowley's *Spanish Gipsy* and Fletcher's *Beggars' Bush*, both involving characters disguised as gipsies.

A Jovial Crew was enthusiastically revived during the Restoration—Samuel Pepys saw it with pleasure four times between 1661 and 1669—and it enjoyed almost a century more of popularity. Regrettably it has not been produced in modern times. Yet it is one of the great comedies of the Caroline era, combining as it does so skilfully a remembrance of times past and an edge of satire to give the play intensity and pathos. It is not escapist in nature, for Brome was clear-eyed enough to realize that flight to the simplicity of parasitic beggary was not an answer; however, if the play has a message almost explicit, it is that happiness and social stability are possible if forgiveness, generosity, acceptance of responsibility and happy marriage exist.

A JOVIAL CREW

or

The Merry Beggars
by Richard Brome
1641

Mart. *Hic totus volo rideat Libellus.*[1]

---

[1] 'I wish this little book to laugh from end to end.' Martial, *Epigrams* (trans. W. Ker), XI, xv, 3.

To the right noble, ingenious, and judicious gentleman, Thomas Stanley, Esq.[1]

Sir:

I have long since studied in these anti-ingenious times to find out a man that might at once be both a judge and patron to this issue of my old age, which needs both. And my blessed stars have flung me upon you, in whom both those attributes concentre and flourish. Nor can I yet find a reason why I should present it to you, it being below your acceptance or censure, but only my own confidence, which had not grown to this forwardness had it not been encouraged by your goodness.

Yet we all know beggars use to flock to great men's gates, and though my fortune has cast me in that mould, I am poor and proud, and preserve the humour of him who could not beg for anything but great boons, such as are your kind acceptance and protection. I dare not say, as my brethren use, that I present this as a testimonial of my gratitude or recompense for your favours; for I protest I conceive it so far from quitting[2] old engagements that it creates new. So that all that this play can do is but to make more work, and involves me in debts beyond a possibility of satisfaction.

Sir, it were a folly in me to tell you of your worth; the world knows it enough, and are bold to say fortune and nature scarce ever clubb'd so well. You know, sir, I am old and cannot cringe nor court with the powder'd and ribbanded wits of our days; but though I cannot speak so much, I can think as well and as honourably as the best. All the arguments I can use to induce you to take notice of this thing of nothing is that it had the luck to tumble last of all in the epidemical ruin of the scene,[3] and now limps hither with a wooden leg to beg an alms at your hands. I will wind up all with a use of exhortation, that since the times conspire to make us all beggars, let us make ourselves merry, which (if I am not mistaken) this drives at. Be pleased therefore, sir, to lodge these harmless beggars in the outhouses of your thoughts and among the rest, him that in this cuckoo-time puts in

[1] Poet, classical scholar, patron to many poets, 1625–78.   [2] Requiting.
[3] Perhaps alluding to *A Jovial Crew* as the last play produced at the Cockpit before the closing of the theatres on 2nd September 1642.

156

for a membership and will fill the choir of those that duly and
truly pray for you, and is,

sir,

Your humble servant,
Richard Brome.

To Master Richard Brome,
on his play called A Jovial Crew, or The Merry Beggars.

Plays are instructive recreations
Which who could write may not expect at once,
No, nor with every breeding, to write well;
And though some itching academics [1] fell
Lately upon this task, their products were
Lame and imperfect, and did grate the ear
So that they mock'd the stupid stationer's care,
That both with gelt [2] and cringes did prepare
Fine copper cuts,[3] and gather'd verses too,
To make a shout before the idle show.
Your fate is other; you do not invade,
But by great Jonson were made free o' th' trade,[4]
So that we must in this your labour find
Some image and fair relic of his mind.

John Hall.[5]

To Master Richard Brome,
on his comedy of A Jovial Crew, or The Merry Beggars.

Not to commend or censure thee or thine,
Nor like a bush to signify good wine,
Nor yet to publish to the world or thee
Thou merit'st bays by wit and poetry
Do I stand here. Though I do know there comes
A shoal, with regiments of encomiums
On all occasions, whose astronomy
Can calculate a praise to fifty-three,
And write blank copies such as, being view'd,
May serve indifferently each altitude,
And make books, like petitions, whose commands

---

[1] Undistinguished dilettante playwrights.   [2] Payments of money, probably bribes.   [3] Engravings.   [4] i.e. a freeman.   [5] A popular author
(1627–56) of poems and pamphlets.

Are not from worth, but multitude of hands.[1]
Those will prove wit by power and make a trade
To force by number when they can't persuade.
Here's no such need, for books, like children, be
Well christ'ned when their sureties are but three,
And those which to twelve godfathers [2] do come
Signify former guilt or speedy doom.
  Nor need the stationer, when all th' wits are past,
Bring his own periwig poetry at last.
All this won't do, for when their labour's done
The reader's rul'd, not by their tastes, but's own;
And he that for encomiastics looks
May find the bigger not the better books.
So that the most our levers serve for shows
Only that we're his friends and do suppose
'Tis good, and that is all that I shall say.
In truth I love him well and like his play,
And if there's any that don't think so too,
Let them let it alone for them that do.
                                        J. B.[3]

To his worthy friend Master Richard Brome,
upon his comedy called *A Jovial Crew, or The Merry Beggars*.

This comedy, ingenious friend, will raise
Itself a monument without a praise
Begg'd by the stationer, who with strength of purse
And pens takes care to make his book sell worse.
And I dare calculate thy play, although
Not elevated unto fifty-two,
It may grow old as time or wit, and he
That dares despise may after envy thee.
  Learning, the file of poesy,[4] may be
Fetch'd from the arts and university,
But he that writes a play, and good, must know,
Beyond his books, men and their actions too.
Copies of verse, that make the new men sweat,
Reach not a poem nor the muses' heat;
Small bavin [5] wits, and wood, may burn awhile,

---

[1] William Cartwright's *Works* (1651) were prefaced with approximately fifty-three commendatory verses. (The number varies in different printings and editions.)   [2] i.e. a jury.   [3] Sir John Birkenhead, 1616–79, poet, editor of political journals, royalist.   [4] i.e. learning smooths the roughness of poetry.   [5] Short-lived (lit. a bundle of brush for a quick fire).

And make more noise than forests on a pile,
Whose fibres shrunk, ma'invite a piteous stream,
Not to lament, but to extinguish them.
Thy fancy's metal,[1] and thy strain's much higher
Proof 'gainst their wit and what that dreads, the fire.

James Shirley.[2]

To my worthy friend, Master Richard Brome, on his excellent play called *A Jovial Crew, or The Merry Beggars.*

There is a faction, friend, in town that cries,
Down with the dagon[3]-poet, Jonson dies.
His work were too elaborate, not fit
To come within the verge or face of wit.
Beaumont and Fletcher, they say, perhaps might
Pass well for current coin in a dark night,
But Shakespeare, the plebeian driller,[4] was
Founder'd in's *Pericles,*[5] and must not pass.
And so at all men fly that have but been
Thought worthy of applause; therefore their spleen.
Ungrateful Negro-kind, dart you your rage
Against the beams that warm'd you and the stage?
This malice shows it is unhallowed heat
That boils your raw brains and your temples beat.
Adulterate pieces may retain the mould
Or stamp, but want the pureness of the gold;
But the world's mad; those jewels that were worn
In high esteem by some laid by in scorn,
Like Indians, who their native wealth despise
And dote on strangers' trash and trumperies.
Yet, if it be not too far spent, there is
Some hopes left us that this, thy well-wrought piece,
May bring it cure, reduce it to its sight,
To judge th' difference 'twixt the day and night.
Draw the curtain of their errors, that their sense
May be conformable to Ben's influence,
And finding here nature and art agree
May swear thou liv'st in him and he in thee.

Jo[hn] Tatham.[6]

---

[1] i.e. made of metal, solid.   [2] 1596–1666; successively clergyman, school-master, prolific playwright (1625–42).   [3] Idolized.   [4] Enticer.
[5] 1609, one of Shakespeare's least satisfactory plays.   [6] Poet, composer of city pageants, playwright; *c.* 1610–*c.* 1664.

To Master Richard Brome
upon his comedy called *A Jovial Crew, or The Merry Beggars.*

Something I'd say, but not to praise thee, friend,
For thou thyself dost best thyself commend,
And he that with an eulogy doth come
May to's own wit raise an encomium,
But not to thine. Yet I'll before thee go,
Though whiffler-like,[1] to usher in the show.
And like a quarter-clock[2] foretell the time
Is come about for greater bells to chime.
  I must not praise thy poetry nor wit,
Though both are very good, yet that's not it.
The reader in his progress will find more
Wit in a line than I praise in a score.
I shall be read with prejudice, for each line
I write of thee or anything that's thine,
Be't name or muse, will all be read of me,
As if I claw'd[3] myself by praising thee.
  But though I may not praise, I hope I may
Be bold to love thee, and the world shall say
I've reason for't. I love thee for thy name;
I love thee for thy merit and thy fame;
I love thee for thy neat and harmless wit,
Thy mirth that does so clean and closely hit;
Thy luck to please so well—who could go faster,
At first to be the envy of thy master?[4]
I love thee for thyself, for who can choose
But like the fountain of so brisk a muse?
I love this comedy and every line,
Because 'tis good, as well's because 'tis thine.
  Thou tell'st the world the life that beggars lead;
'Tis seasonable; 'twill become our trade.[5]
'T must be our study too, for in this time
Who'll not be innocent, since wealth's a crime?
Thou'rt th'age's doctor now, for since all go
To make us poor, thou mak'st us merry too.
  Go on, and thrive; may all thy sportings be

---

[1] An armed attendant who preceded a procession. [2] A clock which strikes the quarter hours. [3] Flattered. [4] Jonson was annoyed by the success of Brome's *Lovesick Maid* (1629) shortly after the failure of his own *New Inn*. [5] The lines that follow include several allusions to the Puritan prohibition of play-acting.

Delightful unto all, as th'are to me.
May this so please, t'encourage thee, that more
May be made public which thou keep'st in store,
That though we've lost their dress, we may be glad
To see and think on th' happiness we had.
　　And thou thereby may'st make our name to shine;
　　'Twas royal [1] once, but now 'twill be divine.
　　　　　　　　　　　　　　　　Alex. Brome. [2]

[1] An oblique pun on 'broom', *planta genista*, i.e. Plantagenet (Haaker).
[2] Poet, playwright, 1620–60. Not related to Richard Brome, but edited two collections of his plays, 1653 and 1659.

Prologue

The title of our play, *A Jovial Crew,*
May seem to promise mirth, which were a new
And forc'd thing in these sad and tragic days
For you to find or we express in plays.
We wish you then would change that expectation,
Since jovial mirth is now grown out of fashion;
Or much not to expect, for now it chances,—
Our comic writer finding that romances [1]
Of lovers, through much travail and distress,
Till it be thought no power can redress
Th'afflicted wanderers, though stout chivalry
Lend all his aid for their delivery,
Till lastly some impossibility
Concludes all strife and makes a comedy—
Finding, he says, such stories bear the sway,
Near as he could he has compos'd a play
Of fortune-tellers, damsels, and their squires
Expos'd to strange adventures through the briars
Of love and fate. But why need I forestall
What shall so soon be obvious to you all,
But wish the dulness may make no man sleep,
Nor sadness of it any woman weep.

[1] Popular romantic dramas.

The Persons of the Play

Oldrents,[1] *an ancient esquire*
Hearty, *his friend and merry companion, but a decay'd gentleman*
Springlove, *steward to* Master Oldrents
Vincent, }
Hilliard, } *two young gentlemen*
Randal, *a groom, servant to* Oldrents
Master Sentwell *and* two other gentlemen, *friends to* Justice Clack
Oliver, *the justice's son*
Master Clack,[2] *the justice himself*
Master Talboy, *lover to the justice's niece*
Martin, *the justice's clerk*
Chaplain }
Usher }
Butler } *to* Oldrents
Cook }
Rachel, } Oldrents*'s daughters*
Meriel, }
Amie, Justice Clack*'s niece*
Autem mort,[3] *an old beggar-woman*
Patrico,[4] }
Soldier, }
Lawyer, } *four especial beggars*
Courtier, }
Scribble, *their poet*
Divers other beggars, fiddlers, and mutes.[5]

[Scene: Rural Kent and vicinity(?)] [6]

[1] The name is an implicit tribute, indicating the squire's refusal to use contemporary inflation to justify the raising of his rents.   [2] A clack is (*a*) the noisemaker struck on a begging bowl and (*b*) the tongue of a garrulous woman.   [3] In beggars' cant, a married woman; 'mort' means church.   [4] Hedge-priest.   [5] Actors in non-speaking roles.   [6] Act I refers to Mapledown, Kent, being three miles from Oldrents's home, but at Act V, Randal alludes to his master's house in Nottinghamshire.

ACT I

[Oldrents's *house*]

[*Enter*] Oldrents [*and*] Hearty

OLD. It has indeed, friend, much afflicted me.

HEARTY. And very justly, let me tell you, sir,
That could so impiously be curious [1]
To tempt a judgment on you; to give ear
And faith too, by your leave, to fortune-tellers,
Wizards and gipsies!

OLD.   I have since been frighted
With't in a thousand dreams.

HEARTY.   I would be drunk
A thousand times to bed, rather than dream
Of any of their riddlemy riddlemies.

10 If they prove happy, so; if not, let't go.
You'll never find their meaning till the event,
If you suppose there was, at all, a meaning,
As the equivocating devil had, when he
Cozen'd the monk to let him live soul-free,
Till he should find him sleeping between sheets;
The wary monk, abjuring all such lodging,
At last, by over-watching in his study,
The foul fiend took him napping with his nose
Betwixt the sheet-leaves of his conjuring book.

20 There was the whim [2] or double meaning on't.
But these fond fortune-tellers, that know nothing,
Aim to be thought more cunning than their master,
The foresaid devil, though truly not so hurtful;
Yet, trust 'em, hang 'em! Wizards! Old blind buzzards!
For once they hit, they miss a thousand times;
And most times give quite contrary, bad for good,
And best for worst. One told a gentleman
His son should be a man-killer, and hang'd for't,
Who after prov'd a great and rich physician,

30 And with great fame i' th'university
Hang'd up in picture for a grave example.
There was the whim of that. Quite contrary!

<hr>

[1] Eager. [2] Play on words.

OLD. And that was happy. Would mine could so deceive my
fears!

HEARTY. They may, but trust not to't. Another schemist [1]
Found that a squint-ey'd boy should prove a notable
Pick-purse, and afterwards a most strong thief;
When he grew up to be a cunning lawyer,
And at last died a judge. Quite contrary!
How many have been mark'd out by these wizards
40   For fools, that after have been prick'd [2] for sheriffs?
Was not a shepherd-boy foretold to be
A drunkard, and to get his living from
Bawds, whores, thieves, quarrellers, and the like?
And did he not become a suburb justice, [3]
And live in wine and worship by the fees
Rack'd [4] out of such delinquents? There's the whim on't.
Now I come to you: Your figure-flinger finds
That both your daughters, notwithstanding all
Your great possessions, which they are co-heirs of,
50   Shall yet be beggars; may it not be meant,
(If, as I said, there be a meaning in it)
They may prove courtiers, or great courtiers' wives,
And so be beggars in law? Is not that the whim
On't, think you? You shall think no worse on't.
OLD. Would I had your merry heart!
HEARTY.   I thank you, sir.
OLD. I mean the like.
HEARTY.   I would you had; and I
Such an estate as yours. Four thousand yearly,
With such a heart as mine, would defy fortune,
And all her babbling soothsayers. I'd as soon
60   Distrust in Providence as lend a fear
To such a destiny for a child of mine,
While there be sack and songs in town or country.
Think like a man of conscience—now I am serious—
What justice can there be for such a curse
To fall upon your heirs? Do you not live
Free, out of law or grieving any man?
Are you not th'only rich man lives unenvied?
Have you not all the praises of the rich
And prayers of the poor? Did ever any
70   Servant or hireling, neighbour, kindred curse you,

---

[1] A framer of schemes or horoscopes.   [2] Nominated.   [3] The suburbs
of London were notorious for licentiousness.   [4] Extorted.

Or wish one minute shorten'd of your life?
Have you one grudging tenant? Will they not all
Fight for you? Do they not teach their children,
And make 'em too, pray for you morn and evening,
And in their graces too, as duly as
For king and realm? The innocent things would think
They ought not eat else.
OLD.   'Tis their goodness.
HEARTY. It is your merit. Your great love and bounty
Procures from Heaven those inspirations in 'em.
Whose rent did ever you exact? Whose have
You not remitted, when by casualties
Of fire, of floods, of common dearth, or sickness,
Poor men were brought behindhand? Nay, whose losses
Have you not piously repair'd?
OLD.   Enough.
HEARTY. What heriots[1] have you ta'en from forlorn widows?
What acre of your thousands have you rack'd?
OLD. Good friend, no more.
HEARTY.   These are enough, indeed,
To fill your ears with joyful acclamations
Where'er you pass: 'Heaven bless our landlord Oldrent[s],
Our master Oldrent[s], our good patron Oldrent[s]!'
Cannot these sounds conjure that evil spirit
Of fear out of you, that your children shall
Live to be beggars? Shall Squire Oldrents' daughters
Wear old rents in their garments—there's a whim too—
Because a fortune-teller told you so?
OLD. Come, I will strive to think no more on't.
HEARTY. Will you ride forth for air then and be merry?
OLD. Your counsel and example may instruct me.
HEARTY. Sack must be had in sundry places too;
For songs I am provided.

Enter Springlove *with books and papers;*
he lays them on the table

OLD. Yet here comes one brings me a second fear,
Who has my care the next unto my children.
HEARTY. Your steward, sir, it seems has business with you.
I wish you would have none.
OLD.   I'll soon dispatch it,
And then be for our journey instantly.

[1] Payments due to a landlord from the estate of a deceased tenant.

HEARTY. I'll wait your coming down, sir.   *Exit.*
OLD.   But why, Springlove,
   Is now this expedition?[1]
SPRING.   Sir, 'tis duty.
OLD. Not common among stewards, I confess,
   To urge in their accompts[2] before the day
110 Their lords have limited.[3] Some that are grown
   To hoary hairs and knighthoods are not found
   Guilty of such an importunity.
   'Tis yet but thirty days, when I give forty
   After the half-year day, our Lady last.[4]
   Could I suspect my trust were lost in thee,
   Or doubt thy youth had not ability
   To carry out the weight of such a charge,
   I then should call on thee.
SPRING.   Sir, your indulgence,
   I hope, shall ne'er corrupt me. Ne'ertheless,
120 The testimony of a fair discharge
   From time to time will be encouragement

   Springlove *turns over the several books to his master*

   To virtue in me. You may then be pleas'd
   To take here a survey of all your rents
   Receiv'd, and all such other payments as
   Came to my hands since my last audit, for
   Cattle, wool, corn, all fruits of husbandry.
   Then, my receipts on bonds and some new leases,
   With some old debts, and almost desperate ones,
   As well from country cavaliers as courtiers.
130 Then here, sir, are my several disbursements,
   In all particulars, for yourself and daughters,
   In charge of housekeeping, buildings and repairs,
   Journeys, apparel, coaches, gifts, and all
   Expenses for your personal necessaries.
   Here servants' wages, liveries, and cures.
   Here for supplies of horses, hawks, and hounds.
   And lastly, not the least to be rememb'red,
   Your large benevolences to the poor.
OLD. Thy charity there goes hand in hand with mine.
140 And, Springlove, I commend it in thee that,
   So young in years, art grown so ripe in goodness.

---

[1] Haste.   [2] Accounts.   [3] Appointed.   [4] i.e. it is now thirty days (23rd April) past Lady Day, the Feast of the Annunciation, 25th March, the traditional time for paying half-yearly rentals.

May their Heaven-piercing prayers bring on thee
Equal rewards with me.
SPRING.   Now here, sir, is
  The balance of the several accompts
  Which shows you what remains in cash; which, added
  Unto your former bank,[1] makes up in all—
                                    [*Shows him a paper*]
OLD. Twelve thousand and odd pounds.
SPRING.   Here are the keys
  Of all. The chests are safe in your own closet.
OLD. Why in my closet? Is not yours as safe?
SPRING. Oh, sir, you know my suit.
OLD.   Your suit? What suit?
SPRING. Touching the time of year.
OLD.   'Tis well-nigh May.
  Why, what of that, good Springlove?
                                    Nightingale sings
SPRING. Oh, sir, you hear I am call'd.
OLD.   Fie, Springlove, fie!
  I hop'd thou hadst abjur'd that uncouth practice.
SPRING. You thought I had forsaken nature then.
OLD. Is that disease of nature still in thee
  So virulent? And, notwithstanding all
  My favours, in my gifts, my cares, and counsels,
  Which to a soul ungrateful might be boasted,
  Have I first bred thee, and then preferr'd thee—from
  I will not say how wretched a beginning—
  To be a master over all my servants,
  Planted thee in my bosom, and canst thou
  There slight me for the whistling of a bird?
SPRING. Your reason, sir, informs you that's no cause.
  But 'tis the season of the year that calls me;
  What moves her notes provokes my disposition
  By a more absolute power of nature than
  Philosophy can render an accompt for.
OLD. I find there's no expelling it; but still
  It will return. I have tried all the means,
  As I may safely think, in human wisdom,
  And did, as near as reason could, assure me
  That thy last year's restraint had stopp'd for ever
  That running sore on thee, that gadding humour;

[1] Capital.

When, only for that cause, I laid the weight
Of mine estate in stewardship upon thee;
Which kept thee in that year, after so many
Summer vagaries thou hadst made before.
180 SPRING. You kept a swallow in a cage that while.
I cannot, sir, endure another summer
In that restraint, with life; 'twas then my torment,
But now my death. Yet, sir, my life is yours,
Who are my patron; freely may you take it.
Yet pardon, sir, my frailty, that do beg
A small continuance of it on my knees.
OLD. Can there no means be found to preserve life
In thee but wand'ring like a vagabond?
Does not the sun as comfortably shine
190 Upon my gardens as the opener fields?
Or on my fields as others far remote?
Are not my walks and greens as delectable
As the highways and commons? Are the shades
Of sycamore and bowers of eglantine
Less pleasing than of bramble or thorn hedges?
Or of my groves and thickets than wild woods?
Are not my fountain waters fresher than
The troubled streams where every beast does drink?
Do not the birds sing here as sweet and lively
200 As any other where? Is not thy bed more soft
And rest more safe than in a field or barn?
Is a full table which is call'd thine own
Less curious [1] or wholesome than the scraps
From others' trenchers,[2] twice or thrice translated?[3]
SPRING. Yea, in the winter season, when the fire
Is sweeter than the air.
OLD.   What air is wanting?
SPRING. Oh, sir, y'have heard of pilgrimages and
The voluntary travels of good men.
OLD. For penance or to holy ends. But bring
210 Not those into comparison, I charge you.
SPRING. I do not, sir. But pardon me to think
Their sufferings are much sweet'ned by delights
Such as we find by shifting place and air.
OLD. Are there delights in beggary? Or, if to take
Diversity of air be such a solace,

[1] Carefully supplied.   [2] Serving-dishes or plates, usually of wood.
[3] Altered, by being passed from hand to hand.

Travel the kingdom over; and if this
Yield not variety enough, try further,
Provided your deportment be genteel.
Take horse, and man, and money; you have all,
Or I'll allow enough.   *Sing nightingale, cuckoo, etc.*
SPRING. [*Aside*]   Oh, how am I confounded!—
Dear sir, retort me [1] naked to the world
Rather than lay those burdens on me which
Will stifle me. I must abroad or perish.
OLD. [*Aside*] I will no longer strive to wash this Moor,[2]
Nor breathe more minutes so unthriftily
In civil argument against rude wind,
But rather practise to withdraw my love
And tender care, if it be possible,
From that unfruitful breast, incapable
Of wholesome counsel.
SPRING.   Have I your leave, sir?
OLD. I leave you to dispute it with yourself.
I have no voice to bid you go or stay.
My love shall give thy will pre-eminence,
And leave th'effect to time and Providence.   *Exit.*
SPRING. I am confounded in my obligation
To this good man: his virtue is my punishment,
When 'tis not in my nature to return
Obedience to his merits. I could wish
Such an ingratitude were death by th' law,
And put in present execution on me,
To rid me of my sharper suffering.
Nor but by death can this predominant sway
Of nature be extinguish'd in me. I
Have fought with my affections,[3] by th'assistance
Of all the strengths of art and discipline—
All which I owe him for in education too—
To conquer and establish my observance,[4]
As in all other rules, to him in this,
This inborn strong desire of liberty
In that free course, which he detests as shameful,
And I approve [5] my earth's felicity,
But find the war is endless, and must fly.
What must I lose then? A good master's love.
What loss feels he that wants not what he loses?

[1] Cast me out.   [2] To labour in vain.   [3] Passions.   [4] Duty.
[5] Confirm.

They'll say I lose all reputation.
What's that, to live where no such thing is known?
My duty to a master will be question'd.
Where duty is exacted it is none,
And among beggars, each man is his own.

Enter Randal *and three or four servants with a great kettle and black jacks* [1] *and a baker's basket, all empty. Exeunt with all; manet* Randal

260 Now, fellows, what news from whence you came?

RAN. The old wonted news, sir, from your guesthouse, the old barn. We have unloaden the breadbasket, the beef-kettle, and the beer-bumbards there, amongst your guests, the beggars. And they have all prayed for you and our master, as their manner is, from the teeth outward; marry, from the teeth inwards 'tis enough to swallow your alms; from whence I think their prayers seldom come.

SPRING. Thou should'st not think uncharitably.

RAN. Thought's free, Master Steward, and it please you. But

270 your charity is nevertheless notorious, I must needs say.

SPRING. Meritorious, thou meant'st to say.

RAN. Surely, sir, no; 'tis out of our curate's book. [2]

SPRING. But I aspire no merits nor popular thanks; 'tis well if I do well in it.

RAN. It might be better though, if old Randal, whom you allow to talk, might counsel, to help to breed up poor men's children, or decayed labourers past their work or travail; or towards the setting up of poor young married couples than to bestow an hundred pound a year—at least you do that, if not all you get—

280 besides our master's bounty, to maintain in begging such wanderers as these, that never are out of their way, [3] that cannot give account from whence they came, or whither they would, nor of any beginning they ever had, or any end they seek, but still to stroll and beg till their bellies be full, and then sleep till they be hungry.

SPRING. Thou art ever repining at [4] those poor people! They take nothing from thee but thy pains, and that I pay thee for too. Why should'st thou grudge?

RAN. Am I not bitten to it every day, by the six-footed blood-

290 hounds that they leave in their litter, when I throw out the old, to lay fresh straw for the newcomers at night? That's one part

[1] Leather jugs for beer.   [2] Beyond biblical precept or admonition.
[3] Miss the point.   [4] Complaining of.

of my office. And you are sure, that though your hospitality be but for a night and a morning for one rabble, to have a new supply every evening. They take nothing from me indeed; they give too much.

SPRING. Thou art old Randal still! Ever grumbling, but still officious for 'em.

RAN. Yes, hang 'em! They know I love 'em well enough; I have had merry bouts with some of 'em.

SPRING. What say'st thou, Randal?

RAN. They are indeed my pastime. I left the merry grigs, as their provender has prick'd[1] 'em, in such a hoigh[2] yonder! Such a frolic! You'll hear anon, as you walk nearer 'em.

SPRING. Well, honest Randal, thus it is: I am for a journey. I know not how long will be my absence, but I will presently take order with the cook, pantler,[3] and butler for my wonted allowance to the poor; and I will leave money with thee to manage the affair till my return.

RAN. Then up rise Randal, bailie[4] of the beggars!

SPRING. And if our master shall be displeas'd, although the charge be mine, at the openness of the entertainment, thou shalt then give it proportionably in money, and let them walk farther.

RAN. Pseugh! That will never do't, never do 'em good. 'Tis the seat, the habitation, the rendezvous, that cheers their hearts. Money would clog their consciences. Nor must I lose the music of 'em in their lodging.

SPRING. We will agree upon't anon. Go now about your business.

RAN. I go. Bailie? Nay, steward and chamberlain of the rogues and beggars.   *Exit.*

SPRING. I cannot think but with a trembling fear
On this adventure, in a scruple which
I have not weighed with all my other doubts.
I shall, in my departure, rob my master.
Of what? Of a true servant; other theft
I have committed none. And that may be supply'd,
And better too, by some more constant to him.
But I may injure many in his trust,
Which now he cannot be but sparing of.
I rob him too of the content and hopes
He had in me, whom he had built and rais'd
Unto that growth in his affection

---

[1] Urged.   [2] State of excitement.   [3] Supervisor of the pantry.
[4] Steward.

That I became a gladness in his eye,
And now must be a grief or a vexation
                    A noise and singing within
Unto his noble heart. But hark! Ay, there's
The harmony that drowns all doubts and fears.
A little nearer—

                    Song.[1]

From hunger and cold who lives more free,
    Or who more richly clad than we?
340   Our bellies are full, our flesh is warm,
        And against pride our rags are a charm.
    Enough is our feast, and for tomorrow
        Let rich men care, we feel no sorrow.
            No sorrow, no sorrow, no sorrow, no sorrow.
            Let rich men care, we feel no sorrow.

SPRING. The emperor hears no such music, nor feels content
like this!

    Each city, each town, and every village
        Afford us either an alms or pillage;
    And if the weather be cold and raw
350   Then in a barn we tumble in straw.
    If warm and fair, by yea-cock and nay-cock
        The fields will afford us a hedge or a hay-cock.
            A hay-cock, a hay-cock, a hay-cock, a hay-cock,
            The fields will afford us a hedge or a hay-cock.

SPRING. Most ravishing delight! But in all this
Only one sense is pleas'd: Mine ear is feasted;
Mine eye too must be satisfied with my joys.
The hoarding usurer cannot have more
Thirsty desire to see his golden store,
360 When he unlocks his treasury, than I
The equipage in which my beggars lie.

        He opens the scene; [2] *the beggars are discovered in*
        their postures; then they issue forth, and last
                    the Patrico

ALL. Our master, our master! Our sweet and comfortable master!
SPRING. How cheer my hearts?
1 BEG.   Most crowse, [3] most cap'ringly.
Shall we dance, shall we sing, to welcome our king?
Strike up, piper, a merry, merry dance,

[1] In *Select Ayres and Dialogue . . .* (1659).   [2] The inner stage or recess.
[3] Jolly.

That we on our stampers [1] may foot it and prance,
To make his heart merry as he has made ours,
As lustick [2] and frolic as lords in their bowers.

Music. Dance

SPRING. Exceeding well perform'd.

1 BEG. 'Tis well if it like you, master. But we have not that rag among us that we will not dance off, to do you service, we being all and only your servants, most noble sir. Command us therefore and employ us, we beseech you.

SPRING. Thou speak'st most courtly.

2 BEG. Sir, he can speak, and could have writ as well. He is a decay'd poet, newly fallen in among us, and begs as well as the best of us. He learnt it pretty well in his own profession before, and can the better practise it in ours now.

SPRING. Thou art a wit too, it seems.

3 BEG. He should have wit and knavery too, sir, for he was an attorney till he was pitch'd over the bar.[3] And, from that fall, he was taken up [4] a knight o' the post; [5] and so he continued, till he was degraded at the whipping-post; and from thence he ran resolutely into this course. His cunning in the law, and the other's labour with the muses are dedicate to your service; and for myself, I'll fight for you.

SPRING. Thou art a brave fellow, and speak'st like a commander. Hast thou borne arms?

4 BEG. Sir, he has borne the name of a Netherland soldier,[6] till he ran away from his colours, and was taken lame with lying in the fields by a sciatica; I mean, sir, the strappado.[7] After which, by a second retreat, indeed, running away, he scambled [8] into this country, and so scap'd the gallows, and then snapp'd up his living in the city by his wit in cheating, pimping, and such like arts, till the cart [9] and the pillory [10] showed him too publicly to the world. And so, begging the last refuge, he enter'd into our society, and now lives honestly, I must needs say, as the best of us.

SPRING. Thou speak'st good language too.

1 BEG. He was a courtier born, sir, and begs on pleasure, I

---

[1] Shoes. [2] Merry. [3] Disbarred. [4] Promoted. [5] A perjurer. [6] English troops, recruited by the Dutch, served in several campaigns of the Dutch wars with Spain during the 1630s. [7] A device for torture in which the victim was elevated by means of his arms tied behind his back and abruptly dropped. [8] Stumbled. [9] Before punishment, criminals were often taken through the streets in a cart as a public example. [10] A framework which held fast the hands and head of an offender, usually punished in the market place.

assure you, refusing great and constant means from able friends to make him a staid [1] man. Yet, the want of a leg notwithstanding, he must travel in this kind [2] against all common reason, by the special policy of Providence.

SPRING. As how, I prithee?

1 BEG. His father, sir, was a courtier, a great court beggar, I assure you; I made these verses of him and his son here.

'A courtier begg'd by covetise, not need,
From others that which made them beg indeed.

410 He begg'd till wealth had laden him with cares
To keep for's children and their children shares;
While the oppress'd, that lost that great estate,
Sent curses after it unto their fate.
The father dies, the world says, very rich;
The son, being gotten while, it seems, the itch
Of begging was upon the courtly sire,
Or bound by Fate, will to no wealth aspire,
Tho' offer'd him in money, clothes, or meat,
More than he begs, or instantly must eat.

420 Is not he heavenly bless'd that hates earth's treasure,
And begs with, "What's a gentleman but's pleasure?"
Or say it be upon the heir a curse;
What's that to him? The beggar's ne'er the worse;
For of the general store that Heaven has sent
He values not a penny till't be spent.'

ALL. A scribble, a scribble!

2 BEG. What city or court poet could say more than our hedge muse-monger here?

3 BEG. What say, sir, to our poet scribble here?

430 SPRING. I like his vein exceeding well, and the whole consort of you.

2 BEG. Consort,[3] sir? We have musicians too among us; true merry beggars indeed, that, being within the reach of the lash for singing libellous songs at London, were fain to fly into our covey,[4] and here they sing all our poet's ditties. They can sing anything most tunably, sir, but psalms. What they may do hereafter under a triple tree [5] is much expected.[6] But they live very civilly and genteelly among us.

SPRING. But what is he there, that solemn old fellow that
440 neither speaks of himself nor any body for him?

---

[1] Settled.　　　　[2] Manner.　　　　[3] Punning on 'company' and 'band of
musicians'.　　　[4] Brood.　　　[5] Gallows (from its three upright parts).
[6] Awaited.

2 BEG. Oh, sir, the rarest man of all. He is a prophet. See how he
  holds up his prognosticating nose. He is divining now.

SPRING. How? A prophet?

2 BEG. Yes, sir, a cunning man and a fortune-teller. 'Tis thought
  he was a great clerk before his decay, but he is very close, will
  not tell his beginning, nor the fortune he himself is fall'n
  from; but he serves us for a clergyman still, and marries us, if
  need be, after a new way of his own.

SPRING. How long have you had his company?

2 BEG. But lately come amongst us, but a very ancient stroll [1]
  all the land over, and has travell'd with gipsies, and is a patrico.
  Shall he read your fortune, sir?

SPRING. If it please him.

PAT. Lend me your hand, sir.
    By this palm I understand,
      Thou art born to wealth and land;
    And after many a bitter gust,
      Shalt build with thy great-grandsire's dust.

SPRING. Where shall I find it? But come, I'll not trouble my
  head with the search.

2 BEG. What say, sir, to our crew? Are we not well congregated?

SPRING. You are a jovial crew; the only people
    Whose happiness I admire.

3 BEG. Will you make us happy in serving you? Have you any
  enemies? Shall we fight under you? Will you be our captain?

2 BEG. Nay, our king.

3 BEG. Command us something, sir.

SPRING. Where's the next rendezvous?

1 BEG. Neither in village nor in town,
    But three mile off at Mapledown. [2]

SPRING. At evening there I'll visit you.

Song [3]

    Come, come, away! The spring,
    By every bird that can but sing
    Or chirp a note, doth now invite
    Us forth, to taste of his delight.
    In field, in grove, on hill, in dale,
    But above all the nightingale,

---

[1] Wanderer.   [2] North-west of Wrotham, Kent.   [3] No other publication of these words is known, but the music appears in *Wit and Mirth, IV*
(1719), p. 142, with later words that are included in two eighteenth-century
editions of the play.

Who in her sweetness strives t' outdo
The loudness of the hoarse cuckoo.
480   'Cuckoo,' cries he, 'Jug, jug, jug,' sings she,
From bush to bush, from tree to tree,
Why in one place then tarry we?

Come away; why do we stay?
We have no debt or rent to pay.
No bargains or accounts to make;
Nor land or lease to let or take;
Or if we had, should that remore [1] us,
When all the world's our own before us?
And where we pass and make resort, [2]
490   It is our kingdom and our court.
'Cuckoo,' cries he, etc.   *Exeunt cantantes.*

SPRING. So, now away.
They dream of happiness that live in state,
But they enjoy it that obey their fate.   *Exit.*

ACT II [SCENE 1]

[Oldrents's *house*]

[*Enter*] Vincent, Hilliard, Meriel, Rachel

VINC. I am overcome with admiration [3] at the felicity they take!
HILL. Beggars! They are the only people can boast the benefit
of a free state, in the full enjoyment of liberty, mirth, and ease,
having all things in common and nothing wanting of nature's
whole provision within the reach of their desires. Who would
have lost this sight of their revels?
VINC. How think you, ladies? Are they not the only happy in a
nation?
MERIEL. Happier than we I'm sure, that are pent up and tied by
10   the nose to the continual steam of hot hospitality, here in our
father's house, when they have the air at pleasure in all variety.
RACHEL. And though I know we have merrier spirits than they,
yet to live thus confin'd stifles us.

---

[1] Hinder.   An assemblage.   [3] Wonder.

HILL. Why, ladies, you have liberty enough, or may take what you please.

MERIEL. Yes, in our father's rule and government, or by his allowance. What's that to absolute freedom, such as the very beggars have, to feast and revel here today and yonder tomorrow, next day where they please, and so on still, the whole country or kingdom over? There's liberty! The birds of the air can take no more.

RACHEL. And then at home here, or wheresoever he comes, our father is so pensive—what muddy spirit soe'er possesses him, would I could conjure't out—that he makes us even sick of his sadness, that were wont to see my gossip's cock today, mould cocklebread, dance clutterdepouch and hannykinbooby, bind barrels,[1] or do anything before him and he would laugh at us.

MERIEL. Now he never looks upon us but with a sigh, or tears in his eyes, though we simper never so sanctifiedly. What tales have been told him of us, or what he suspects I know not. God forgive him; I do, but I am weary of his house.

RACHEL. Does he think us whores, trow, because sometimes we talk as lightly as great ladies? I can swear safely for the virginity of one of us, so far as word and deed goes; marry, thought's free.

MERIEL. Which is that one of us, I pray? Yourself or me?

RACHEL. Good sister Meriel, charity begins at home. But I'll swear I think as charitably of thee, and not only because thou art a year younger neither.

MERIEL. I am beholden to you. But for my father, I would I knew his grief and how to cure him, or that we were where we could not see it. It spoils our mirth, and that has been better than his meat to us.

VINC. Will you hear our motion,[2] ladies?

MERIEL. Pseugh, you would marry us presently out of his way, because he has given you a foolish kind of promise, but we will see him in a better humour first, and as apt to laugh as we to lie down, I warrant him.

HILL. 'Tis like that course will cure him, would you embrace it.

RACHEL. We will have him cur'd first, I tell you, and you shall wait that season and our leisure.

MERIEL. I will rather hazard my being one of the devil's ape-leaders [3] than to marry while he is melancholy.

RACHEL. Or I to stay in his house; to give entertainment to

---

[1] A series of country dances.   [2] Proposal.   [3] An old maid was traditionally destined to lead apes in Hell.

this knight or tother coxcomb, that comes to cheer him up with eating of his cheer; when we must fetch 'em sweetmeats, and they must tell us, 'Ladies, your lips are sweeter', and then fall into courtship, one in a speech taken out of old Britain's works,[1] another with verses out of *The Academy of Complements*,[2]
60 or some or other of the new poetical pamphleteers,[3] ambitious only to spoil paper and publish their names in print. And then to be kissed, and sometimes slaver'd—Faugh!

MERIEL. 'Tis not to be endur'd! We must out of the house. We cannot live but by laughing, and that aloud, and nobody sad within hearing.

VINC. We are for any adventure with you, ladies. Shall we project a journey for you? Your father has trusted you, and will think you safe in our company; and we would fain be abroad upon some progress [4] with you. Shall we make a fling
70 to London, and see how the spring appears there in the Spring Garden;[5] and in Hyde Park, to see the races, horse and foot; to hear the jockeys crack;[6] and see the Adamites run naked afore the ladies? [7]

RACHEL. We have seen all already there, as well as they, last year.

HILL. But there ha' been new plays since.

RACHEL. No, no, we are not for London.

HILL. What think you of a journey to the Bath then?

RACHEL. Worse than tother way. I love not to carry my health
80 where others drop their diseases. There's no sport i' that.

VINC. Will you up to the hill-top of sports, then, and merriments: Dover's Olympics or the Cotswold Games? [8]

MERIEL. No, that will be too public for our recreation. We would have it more within ourselves.

HILL. Think of some course yourselves then. We are for you upon any way, as far as horse and money can carry us.

VINC. Ay, and if those means fail us, as far as our legs can bear or our hands can help us.

[1] Nicholas Breton, *c.* 1545–*c.* 1626; perhaps an allusion to *The Passionate Shepherd* (1604), a collection of his sonnets and lyrics.   [2] *. . . Wherein Ladyes, Gentlewomen, Schollers, and Strangers may accommodate their Courtly Practice with most Curious Ceremonies, Complementall, Amorous, High Expressions, and formes of speaking, or writing* (1640).
[3] An aristocratic vogue for love poetry in pamphlet form.   [4] Excursion.
[5] A seventeenth-century pleasure garden near St James's Park, London.
[6] To hear the horse-dealers boast.   [7] The sentence combines allusions to the notorious eccentric religious sect which abjured clothes and the nude participants in contemporary foot-races.   [8] Annual games of strength and skill organized by Robert Dover (1575–1641), held during Whitsun week near Evesham, Worcs., 1604–44.

RACHEL. And we will put you to't. Come aside, Meriel.

[Rachel *and* Meriel *speak*] *aside*

VINC. Some jeer, perhaps, to put upon us.

HILL. What think you of a pilgrimage to Saint Winifride's Well?[1]

VINC. Or a journey to the wise woman at Nantwich,[2] to ask if we be fit husbands for 'em?

HILL. They are not scrupulous in that, we having had their growing loves up from our childhoods and the old squire's good will before all men.

RACHEL, MERIEL. Ha, ha, ha!

VINC. What's the conceit, I marvel?

RACHEL, MERIEL. Ha, ha, ha, ha!

HILL. Some merry one, it seems.

RACHEL. And then, sirrah[3] Meriel—Hark again—Ha, ha, ha!

VINC. How they are taken with it!

MERIEL. Ha, ha, ha!—Hark again, Rachel.

HILL. Some wonderful nothing sure. They will laugh as much to see a swallow fly with a white feather imp'd[4] in her tail.

VINC. They were born laughing, I think.

RACHEL, MERIEL. Ha, ha, ha!

VINC. If it be not some trick upon us, which they'll discover in some monstrous shape, they cozen me. Now, ladies, is your project ripe? Possess us with the knowledge of it.

RACHEL. It is more precious than to be imparted upon a slight demand.

HILL. Pray let us hear it. You know we are your trusty servants.

VINC. And have kept all your counsels ever since we have been infant playfellows.

RACHEL. Yes, you have played at all kinds of small game with us; but this is to the purpose. Ha, ha, ha!

HILL. It seems so by your laughing.

RACHEL. And asks a stronger tongue-tie than tearing of books, burning of samplers, making dirt-pies, or piss and paddle in't.

VINC. You know how and what we have vow'd: to wait upon you any way, any how, and any whither.

MERIEL. And you will stand to't?

HILL. Ay, and go to't with you, wherever it be.

MERIEL. Pray tell't 'em, sister Rachel.

[1] A miraculous shrine and well at Holywell, Wales.   [2] Twenty miles south-east of Chester.   [3] A casual form of address used by a superior, only occasionally alluding to females. Rachel is the elder of the sisters.   [4] Grafted (a term in falconry).

RACHEL. Why, gentlemen—Ha, ha!—Thus it is—Tell it you, Meriel.

VINC. Oh, is that all?

130 MERIEL. You are the elder. Pray tell it you.

RACHEL. You are the younger. I command you tell it. Come, out with it. They long to have it.

HILL. When?[1]

VINC. When?

MERIEL. In troth, you must tell it, sister; I cannot. Pray begin.

RACHEL. Then, gentlemen, stand your ground.

VINC. Some terrible business sure!

RACHEL. You seem'd e'en now to admire the felicity of beggars.

MERIEL. And have engag'd yourselves to join with us in any
140 course.

RACHEL. Will you now with us, and for our sakes turn beggars?

MERIEL. It is our resolution and our injunction on you.

RACHEL. But for a time and a short progress.

MERIEL. And for a spring-trick of youth now, in the season.

VINC. Beggars! What rogues are these?

HILL. A simple trial of our loves and service!

RACHEL. Are you resolv'd upon't? If not, God b'w'y'. We are resolv'd to take our course.

MERIEL. Let yours be to keep counsel.

150 VINC. Stay, stay. Beggars! Are we not so already?
Do we not beg your loves and your enjoyings?
Do we not beg to be receiv'd your servants,
To kiss your hands, or, if you will vouchsafe,
Your lips, or your embraces?

HILL.   We now beg
That we may fetch the rings and priest to marry us.
Wherein are we no beggars?

RACHEL. That will not serve. Your time's not come for that yet. You shall beg victuals first.

VINC. Oh, I conceive your begging progress is to ramble out
160 this summer among your father's tenants, and 'tis in request among gentlemen's daughters to devour their cheese-cakes, apple pies, cream and custards, flapjacks, and pan-puddings.

MERIEL. Not so, not so.

HILL. Why, so we may be a kind of civil beggars.

RACHEL. I mean stark, errant, downright beggars, ay, without equivocation, statute [2] beggars.

---

[1] An exclamation of impatience.   [2] Licensed.

MERIEL. Couchant and passant, guardant, rampant [1] beggars.

VINC. Current [2] and vagrant—

HILL. We are most resolutely for you in your course.

VINC. But the vexation is how to set it on foot.

RACHEL. We have projected it. Now if you be perfect and constant lovers and friends, search you the means. [*To* Meriel] We have puzzl'd 'em.

MERIEL. [*To* Rachel] I am glad on't. Let 'em pump.[3]

VINC. Troth, a small stock will serve to set up withal. This doublet sold off o' my back might serve to furnish a camp royal [4] of us.

HILL. But how to enter or arrange ourselves into the crew will be the difficulty. If we light raw and tame amongst 'em, like cage-birds among a flight of wild ones, we shall never pick up a living, but have our brains peck'd out.

VINC. We want instruction dearly.

Enter Springlove

HILL. Oh, here comes Springlove. His great benefactorship among the beggars might prefer [5] us with authority into a ragged regiment presently. Shall I put it to him?

RACHEL. Take heed what you do. His greatness with my father will betray us.

VINC. I will cut his throat then.—My noble Springlove, the great commander of the maunders [6] and king of canters,[7] we saw the gratitude of your loyal subjects in the large tributary content they gave you in their revels.

SPRING. Did you, sir?

HILL. We have seen all with great delight and admiration.

SPRING. I have seen you too, kind gentlemen and ladies, and overheard you in your quaint design, to new-create yourselves out of the worldly blessings and spiritual graces Heaven has bestow'd upon you, to be partakers and co-actors too in those vile courses, which you call delights, ta'en by those despicable and abhorred creatures.

VINC. Thou art a despiser, nay a blasphemer
Against the Maker of those happy creatures,
Who, of all human, have priority
In their content, in which they are so blest
That they enjoy most in possessing least.
Who made 'em such, dost think? Or why so happy?

[1] Terms from heraldry, echoed in puns by Vincent and Hilliard.
[2] Genuine.   [3] Achieve by persistent effort.   [4] The main body of an army.   [5] Promote.   [6] Beggars.   [7] Vagabonds.

RACHEL. He grows zealous in the cause; sure he'll beg indeed.

HILL. Art thou an hypocrite, then, all this while?
Only pretending charity, or using it
To get a name and praise unto thyself,
210 And not to cherish and increase those creatures
In their most happy way of living? Or
Dost thou bestow thine alms with a foul purpose
To stint their begging, and with loss to buy
And slave those free souls from their liberty?

MERIEL. [*To* Rachel] They are more zealous in the cause than
we.

SPRING. But are you, ladies, at defiance too
With reputation and the dignity
Due to your father's house and you?

220 RACHEL. Hold thy peace, good Springlove, and, though you
seem to dislike this course and reprove us for it, do not betray us
in it; your throat's in question. I tell you for good will, good
Springlove.

MERIEL. What wouldst thou have us do? Thou talk'st o' th'
house. 'Tis a base melancholy house. Our father's sadness
banishes us out on't. And, for the delight thou tak'st in beggars
and their brawls, thou canst not but think they live a better
life abroad than we do in this house.

SPRING. I have sounded your faith, and I am glad I find you all
230 right. And for your father's sadness, I'll tell you the cause on't.
I overheard it but this day in his private discourse with his
merry mate, Master Hearty. He has been told by some wizard
that you both were born to be beggars.

ALL. How! How!

SPRING. For which he is so tormented in mind that he cannot
sleep in peace, nor look upon you but with heart's grief.

VINC. This is most strange.

RACHEL. Let him be griev'd then till we are beggars;
We have just reason to become so now,
240 And what we thought on but in jest before,
We'll do in earnest now.

SPRING. Oh, I applaud this resolution in you, would have
persuaded it, will be your servant in't. For, look ye, ladies: The
sentence of your fortune does not say that you shall beg for
need, hungry or cold necessity. If therefore you expose yourselves on pleasure into it, you shall absolve your destiny
nevertheless, and cure your father's grief. I am overjoy'd to
think on't, and will assist you faithfully.

ALL. A Springlove! A Springlove!

50 SPRING. I am prepar'd already for th'adventure,
　　And will with all conveniences furnish
　　And set you forth, give you your dimensions,[1]
　　Rules, and directions; I will be your guide,
　　Your guard, your convoy, your authority.
　　You do not know my power, my command
　　I' th' beggars' commonwealth.

VINC. But how, but how, good Springlove?

SPRING. I'll confess all. In my minority
　　My master took me up a naked beggar,
60 Bred me at school; then took me to his service—
　　You know in what good fashion—and you may
　　Collect to memory for seven late summers,
　　Either by leave, pretending friends to see
　　At far remote parts of the land, or else
　　By stealth, I would absent myself from service
　　To follow my own pleasure, which was begging,
　　Led to't by nature. My indulgent master,
　　Yet ignorant of my course, on my submission,
　　When cold and hunger forc'd me back at winter,
70 Receiv'd me still again. Till, two years since,
　　He being drawn by journey towards the north,
　　Where then I quarter'd with a ragged crew;
　　On the highway, not dreaming of him there,
　　I did accost him, with a 'Good your worship,
　　The gift o' one small penny to a creeple'—
　　For here I was with him—'and the good Lord　　　　　*Halts* [2]
　　To bless you and restore it you in Heaven'.

ALL. Ha, ha, ha!

SPRING. My head was dirty clouted,[3] and this leg
80 Swaddl'd with rags, the other naked, and
　　My body clad like his upon the gibbet.
　　Yet he, with searching eyes, through all my rags
　　And counterfeit postures made discovery
　　Of his man Springlove, chid me into tears
　　And a confession of my forespent life.
　　At last, upon condition that vagary
　　Should be the last, he gave me leave to run
　　That summer out. In autumn home came I
　　In my home clothes again and former duty.

---

[1] Dimensum, a fixed allowance.　　　　[2] Limps (to illustrate his deportment).
[3] Wrapped.

290 My master not alone conserv'd my counsel,[1]
     But lays more weighty trust and charge upon me.
     Such was his love, to keep me a home-man,
     That he conferr'd his steward's place upon me,
     Which clogg'd me the last year from those delights
     I would not lose again to be his lord.
     ALL. A Springlove! A Springlove!
     SPRING. Pursue the course you are on then, as cheerfully
     As the inviting season smiles upon you.
     Think how you are necessitated to it,
300 To quit [2] your father's sadness and his fears
     Touching your fortune. Till you have been beggars
     The sword hangs over him. You cannot think
     Upon an act of greater piety
     Unto your father than t'expose yourselves
     Brave volunteers, unpress'd by common need
     Into this meritorious warfare, whence,
     After a few days, or short season spent,
     You bring him a perpetual peace and joy
     By expiating the prophecy that torments him.
310 'Twere worth your time in painful, woeful steps,
     With your lives hazard in a pilgrimage,
     So to redeem a father. But you'll find
     A progress of such pleasure, as I'll govern't,
     That the most happy courts could never boast
     In all their tramplings on the country's cost,[3]
     Whose envy we shall draw when they shall read
     We outbeg them, and for as little need.
     ALL. A Springlove! A Springlove!
     SPRING. Follow me, gallants, then, as cheerfully
     As—Hark!—we are summon'd forth.   *Birds singing*
320 ALL.   We follow thee! *Exeunt.*

---

[1] Not only kept my secret.   [2] Absolve.   [3] Casual rural progresses by
the aristocracy, with little regard for fields and crops.

[ACT II SCENE 2]

[*Near* Oldrents's *house*]

Enter Randal, *a purse in his hand*

RAN. Well, go thy ways. If ever any just or charitable steward
was commended, sure thou shalt be at the last quarter-day.[1]
Here's five-and-twenty pounds for this quarter's beggar-
charge, and, if he return not by the end of this quarter, here's
order to a friend to supply for the next. If I now should venture
for the commendation of an unjust steward, and turn this money
to mine own use! Ha! Dear devil, tempt me not! I'll do thee
service in a greater matter. But to rob the poor! A poor trick;
every churchwarden can do't.[2] Now something whispers me
that my master, for his steward's love, will supply the poor, as I
may handle the matter. Then I rob the steward if I restore him
not the money at his return. Away, temptation, leave me. I am
frail flesh; yet I will fight with thee. But say the steward never
return. Oh, but he will return. Perhaps he may not return.
Turn from me, Satan; strive not to clog my conscience. I would
not have this weight upon't for all thy kingdom.[3]

Enter Hearty, *singing, and* Oldrents

HEARTY. Hey down, hey down a down, *etc.*
Remember, sir, your covenant to be merry.

OLD. I strive, you see, to be so, yet something pricks me within
methinks.

HEARTY. No further thought, I hope, of fortune's tell-tales.

OLD. I think not of 'em. Nor will I presage
That when a disposition of sadness
O'erclouds my spirits I shall therefore hear
Ill news or shortly meet with some disaster.

HEARTY. Nay, when a man meets with bad tidings, why
May not he then compel his mind to mirth,
As well as puling stomachs are made strong
By eating against appetite?[4]

OLD. Forc'd mirth, though, is not good.

HEARTY. It relishes[5] not, you'll say. No more does meat
That is most savory to a long-sick stomach,
Until by strife and custom 'tis made good.

---

[1] One of the four days in the year designated for payment of rentals, etc.;
here the Day of Judgment.   [2] A serious contemporary grievance.
[3] This speech is reminiscent of Launcelot Gobbo's in Shakespeare's *Merchant of Venice* (1596), II, ii, 1–33.   [4] Desire.   [5] Pleases.

OLD. You argue well. But do you see yond fellow?

HEARTY. I never noted him so sad before;
He neither sings nor whistles.

OLD.   Something troubles him.
Can he force mirth out of himself now, think you?

HEARTY. What? Speak you of a clod of earth, a hind,[1]
But one degree above a beast, compar'd

40   To th'aery spirit of a gentleman?

OLD. He looks,[2] as he came laden with ill news,
To meet me on my way.

HEARTY.   'Tis very pretty.
Suppose the ass be tir'd with sadness; will you disburden him
to load yourself? Think of your covenant to be merry in spite
of fortune and her riddle-makers.

OLD. Why, how now, Randal? Sad? Where's Springlove?

HEARTY. [Aside] He's ever in his care. But that I know
The old squire's virtue, I should think Springlove
Were sure his bastard.

RAN.   Here's his money, sir.

50   I pray that I be charg'd with it no longer. The devil and I have
strain'd courtesy these two hours about it. I would not be
corrupted with the trust of more than is mine own. Mr[3]
Steward gave it me, sir, to order it for the beggars. He has made
me steward of the barn and them while he is gone, he says, a
journey, to survey and measure lands abroad about the
countries. Some purchase, I think, for your worship.

OLD. I know his measuring of land. He is gone his old way. And
let him go. Am not I merry, Hearty?

HEARTY. Yes, but not hearty merry. There's a whim now!

60   OLD. The poor's charge shall be mine. Keep you the money for
him.

RAN. Mine is the greater charge then.
Knew you but my temptations and my care,
You would discharge me of it.

OLD. Ha, ha, ha!

RAN. I have not had it so many minutes, as I have been in
several minds about it; and most of them dishonest.

OLD. Go then, and give it to one of my daughters to keep for
Springlove.

70   RAN. Oh, I thank your worship.   *Exit.*

OLD. Alas, poor knave! How hard a task it is to alter custom!

---

[1] Labourer.   [2] Makes sure.   [3] Pronounced 'master'.

HEARTY. And how easy for money to corrupt it. What a pure
    treasurer would he make!
OLD. All were not born for weighty offices.
    Which makes me think of Springlove. He might have ta'en his
    leave though.
HEARTY. I hope he's run away with some large trust;
    I never lik'd such demure, down-look'd fellows.
OLD. You are deceiv'd in him.
HEARTY.   If you be not,
    'Tis well. But this is from the covenant.
OLD. Well, sir, I will be merry. I am resolv'd
    To force my spirit only unto mirth.
    Should I hear now my daughters were misled
    Or run away, I would not send a sigh
    To fetch 'em back.
HEARTY.   Tother old song for that!

                    Song [1]

    There was an old fellow at Waltham Cross,
        Who merrily sung when he liv'd by the loss;
    He never was heard to sigh with 'Hey-ho',
    But sent it out with a 'Heigh trolly lo!'
        He cheer'd up his heart when his goods went to wrack
        With a 'Heghm, boy, heghm', and a cup of old sack.

OLD. Is that the way on't? Well, it shall be mine then.

                    Enter Randal

RAN. My mistresses are both abroad, sir.
OLD.   How? Since when?
RAN. On foot, sir, two hours since, with the two gentlemen their
    lovers. Here's a letter they left with the butler. And there's a
    mutt'ring in the house.
OLD. I will not read nor open it, but conceive
    Within myself the worst that can befall them,
    That they are lost and no more mine. What follows?
    That I am happy, all my cares are flown.
    The counsel I anticipated from
    My friend shall serve to set my rest upon,[2]
    Without all further helps, to jovial mirth,
    Which I will force out of my spleen so freely
    That grief shall lose her name where I have being,

---

[1] In *Catch That Catch Can* (1652), p. 31.   [2] To venture one's reserve
stakes (from the card game of primero).

And sadness from my furthest foot of land,
While I have life, be banish'd.

HEARTY. What's the whim now?

OLD. My tenants shall sit rent-free for this twelvemonth,
And all my servants have their wages doubled;
110 And so shall be my charge in housekeeping.
I hope my friends will find and put me to't.

HEARTY. For them I'll be your undertaker, sir.
But this is overdone; I do not like it.

OLD. And for thy news, the money that thou hast
Is now thine own. I'll make it good to Springlove.
Be sad with it and leave me; for I tell thee,
I'll purge my house of stupid melancholy.

RAN. I'll be as merry as the charge that's under me.

*A confused noise within of laughing and singing,
and one crying out*

The beggars, sir. Do'ee hear 'em in the barn?

120 OLD. I'll double their allowance too, that they may
Double their numbers, and increase their noise.
These bear [1] not sound enough, and one, methought,
Cried out among 'em.

RAN. By a most natural cause. For there's a doxy [2]
Has been in labour, sir, and 'tis their custom
With songs and shouts to drown the woman's cries,
A ceremony which they use, not for
Devotion, but to keep off notice of
The work they have in hand. Now she is in
The straw, it seems, and they are quiet.

130 HEARTY. The straw!
That's very proper there. That's Randal's whim.

OLD. We will have such a lying in and such
A christ'ning, such up-sitting [3] and gossiping! [4]
I mean to send forty miles circuit at the least,
To draw in all the beggars can be found,
And such devices we will have for jollity,
As fame shall boast to all posterity.
Am I not merry, Hearty? Hearty merry?

HEARTY. Would you were else! I fear this overdoing.

140 OLD. I'll do't for expiation of a crime
That's charg'd upon my conscience till't be done.

---

[1] Raise.   [2] Strumpet.   [3] A woman's first receiving visitors after a
confinement.   [4] A celebration on the occasion of the birth of a child.

HEARTY. What's that? What says he?

OLD. We will have such a festival month on't, Randal—

RAN. Sir, you may spare the labour and the cost;
They'll never thank you for't. They'll not endure
A ceremony that is not their own,
Belonging either to the child or mother.
A month, sir? They'll not be detain'd so long
For your estate. Their work is done already:
50   The bratling's born, the doxy's in the strummel,[1]
Laid by an autem mort of their own crew
That serv'd for midwife, and the childbed woman
Eating of hasty pudding for her supper,
And the child, part of it for pap
I warrant you by this time; then to sleep,
So to rise early to regain the strength
By travail,[2] which she lost by travail.[3]

HEARTY. There's Randal again.

OLD. Can this be?

60 RAN. She'll have the bantling [4] at her back tomorrow
That was today in her belly, and march a foot-back [5] with it.

HEARTY. Art there again, old Randal?

RAN. And for their gossiping, now you are so nigh,
If you'll look in, I doubt not but you'll find 'em
At their high feast already.

HEARTY.   Pray let's see 'em, sir.

Randal *opens the scene: the beggars discovered at
their feast. After they have scrambled a while
at their victuals, this song:*

Here, safe in our skipper,[6] let's cly off [7] our peck,[8]
And bowse [9] in defiance o' th' harman-beck.[10]
Here's pannum [11] and lap,[12] and good poplars of yarrum,[13]
To fill up the crib,[14] and to comfort the quarron.[15]
70   Now bowse a round health to the go-well and come-well
Of Cisley Bumtrincket [16] that lies in the strummel.
Now bowse a round health to the go-well and come-well
Of Cisley Bumtrincket that lies in the strummel.
Here's ruffpeck [17] and casson,[18] and all of the best,
And scraps of the dainties of gentry cofe's [19] feast.

---

[1] Straw.   [2] i.e. travel.   [3] Parturition.   [4] Bastard.   [5] On foot (as opposed to horse-back).   [6] Barn.   [7] Seize.   [8] Meat.   [9] Tipple.   [10] Constable (harmans are stocks).   [11] Bread.   [12] Whey.   [13] Butter-milk.   [14] Stomach.   [15] Body.   [16] Referred to in Dekker's *Shoemakers Holiday* (1599), I, i, 161; I, iv, 34–5.   [17] Bacon.   [18] Cheese.   [19] A gentleman's.

Here's grunter [1] and bleater,[2] with Tib of the butt'ry,[3]
And Margery Prater,[4] all dress'd without slutt'ry.[5]
  For all this bene cribbing [6] and peck let us then
  Bowse a health to the gentry cofe of the ken.[7]
180 Now bowse a round health to the go-well and come-well
  of Cisley Bumtrincket that lies in the strummel.

OLD. Good Heaven! How merry they are!
HEARTY.   Be not you sad at that.
OLD. Sad, Hearty? No; unless it be with envy
  At their full happiness. What is an estate
  Of wealth and power, balanc'd with their freedom,
  But a mere load of outward complement,[8]
  When they enjoy the fruits of rich content?
  Our dross but weighs us down into despair,
  While their sublimed spirits dance i' th'air.
190 HEARTY. I ha' not so much wealth to weigh me down,
  Nor so little, I thank chance, as to dance naked.
OLD. True, my friend Hearty. Thou having less than I—
  Of which I boast not—art the merrier man.
  But they exceed thee in that way so far
  That should I know my children now were beggars—
  Which yet I will not read [9]—I must conclude
  They were not lost, nor I to be aggriev'd.
HEARTY. If this be madness, 'tis a merry fit.
     Enter Patrico. *Many of the beggars look out*
PAT. Toure [10] out with your glasiers! [11] I swear by the ruffin [12]
200 That we are assaulted by a quire cuffin.[13]
RAN. Hold! What d'e mean, my friends? This is our master,
  The master of your feast and feasting-house.
PAT. Is this the gentry cofe?
ALL THE BEGGARS. Lord bless his worship, his good worship!
  Bless his worship!   *Exeunt* Beggars. *Manet* Patrico.
PAT. Now, bounteous sir, before you go,
  Hear me, the beggar patrico,
  Or priest, if you do rather choose
  That we no word of canting use.
210 Long may you live, and may your store
  Never decay, nor balk [14] the poor;
  And as you more in years do grow,

---

[1] Pig. [2] Sheep. [3] A goose. [4] A hen. [5] Untidiness. [6] Good
provender. [7] House. [8] Accomplishment. [9] A reference to
Rachel and Meriel's letter; see above, lines 95–7. [10] Look. [11] Eyes.
[12] Devil. [13] Justice of the Peace. [14] Overlook.

May treasure to your coffers flow,
And may your care no more thereon
Be set than ours are, that have none,
But as your riches do increase,
So may your heart's content and peace.
And, after many, many years,
When the poor have quit their fears
20 Of losing you, and that with Heaven
And all the world you have made even,
Then may your blest posterity
Age after age successively,
Until the world shall be untwin'd,
Inherit your estate and mind.
So shall the poor to the last day
For you, in your succession, pray.
HEARTY. 'Tis a good vote,[1] Sir Patrico, but you are too grave.
Let us hear and see something of your merry grigs, that can
30 sing, play gambols,[2] and do feats.
PAT. Sir, I can lay my function by,
And talk as wild and wantonly
As Tom or Tib or Jack or Jill,
When they at bowsing ken [3] do swill.
Will you therefore deign to hear
My autem mort, with throat as clear
As was Dame Aniss's [4] of the name,
How sweet in song her notes she'll frame,
That when she chides, as loud is yawning,
40 As chanticleer wak'd by the dawning?
HEARTY. Yes, pray let's hear her. What is she, your wife?
PAT. Yes, sir. We of our ministry,
As well as those o' th' presbytery,
Take wives and defy dignity.[5]   *Exit.*
HEARTY. A learned clerk in verity!

Enter Patrico *with his old wife,*
with a wooden bowl of drink. She is drunk

PAT. By Salmon,[6] I think my mort is in drink.
I find by her stink and the pretty, pretty pink
Of her neyes [7] that half wink,

---

[1] Wish.   [2] Sport.   [3] Drinking house.   [4] Dame Annis Clare, who
gave her name to a spring at Hoxton, a section of London just north of the
City, by drowning herself there, probably late sixteenth century.
[5] Ecclesiastical authority; an allusion to the Catholic law of priestly
celibacy.   [6] By the mass.   [7] Eyes.

That the tippling feast with the doxy in the nest
250   Hath turn'd her brain to a merry, merry vein.
AUT. Go fiddle, patrico, and let me sing. First, set me down here
on both my prats.[1] Gently, gently, for cracking of my wind, now
I must use it. Hem, hem!

She sings [2]

This is bien bowse,[3] this is bien bowse,
    Too little is my skew.[4]
I bowse no lage,[5] but a whole gage [6]
    Of this I'll bowse to you,
This bowse is better than rum bowse;[7]
    It sets the gan [8] a-giggling.
260   The autem mort finds better sport
    In bowsing than in niggling.[9]
    This is bien bowse, etc.
    She tosses off her bowl, falls back, and is carried out
PAT. So, so; your part is done.   *Exit with her.*
HEARTY. How find you, sir, yourself?
OLD. Wondrous merry, my good Hearty!

Enter Patrico

PAT. I wish we had, in all our store,
    Something that could please you more.
    The old or autem mort's asleep;
    But before the young ones creep
270   Into the straw, sir, if you are—
    As gallants sometimes love coarse fare,
    So it be fresh and wholesome ware—
    Dispos'd to doxy or a dell [10]
    That never yet with man did mell,[11]
    Of whom no upright man [12] is taster,
    I'll present her to you, master.
OLD. Away! You would be punish'd. Oh!
HEARTY. How is it with you, sir?
OLD. A sudden qualm overchills my stomach, but 'twill away.

Enter dancers

280 PAT. See, in their rags, then, dancing for your sports,

---

[1] Buttocks.   [2] This song is in *The English Rogue*, Part II (1671, 1928),
p. 340.   [3] Good drink.   [4] Cup.   [5] Water.   [6] Quart.   [7] Wine.
[8] Mouth.   [9] Lying with a man.   [10] Virgin.   [11] Have a sexual
relationship.   [12] A leader among a band of beggars; he had the privilege
of taking the virginity of nubile girls in the group.

Our clapper-dudgeons [1] and their walking morts.[2] [*They*] *dance*
You have done well. Now let each tripper
Make a retreat into the skipper
And couch a hogshead [3] till the darkman's [4] past;
Then all with bag and baggage bing awast.[5] *Exeunt* Beggars.

RAN. I told you, sir, they would be gone tomorrow;
  I understand their canting.
OLD.   Take that amongst you. *Gives money*
PAT. May rich plenty so you bless,
  Though you still give, you ne'er have less.   *Exit.*
90 HEARTY. And as your walks may lead this way,
  Pray strike in here another day.
  So you may go, Sir Patrico—
  How think you, sir? Or what? Or why do you think at all,
  unless on sack and supper-time? Do you fall back? Do you not
  know the danger of relapses?
OLD. Good Hearty, thou mistak'st me. I was thinking upon this
  patrico, and that he has more soul than a born beggar in him.
HEARTY. Rogue enough though, to offer us his what-d'ee-call'ts,
  his doxies! Heart, and a cup of sack! Do we look like old
00 beggar-nigglers? [6]
OLD. Pray forbear that language.
HEARTY. Will you then talk of sack, that can drown sighing?
  Will you in to supper, and take me there your guest, or must
  I creep into the barn among your welcome ones?
OLD. You have rebuk'd me timely and most friendly.   *Exit.*
HEARTY. Would all were well with him.   *Exit.*
RAN.   It is with me.
  For now these pounds are, as I feel them swag,[7]
  Light at my heart, though heavy in the bag.   *Exit.*

ACT III

[*Near the beggars' camp*]

[*Enter*] Vincent *and* Hilliard *in their rags*

VINC. Is this the life that we admir'd in others, with envy at their
  happiness?

---

[1] Beggars (from the sound made by striking a beggar's dish with a dudgeon
or knife-handle).   [2] Unmarried women who pretended to be widows.
[3] Sleep.   [4] Night.   [5] Haste away.   [6] Those who are intimate with
beggar-women.   [7] Sway.

HILL. Pray let us make virtuous use of it, and repent us of that
deadly sin, before a greater punishment than famine and lice
fall upon us, by steering our course homeward. Before I'll
endure such another night—

VINC. What? What wouldst thou do? I would thy mistress heard
thee.

HILL. I hope she does not, for I know there is no altering our
10   course before they make the first motion.

VINC. Is't possible we should be weary already, and before their
softer constitutions of flesh and blood?

HILL. They are the stronger in will, it seems.

Enter Springlove

SPRING. How now, comrades? Repining already at your fullness
of liberty? Do you complain of ease?

VINC. Ease, call'st thou it? Didst thou sleep tonight?

SPRING. Not so well these eighteen months, I swear, since my
last walks!

HILL. Lightning and tempest is out of thy litany. Could not the
20   thunder wake thee?

SPRING. Ha, ha, ha!

VINC. Nor the noise of the crew in the quarter by us?

HILL. Nor the hogs in the hovel, that cried till they drown'd
the noise of the wind? If I could but once ha' dreamt in all my
former nights that such an affliction could have been found
among beggars, sure I should never have travell'd to the proof
on't.

VINC. We look'd upon them in their jollity, and cast no
further.

30   HILL. Nor did that only draw us forth, by your favour, Vince,
but our obedience to our loves, which we must suffer till they
cry home again. Are they not weary yet, as much as we, dost
think, Springlove?

SPRING. They have more moral understanding than so. They
know, and so may you, this is your birth-night into a new world.
And we all know, or have been told, that all come crying into
the world, when the whole world of pleasures is before us.
The world itself had ne'er been glorious had it not first been a
confused chaos.

40   VINC. Well, never did knight-errants in all adventures merit
more of their ladies than we beggar-errants, or errant beggars,
do in ours!

SPRING. The greater will be your reward. Think upon that, and show no manner of distaste to turn their hearts from you. Y'are undone then.

HILL. Are they ready to appear out of their privy lodgings, in the pigs' palace of pleasure? Are they coming forth?

SPRING. I left 'em almost ready, sitting on their pads of straw, helping to dress each other's heads—the one's eye is the tother's looking-glass—with the prettiest coil [1] they keep to fit their fancies in the most graceful way of wearing their new dressings, that you would admire.

VINC. I hope we are as gracefully set out. Are we not?

SPRING. Indifferent well. But will you fall to practise? Let me hear how you can maund [2] when you meet with passengers.[3]

HILL. We do not look like men, I hope, too good to learn.

SPRING. Suppose some persons of worth or wealth passing by now. Note me. 'Good your good worship, your charity to the poor, that will duly and truly pray for you day and night—

VINC. Away, you idle rogue! You would be set to work and whipp'd—

SPRING. That is lame and sick, hungry and comfortless,—

VINC. If you were well serv'd—

SPRING. And even to bless you and reward you for it—'

HILL. Prithee hold thy peace—here be doleful notes indeed—and leave us to our own genius. If we must beg, let's let it go, as it comes, by inspiration. I love not your set form of begging.

SPRING. Let me instruct ye though.

Enter Rachel *and* Meriel *in rags*. [*They remain aside*]

RACHEL. Have a care, good Meriel, what hearts or limbs soever we have, and though never so feeble, let us set our best faces on't, and laugh our last gasp out before we discover any dislike or weariness to them. Let us bear it out till they complain first, and beg to carry us home a pick pack.[4]

MERIEL. I am sorely surbated [5] with hoofing already though, and so crupper-cramp'd [6] with our hard lodging, and so bumfiddled [7] with the straw, that—

RACHEL. Think not on't. I am numb'd i' the bum and shoulders too a little, and have found the difference between a hard floor with a little straw and a down bed with a quilt upon't. But no words nor a sour look, I prithee.

HILL. Oh, here they come now, Madam Fewclothes and my Lady Bonnyrag.

VINC. Peace, they see us.

[1] Fuss. [2] Beg. [3] Travellers. [4] On their backs. [5] Foot-sore.
[6] Lamed in the buttocks. [7] Bruised.

RACHEL, MERIEL. Ha, ha, ha!

VINC. We are glad the object pleases ye.

RACHEL.   So does the subject.
Now you appear the glories of the spring.
Darlings of Phoebus,[1] and the summer's heirs.

HILL. How fairer than fair Flora's self [2] appear,
To deck the spring, Diana's darlings [3] dear!

90   Oh, let us not, Actaeon-like, be struck,
With greedy eyes while we presume to look
On your half nakedness, since courteous rags
Cover the rest, into the shape of stags.[4]

RACHEL, MERIEL. Ha, ha, ha! We are glad you are so merry.

VINC. Merry and lusty too. This night will we lie together as
well as the proudest couple in the barn.

HILL. And so will we. I can hold out no longer.

RACHEL. Does the straw stir up your flesh to't, gentlemen?

MERIEL. Or does your provender prick you?

100 SPRING. What! Do we come for this? Laugh and lie down
When you bellies are full. Remember, ladies,
You have not begg'd yet, to quit your destiny,
But have liv'd hitherto on my endeavours.
Who got your suppers, pray, last night, but I?
Of dainty trencher-fees [5] from a gentleman's house,
Such as the serving-men themselves sometimes
Would have been glad of. And this morning now,
What comfortable chippings [6] and sweet buttermilk
Had you to breakfast?

110 RACHEL. Oh, 'twas excellent! I feel it good still, here.

MERIEL. There was a brown crust amongst it, that has made my
neck so white methinks. Is it not, Rachel?

RACHEL. Yes, you ga' me none on't.
You ever covet to have all the beauty.
'Tis the ambition of all younger sisters.

VINC. [To Hilliard] They are pleas'd, and never like to be weary.

HILL. [To Vincent] No more must we, if we'll be theirs.

SPRING. Peace! Here come passengers. Forget not your rules,
and quickly disperse yourselves, and fall to your calling.
Exeunt Rachel, Meriel, *and* Hilliard. [Vincent *and* Springlove
stand aside]

---

[1] Apollo, the god of the sun.   [2] The Roman goddess of spring.
[3] Protected by Diana, goddess of virginity, etc.   [4] Actaeon was turned
into a stag after watching Diana whilst she was bathing.   [5] Remnants of
food given to beggars.   [6] Crusts.

Enter two Gentlemen

20 1 GENT. Lead the horses down the hill. The heat of our speed is
over, for we have lost our journey.[1]

2 GENT. Had they taken this way, we had overtaken 'em, or
heard of 'em at least.

1 GENT. But some of our scouts will light on 'em, the whole
country being overspread with 'em.

2 GENT. There was never such an escape else.

VINC. [*To* Springlove] A search for us perhaps. Yet I know not
them, nor they me, I am sure. I might the better beg of 'em.
But how to begin, or set the worst leg forwards, would I were
30 whipp'd if I know now.

1 GENT. That a young gentlewoman of her breeding, and heir to
such an estate, should fly from so great a match, and run away
with her uncle's clerk!

2 GENT. The old justice will run mad upon't, I fear.

VINC. If I were to be hang'd now, I could not beg for my life.

SPRING. Step forwards, and beg handsomely. I'll set my goad
i' your breech else.

VINC. What shall I say?

SPRING. Have I not told you? Now begin.

40 VINC. After you, good Springlove.

SPRING. Good, your good worships—

1 GENT. Away, you idle vagabond!

SPRING. Your worships' charity to a poor crytur welly [2] starv'd.

VINC. That will duly and truly prea for ye.

2 GENT. You counterfeit villains, hence!

SPRING. Good masters' sweet worship, for the tender mercy
of—

VINC. Duly and truly prea for you.

1 GENT. You would be well whipp'd and set to work, if you
50 were duly and truly serv'd.

VINC. [*Aside*] Did not I say so before?

SPRING. Good worshipful masters' worship, to bestow your
charity, and to maintain your health and limbs—

VINC. Duly and truly pray for you.

2 GENT. Begone, I say, you impudent lusty young rascals!

1 GENT. I'll set you going else. [*They*] *switch* 'em.

SPRING. Ah, the goodness of compassion to soften your hearts
to the poor—

VINC. [*To* Springlove] Oh, the devil! Must we not beat 'em now?
60 'Steth,[3]—

---

[1] Direction.   [2] Well nigh.   [3] By God's death'.

SPRING. [*To* Vincent] Nor show an angry look for all the skin of our backs.—Ah, the sweetness of that mercy that gives to all, to move your compassion to the hungry, when it shall seem good unto you, and night and day to bless all that you have. Ah, ah,—

2 GENT. Come back, sirrah.—[*To* 1 Gentleman] His patience and humility has wrought upon me.

VINC. Duly and—

2 GENT. Not you, sirrah. The tother. You look like a sturdy
170 rogue.

SPRING. Lord bless your master's worship!

2 GENT. There's a half-penny for you. Let him have no share with you.

VINC. [*Aside*] I shall never thrive o' this trade.

1 GENT. They are of a fraternity, and will share, I warrant you.

SPRING. Never in our lives truly. He never begg'd with me before.

1 GENT. But if hedges or hen-roosts could speak, you might be found sharers in pillage, I believe.

180 SPRING. Never saw him before, bless you good master, in all my life.—[*To* Vincent] Beg for yourself. Your credit's gone else.—Good Hea'n to bliss and prosper yea! *Exit.*

2 GENT. Why dost thou follow us? Is it your office to be privy to our talk?

VINC. Sir, I beseech you hear me.—[*Aside*] 'Slife, what shall I say?—I am a stranger in these parts, and destitute of means and apparel.

1 GENT. So methinks. And what o' that?

VINC. Will you therefore be pleas'd, as you are worthy gentle-
190 men, and bless'd with plenty,—

2 GENT. This is courtly!

VINC. Out of your abundant store, towards my relief in extreme necessity, to furnish me with a small parcel of money, five or six pieces,[1] or ten, if you can presently spare it.

1 AND 2 GENT. Stand off! [*They*] *draw*

VINC. [*Aside*] I have spoil'd all, and know not how to beg otherwise.

1 GENT. Here's a new way of begging!

VINC. [*Aside*] Quite run out of my instructions.

200 2 GENT. Some highway thief, o' my conscience, that forgets he is weaponless.

---

[1] Unites, a coin worth £1.10.

vinc. Only to make you merry, gentlemen, at my unskilfulness
in my new trade. I have been another man i' my days. So I kiss
your hands.   *Exit.*

1 gent. With your heels, do you?

2 gent. It had been good to have apprehended the rakeshame.[1]
There is some mystery in his rags. But let him go.

Enter Oliver, *putting up his sword*

oliver. [*To* Hilliard, *offstage*] You found your legs in time. I
had made you halt for something else.

10 1 gent. Master Oliver, well return'd. What's the matter, sir?

oliver. Why, sir, a counterfeit lame rogue begg'd of me, but in
such language, the high sheriff's son o' the shire could not have
spoke better, nor to have borrowed a greater sum. He ask'd me
if I could spare him ten or twenty pound! I switch'd him; his
cudgel was up; I drew, and into the wood he scap'd me, as
nimbly—But first he told me I should hear from him by a
gentleman, to require satisfaction of me.

2 gent. We had such another begg'd of us. The court goes
a-begging, I think.

20 1 gent. Dropp'd through the clouds, I think; more Lucifers
travelling to Hell, that beg by the way. Met you no news of your
kinswoman, Mistress Amie?

oliver. No. What's the matter with her? Goes her marriage
forwards with young Master Talboy? I hasten'd my journey
from London to be at the wedding.

2 gent. 'Twas to ha' been yesterday morning, all things in
readiness prepar'd for it, but the bride, stolen by your father's
clerk, is slipp'd away. We were in quest of 'em, and so are twenty
more, several ways.

30 oliver. Such young wenches will have their own ways in their
own loves, what matches soever their guardians make for 'em.
And I hope my father will not follow the law so close to hang
his clerk for stealing his ward with her own consent. It may
breed such a grudge may cause some clerks to hang their
masters, that have 'em o' the hip [2] of injustice. Besides, Martin,
though he be his servant, is a gentleman. But, indeed, the
miserablest rascal! He will grudge her meat when he has her.

1 gent. Your father is exceedingly troubled at their escape. I
wish that you may qualify [3] him with your reasons.

40 oliver. But what says Talboy to the matter, the bridegroom
that should ha' been?

---

[1] Scoundrel.   [2] At a disadvantage (a term from wrestling).   [3] Pacify.

2 GENT. Marry, he says little to the purpose, but cries outright.

OLIVER. I like him well for that; he holds his humour. A
miserable wretch too, though rich. I ha' known him cry when
he has lost but three shillings at mumchance.[1] But, gentlemen,
keep on your way to comfort my father. I know some of his
man's private haunts about the country here, which I will
search immediately.

250 1 GENT. We will accompany you, if you please.

OLIVER. No, by no means; that will be too public.

2 GENT. Do your pleasure.   *Exeunt* Gentlemen.

OLIVER. My pleasure, and all the search that I intend, is, by
hovering here, to take a review of a brace of the handsomest
beggar-braches [2] that ever grac'd a ditch or a hedge-side. I
pass'd by 'em in haste, but something so possesses me, that I
must—What the devil must I? A beggar? Why, beggars are
flesh and blood, and rags are no diseases. Their lice are no
French fleas.[3] And there is much wholesomer flesh under
260 country dirt than city painting, and less danger in dirt and rags
than in ceruse [4] and satin. I durst not take a touch [5] at London,
both for the present cost, and fear of an after-reckoning. But,
Oliver, dost thou speak like a gentleman? Fear price or pox, ha?
Marry, do I, sir; nor can beggar-sport be inexcusable in a
young country gentleman short of means, for another respect, a
principal one indeed: to avoid the punishment or charge of
bastardy. There's no commuting [6] with them, or keeping of
children for them. The poor whores, rather than part with their
own, or want [7] children at all, will steal other folks', to travel
270 with and move compassion. He feeds a beggar-wench well that
fills her belly with young bones. And these reasons considered,
good Master Oliver—'Slid, yonder they are at peep![8] And now
sitten down, as waiting for my purpose.

Enter Vincent

Heart! Here's another delay. I must shift [9] him. [*To* Vincent]
Dost hear, honest poor fellow? I prithee go back presently, and
at the hill foot—here's sixpence for thy pains—thou shalt
find a footman with a horse in his hand. Bid him wait there. His
master will come presently, say.

VINC. Sir, I have a business of another nature to you, which—

---

[1] A dicing game played in silence.   [2] Beggar-bitches.   [3] An allusion
to syphilis.   [4] White lead, used as a cosmetic.   [5] Engage in sexual
intercourse.   [6] Bargaining.   [7] Lack.   [8] Peering surreptitiously.
[9] Get rid of.

80 as I presume you are a gentleman of right noble spirit and
    resolution—you will receive without offence and in that temper
    as most properly appertains to the most heroic natures.

OLIVER. Thy language makes me wonder at thy person. What's
    the matter with thee? Quickly!

VINC. You may be pleas'd to call to mind a late affront, which,
    in your heat of passion, you gave a gentleman.[1]

OLIVER. What, such a one as thou art, was he?

VINC. True, noble sir. Who could no less in honour than direct
    me, his chosen friend, unto you, with the length of his sword or
90 to take the length of yours. The place, if you please, the ground
    whereon you parted; the hour, seven the next morning; or, if
    you like not these in part or all, to make your own appoint-
    ments.

OLIVER. [Aside] The bravest method in beggars that ever was
    discovered! I would be upon the bones of this rogue now, but
    for crossing my other design, which fires me. I must therefore
    be rid of him on any terms.—Let his own appointments stand.
    Tell him I'll meet him.

VINC. You shall most nobly engage his life to serve you, sir.

100 OLIVER. You'll be his second, will you?

VINC. To do you further service, sir, I have undertaken it.

OLIVER. I'll send a beadle [2] shall undertake [3] you both.

VINC. Your mirth becomes the bravery of your mind and
    dauntless spirit. So takes his leave, your servant, sir.

OLIVER. I think, as my friend said, the court goes a-begging
    indeed. But I must not lose my beggar-wenches.

Enter Rachel *and* Meriel

Oh, here they come. They are delicately skinn'd and limb'd.
There, there, I saw above the ham as the wind blew. Now they
spy me.

110 RACHEL. Sir, I beseech you look upon us with the favour of a
    gentleman. We are in a present distress, and utterly un-
    acquainted in these parts, and therefore forc'd by the calamity
    of our misfortune to implore the courtesy, or rather charity, of
    those to whom we are strangers.

OLIVER. [Aside] Very fine, this!

MERIEL. Be therefore pleas'd, right noble sir, not only [4] valuing
    us by our outward habits, which cannot but appear loathsome
    or despicable unto you, but as we are forlorn Christians; and,
    in that estimation, be compassionately moved to cast a handful

---

[1] i.e. Hilliard.   [2] A minor parish official.   [3] Deal with.   [4] Merely.

320 or two of your silver, or a few of your golden pieces unto us, to furnish us with linen, and some decent habiliments.

OLIVER. [*Aside*] They beg as high as the man-beggar I met withal! Sure the beggars are all mad today, or bewitched into a language they understand not. The spirits of some decay'd gentry talk in 'em sure.

RACHEL. May we expect a gracious answer from you, sir?

MERIEL. And that as you can wish our virgin prayers to be propitious for you.

RACHEL. That you never be denied a suit by any mistress.

330 MERIEL. Nay, that the fairest may be ambitious to place their favours on you.

RACHEL. That your virtue and valour may lead you to the most honourable actions, and that the love of all exquisite ladies may arm you.

MERIEL. And that, when you please to take a wife, may honour, beauty, and wealth contend to endow her most with.

RACHEL. And that with her you have a long and prosperous life.

MERIEL. A fair and fortunate posterity.

OLIVER. [*Aside*] This exceeds all that ever I heard, and strikes
340 me into wonder.—Pray tell me, how long have you been beggars, or how chanc'd you to be so?

RACHEL. By influence of our stars, sir.

MERIEL. We were born to no better fortune.

OLIVER. How came you to talk thus, and so much above the beggar's dialect?

RACHEL. Our speech came naturally to us, and we ever lov'd to learn by rote as well as we could.

MERIEL. And to be ambitious above the vulgar, to ask more than common alms, whate'er men please to give us.

350 OLIVER. [*Aside*] Sure some well-disposed gentleman, as myself, got these wenches. They are too well grown to be mine own, and [1] I cannot be incestuous with 'em.

RACHEL. Pray, sir, your noble bounty.

OLIVER. [*Aside*] What a tempting lip that little rogue moves there! And what an enticing eye the tother. I know not which to begin with.—What's this, a flea upon thy bosom?

MERIEL. Is it not a straw-colour'd one, sir?

OLIVER. [*Aside*] Oh, what a provoking skin is there! That very touch inflames me.

360 RACHEL. Sir, are you mov'd in charity towards us yet?

OLIVER. Mov'd? I am mov'd; no flesh and blood more mov'd!

[1] i.e. therefore.

MERIEL. Then pray, sir, your benevolence.

OLIVER. [*Aside*] Benevolence? Which shall I be benevolent to, or which first? I am puzzl'd in the choice. Would some sworn brother of mine were here to draw a cut with me.

RACHEL. Sir, noble sir.

OLIVER. First let me tell you, damsels, I am bound by a strong vow to kiss all of the woman sex I meet this morning.

MERIEL. Beggars and all, sir?

370 OLIVER. All, all! Let not your coyness cross a gentleman's vow, I beseech you.   *Kisses* [*them*]

RACHEL. You will tell now.

OLIVER. Tell, quoth a! I could tell [1] a thousand on those lips, and as many upon those. [*Aside*] What life-restoring breaths they have! Milk from the cow steams not so sweetly. I must lay one of 'em aboard; both, if my tackling hold.

RACHEL, MERIEL. Sir! Sir!

OLIVER. [*Aside*] But how to bargain now will be the doubt.[2] They that beg so high as by the handfuls may expect for price

380 above the rate of good men's wives.

RACHEL. Now will you, sir, be pleas'd?

OLIVER. With all my heart, sweetheart, and I am glad thou knowest my mind. Here is twelve pence apiece for you.

RACHEL, MERIEL. We thank you, sir.

OLIVER. That's but in earnest. I'll jest away the rest with ye. Look here—All this. [*Shows money*] Come, you know my meaning. Dost thou look about thee, sweet little one? I like thy care. There's nobody coming, but we'll get behind these bushes. I know you keep each other's counsels. Must you be drawn

390 to't? Then I'll pull. Come away.

RACHEL, MERIEL. Ah, ah!

Enter Springlove, Vincent, Hilliard

VINC. Let's beat his brains out.

OLIVER. Come; leave your squealing.

RACHEL. Oh, you hurt my hand.

HILL. Or cut the lecher's throat.

SPRING. Would you be hang'd? Stand back. Let me alone.

MERIEL. You shall not pull us so.

SPRING. Oh, do not hurt 'em, master.

OLIVER. Hurt 'em? I meant 'hem but too well. Shall I be so

00 prevented?

SPRING. They be but young and simple, and if they have

[1] Count.   [2] Difficulty.

offended, let not your worship's own hands drag 'em to the law
or carry 'em to punishment. Correct 'em not yourself. It is the
beadle's office.

OLIVER. Do you talk, shake-rag?[1] [*Aside*] Heart, yond's more of
'em! I shall be beggar-mawl'd if I stay.—Thou say'st right,
honest fellow; there's a tester[2] for thee.   *Exit running*.

VINC. He is prevented, and asham'd of his purpose.

SPRING. Nor were we to take notice of his purpose more than
410   to prevent it.

HILL. True, politic Springlove; 'twas better his own fear quit
us of him than our force.

RACHEL. Look you here, gentlemen, twelve pence apiece!

MERIEL. Besides fair offers and large promises. What ha' you
got today, gentlemen?

VINC. More than, as we are gentlemen, we would have taken.

HILL. Yet we put it up[3] in your service.

RACHEL, MERIEL. Ha, ha, ha! Switches and kicks. Ha, ha, ha!

SPRING. Talk not here of your gettings. We must quit this
420   quarter. The eager gentleman's repulse may arm and return
him with revenge upon us. We must therefore leap hedge and
ditch now, through the briars and mires, till we scape out of
this liberty,[4] to our next rendezvous, where we shall meet the
crew, and then hay toss and laugh all night!

MERIEL. [*To* Rachel] As we did last night.

RACHEL. [*To* Meriel] Hold out, Meriel.

MERIEL. [*To* Springlove] Lead on, brave general.

VINC. [*To* Hilliard] What shall we do? They are in heart still.
Shall we go on?

430 HILL. [*To* Vincent] There's no flinching back, you see.

SPRING. [*To* Vincent *and* Hilliard] Besides, if you beg no better
than you begin, in this lofty fashion, you cannot scape the jail
or the whip long.

VINC. [*To* Springlove] To tell you true, 'tis not the least of my
purpose, to work means for our discovery, to be releas'd out of
our trade.

Enter Martin *and* Amie *in poor habits*

SPRING. Stay. Here come more passengers. Single[5] yourselves
again, and fall to your calling discreetly.

HILL. I'll single no more. If you'll beg in full cry I am for you.

440 MERIEL. Ay, that will be fine; let's charm all together.

SPRING. Stay first, and list a little.   [*They stand aside*]

[1] Ragged, disreputable person.   [2] 2.5 pence.   [3] Endure it.   [4] District.
[5] Separate.

MARTIN. Be of good cheer, sweetheart; we have scap'd hitherto,
and I believe that all the search is now retir'd, and we may
safely pass forwards.

AMIE. I should be safe with thee, but that's a most lying proverb
that says, 'Where love is, there's no lack'. I am faint and cannot
travel further without meat, and if you lov'd me, you would get
me some.

MARTIN. We'll venter at the next village to call for some. The
50   best is, we want no money.

AMIE. We shall be taken then, I fear. I'll rather pine to death.

MARTIN. Be not so fearful. Who can know us in these clownish
habits?

AMIE. Our clothes, indeed, are poor enough to beg with. Would
I could beg, so it were of strangers that could not know me,
rather than buy of those that would betray us.

MARTIN. And yonder be some that can teach us.

SPRING. These are the young couple of runaway lovers disguis'd
that the country is so laid [1] for. Observe and follow now.—
60   Now the Lord to come with ye, good loving master and may-
stress, your blessed charity to the poor, lame and sick, weak and
comfortless, that will night and day—

ALL. Duly and truly pray for you, duly and truly pray for you.

SPRING. [*To* companions] Pray hold your peace and let me
alone.—Good young master and mistress, a little comfort
amongst us all, and to bless you where'er you go, and—

ALL. Duly and truly pray for you, duly and truly—

SPRING. [*To* companions] Pray do not use me thus.—Now,
sweet young master and mistress, to look upon your poor, that
70   have no relief or succour, no bread to put in our heads,—

VINC. [*Aside*] Wouldst thou put bread in thy brains?—
No lands or livings.

SPRING. No house nor home, nor covering from the
cold, no health, no help but your sweet charity.

MERIEL. No bands [2] or shirts but lousy on our backs.

HILL. No smocks or petticoats to hide our scratches.

RACHEL. No shoes to our legs or hose to our feet.   *All*
together.

VINC. No skin to our flesh nor flesh to our bones
shortly.

80   HILL. [*Aside*] If we follow the devil that taught us to
beg.

ALL. Duly and truly pray for you.

[1] Searched.   [2] Collars.

SPRING. [*To* companions] I'll run away from you if you beg a
stroke more.—Good worshipful master and mistress,—

MARTIN. Good friend, forbear. Here is no master or mistress.
We are poor folks. Thou seest no worship upon our backs, I
am sure. And for within, we want as much as you, and would
as willingly beg, if we knew how as well.

SPRING. Alack for pity. You may have enough. And what I
490 have is yours, if you'll accept it. 'Tis wholesome food from a
good gentleman's gate. Alas, good mistress! Much good do
your heart. [*Aside*] How savourly [1] she feeds!

MARTIN. What, do you mean to poison yourself?

AMIE. Do you show love in grudging me?

MARTIN. Nay, if you think it hurts you not, fall to, I'll not
beguile [2] you. And here, mine host, something towards your
reckoning.

AMIE. This beggar is an angel sure!

SPRING. Nothing by way of bargain, gentle master. 'Tis against
500 order, and will never thrive. But pray, sir, your reward in
charity.

MARTIN. Here then in charity. [*Aside*] This fellow would never
make a clerk.

SPRING. What! All this, master?

AMIE. What is it? Let me see't.

SPRING. 'Tis a whole silver threepence, mistress.

AMIE. For shame, ungrateful miser. Here, friend, a golden
crown [3] for thee.

SPRING. Bountiful goodness! Gold? If I thought a dear year
510 were coming, I would take a farm now.

AMIE. I have robb'd thy partners of their shares too. There's a
crown for them.

RACHEL, MERIEL, VINCENT, HILLIARD. [4] Duly and truly pray
for you.

MARTIN. [*To* Amie] What have you done? Less would have
serv'd, and your bounty will betray us.

AMIE. [*To* Martin] Fie on your wretched policy! [5]

SPRING. No, no, good master. I knew you all this while, and
my sweet mistress too. And now I'll tell you: The search is
520 every way, the country all laid for you. 'Tis well you stayed
here. Your habits, were they but a little nearer our fashion,
would secure you with us. But are you married, master and
mistress? Are you joined in matrimony? In heart, I know you

[1] With relish.   [2] Deprive.   [3] About twenty-five pence.   [4] Q has '4'.
[5] Craftiness.

are. And I will, if it please you, for your great bounty, bring you
to a curate that lacks no licence nor has any living to lose, that
shall put you together.

MARTIN. Thou art a heavenly beggar!

SPRING. But he is so scrupulous, and severely precise,[1] that
unless you, mistress, will affirm that you are with child by the
gentleman, or that you have, at least, cleft [2] or slept together, as
he calls it, he will not marry you. But if you have lain together,
then 'tis a case of necessity, and he holds himself bound to do
it.

MARTIN. [*To* Amie] You may say you have.

AMIE. I would not have it so, nor make that lie against myself
for all the world.

SPRING. [*Aside*] That I like well, and her exceedingly.—I'll do
my best for you, however.

MARTIN. I'll do for thee, that thou shalt never beg more.

SPRING. That cannot be purchas'd, scarce for the price of your
mistress. Will you walk, master? We use no compliments.

[Exeunt all except Amie.]

AMIE. By enforc'd matches wards are not set free
So oft as sold into captivity;
Which made me, fearless, fly from one I hate,
Into the hazard of a harder fate.   *Exit.*

ACT IV SCENE 1

[Oldrents's *house*]

Enter Talboy [*and*] Oliver, *with riding switches*

TAL. She's gone. Amie is gone. Ay me, she's gone,
And has me left of joy bereft, to make my moan.
Oh me, Amie!

OLIVER. [*Aside*] What the devil ails the fellow, trow?—Why,
why, Master Talboy, my cousin Talboy that should'st ha' been,
art not asham'd to cry at this growth? [3] And for a thing that's
better lost than found, a wench?

---

[1] Puritanical.   [2] Had intercourse.   [3] i.e. at your age.

TAL. Cry? Who cries? Do I cry or look with a crying countenance? I scorn it, and scorn to think on her but in just anger.

10 OLIVER. So; this is brave now if 'twould hold.

TAL. Nay, it shall hold. And so let her go, for a scurvy what-
d'ee-call't; I know not what bad enough to call her. But something of mine goes with her, I am sure. She has cost me in
gloves, ribands, scarfs, rings, and suchlike things more than I
am able to speak of at this time. Oh!

OLIVER. Because thou canst not speak for crying. Fie, Master
Talboy, again?

TAL. I scorn it again, and any man that says I cry or will cry
again. And let her go again, and what she has of mine let her
20 keep, and hang herself, and the rogue that's with her. I have
enough, and am heir of a well-known estate, and that she
knows; and therefore that she should slight me and run away
with a wages-fellow that is but a petty clerk and a serving-man!
There's the vexation of it! Oh, there's the grief and the vexation
of it. Oh!

OLIVER. [*Aside*] Now he will cry his eyes out.—You, sir! This
life have I had with you all our long journey, which now is at an
end here. This is Master Oldrents' house, where perhaps we
shall find old Hearty, the uncle of that rogue Martin that is
30 run away with your sweetheart.

TAL. Ay, 'tis too true, too true, too true. You need not put me in
mind on't. Oh, oh!

OLIVER. Hold your peace and mind me! Leave your bawling,
for fear I give you correction. This is the house, I say, where
it is most likely we shall hear of your mistress and her companion. Make up your face quickly. Here comes one of the
servants, I suppose.

Enter Randal

Shame not yourself for ever, and me for company. Come; be
confident.

40 TAL. As confident as yourself or any man. But my poor heart
feels what lies here. Here. Ay, here it is. Oh!

OLIVER. Good morrow, friend. This is Squire Oldrents' house,
I take it?

RAN. Pray take it not, sir, before it be to be let. It has been my
master's and his ancestors' in that name above these three
hundred years, as our house chronicle doth notify, and not
yet to be let. But as a friend or stranger, in guest-wise, you are

welcome to it, as all other gentlemen are, far and near, to my good master, as you will find anon when you see him.

OLIVER. Thou speak'st wittily and honestly, but I prithee, good friend, let our nags be set up;[1] they are tied up at the post. You belong to the stable, do you not?

RAN. Not so much as the stable belongs to me, sir. I pass through many offices of the house, sir. I am the running bailie of it.

OLIVER. We have rid hard, hoping to find the squire at home at this early time in the morning.

RAN. You are deceiv'd in that, sir; he has been out these four hours. He is no snail, sir. You do not know him, I perceive, since he has been new-moulded, but I'll tell you, because you are gentlemen,—

OLIVER. Our horses, good friend.

RAN. My master is an ancient gentleman and a great house-keeper, and pray'd for by all the poor in the country. He keeps a guest house for all beggars far and near costs him a hundred a year at least, and is as well belov'd among the rich. But of late he fell into a great melancholy, upon what I know not; for he had then more cause to be merry than he has now. Take that by the way.

OLIVER. But, good friend, our horses.

RAN. For he had two daughters that knew well to order a house and give entertainment to gentlemen. They were his house-doves, but now they are flown, and no man knows how, why, or whither.

TAL. My dove is flown too. Oh!

RAN. Was she your daughter, sir? She was a young one then, by the beard you wear.

TAL. What she was, she was, d'ee see? I scorn to think on her, but I do. Oh!

OLIVER. Pray hold your peace or feign some mirth if you can.

TAL. *Sings* Let her go, let her go.
I care not if I have her, I have her, or no.
Ha, ha, ha! Oh, my heart will break! Oh!

OLIVER. Pray think of our horses, sir.

RAN. This is right [2] my master. When he had his daughters he was sad, and now they are gone he is the merriest man alive. Up at five a clock in the morning and out till dinner-time, out again at afternoon, and so till supper-time. Skice [3] out this-a-way and skice out that-a-way. He's no snail, I assure you. And

---

[1] Put up, in a stable. [2] Altogether. [3] Skip.

tantivy [1] all the country over, where hunting, hawking, or any
90   sport is to be made, or good fellowship to be had, and so merry
      upon all occasions that you would even bless yourself if it were
      possible.

OLIVER. Our horses, I prithee.

RAN. And we his servants live as merrily under him, and do all
      thrive. I myself was but a silly lad when I came first, a poor
      turn-spit boy. Gentlemen kept no whirling jacks [2] then to
      cozen poor people of meat. And I have now, without boast,
      forty pounds in my purse, and am the youngest of half a score
      in the house, none younger than myself but one, and he is the
100   steward over all. His name is Master Springlove—bless him
      where'er he is—He has a world of means, and we the under-
      lings get well the better by him, besides the rewards many
      gentlemen give us, that fare well and lodge here sometimes.

OLIVER. Oh, we shall not forget you, friend, if you remember
      our horses before they take harm.

RAN. No hurt, I warrant you; there's a lad walking them.

OLIVER. Is not your master coming, think you?

RAN. He will not be long a-coming. He's no snail, as I told you.

OLIVER. You told me so, indeed.

110   RAN. But of all the gentlemen that toss up the ball, [3] yea, and
      the sack too, commend me to old Master Hearty, a decay'd
      gentleman, lives most upon his own mirth and my master's
      means, and much good do him with it. He is the finest com-
      panion of all; he does so hold my master up with stories and
      songs and catches and tother [4] cup of sack, and such tricks and
      jigs you would admire. He is with him now.

OLIVER. [Aside] That Hearty is Martin's uncle. I am glad he is
      here.—Bear up, Talboy. Now, friend, pray let me ask you a
      question. Prithee, stay.

120   RAN. Nay, marry, I dare not. Your yaudes [5] may take cold, and
      never be good after it.   Exit.

OLIVER. I thought I should never have been rid of him, but no
      sooner desir'd to stay but he is gone. A pretty humour!

Enter Randal

RAN. Gentlemen, my master will be here e'en now, doubt not,
      for he is no snail, as I told you.   Exit.

OLIVER. No snail's a great word with him. Prithee, Talboy, bear
      up.

---

[1] Rush headlong.   [2] A mechanically operated device to turn meat over
a fire.   [3] Promote conversation.   [4] A second.   [5] Jades, worn out horses.

Enter Usher

Here comes another grey fellow.

USHER. Do you stand in the porch, gentlemen? The house is
30   open to you. Pray enter the hall; I am the usher of it.

OLIVER. In good time, sir. We shall be bold here then to attend
your master's coming.

USHER. And he's upon coming, and when he comes he comes
apace. He's no snail, I assure you.

OLIVER. I was told so before, sir. [*Aside*] No snail! Sure, 'tis
the word of the house, and as ancient as the family.

USHER. This gentleman looks sadly methinks.

TAL. Who, I? Not I. Pray pardon my looks for that. But my
heart feels what's what. Ay me!

40 USHER. Pray walk to the butt'ry, gentlemen. My office [1] leads
you thither.

OLIVER. Thanks, good master usher.

USHER. I have been usher these twenty years, sir, and have got
well by my place, for using strangers respectfully.

OLIVER. [*Aside*] He has given the hint too.

USHER. Something has come in by the by, besides standing [2]
wages, which is ever duly paid, thank a good master and an
honest steward. Heaven bless 'hem; we all thrive under 'em.

Enter Butler, *with glasses and a napkin*

Oh, here comes the butler.

50 BUTLER. You are welcome, gentlemen. Please ye draw nearer my
office and take a morning drink in a cup of sack, if it please
you.

OLIVER. In what please you, sir. We cannot deny the courtesy of
the house in the master's absence.

BUTLER. He'll come apace when he comes. He's no snail, sir.
                                                              Going

OLIVER. [*Aside*] Still 'tis the house-word, and all the servants
wear livery beards. [3]

BUTLER. Or perhaps you had rather drink white wine and sugar.
Please yourselves, gentlemen; here you may taste all liquors.
60   No gentleman's house in all this county or the next so well
stor'd—make us all thankful for it. And my master, for his
hospitality to gentlemen, his charity to the poor, and his bounty
to his servants, has not his peer in the kingdom—make us
thankful for it. And 'tis as fortunate a house for servants as

----

[1] Duty.   [2] Fixed.   [3] Beards of a uniform style.

ever was built upon fairy ground. I myself, that have serv'd
here man and boy these four-and-forty years, have gotten
together—besides something more than I will speak of,
distributed among my poor kindred—by my wages, my vails [1]
at Christmas and otherwise, together with my rewards of kind
170   gentlemen that found courteous entertainment here,—

OLIVER. [*Aside*] There is he too.

BUTLER.—Have, I say, gotten together, though in a dangerous
time I speak it, a brace of hundred pounds—make me thankful
for it. And for losses, I have had none. I have been butler these
two-and-thirty years, and never lost the value of a silver spoon,
nor ever broke a glass—make me thankful for it. White wine
and sugar say you, sir?

OLIVER. Please yourself, sir.

BUTLER. This gentleman speaks not. Or had you rather take a
180   drink of brown ale with a toast, or March beer with sugar and
nutmeg? Or had you rather drink without sugar?

OLIVER. Good sir, a cup of your household beer. *Exit* Butler.
I fear he will draw down to that at last.

Enter Butler, *with a silver can of sack*

BUTLER. Here, gentlemen, is a cup of my master's small beer,[2]
but it is good old canary, I assure you. And here's to your
welcome.

Enter Cook

COOK. And welcome the cook says, gentlemen. Brother butler,
lay a napkin; I'll fetch a cut of the sirloin to strengthen your
patience till my master comes, who will not now be long, for he's
190   no snail, gentlemen.

OLIVER. I have often heard so. And here's to you, master cook.
Prithee speak, Master Talboy, or force one laugh more if thou
canst.

COOK. *To* Talboy. Sir, the cook drinks to you.

TAL. Ha, ha, ha!

OLIVER. [*To* Talboy] Well said.

TAL. [*To* Oliver] He is in the same livery beard too.

COOK. But he is the oldest cook, and of the ancientest house,
and the best for housekeeping in this county or the next. And
200   though the master of it write but 'Squire,' I know no lord like
him.

---

[1] Gratuities.   [2] A deprecating phrase; sack is a white wine, often dry,
from Spain; it is similar to canary, which derives from the Canary Islands.

Enter Chaplain

And now he's come. Here comes the Word before him. The parson has ever the best stomach. I'll dish away presently.

Exit.

BUTLER. Is our master come, Sir Dominie?

CHAP. *Est ad manum. Non est ille testudo.*[1]

OLIVER. [*To* Talboy] He has the word too in Latin. Now bear up, Talboy.

CHAP. Give me a preparative of sack. It is a gentle preparative before meat. And so, a gentle touch of it to you, gentlemen.

10 OLIVER. It is a gentle offer, sir, and as gently to be taken.

Enter Oldrents *and* Hearty

OLD. About with it, my lads! And this is as it should be.
[Butler *offers him wine*] Not till my turn, sir, I. Though I confess I have had but three morning-draughts today.

OLIVER. Yet it appears you were abroad betimes, sir.

OLD. I am no snail, sir.

OLIVER. So your men told us, sir.

OLD. But where be my catchers?[2] Come, a round! And so let us drink.

*The catch sung, and they drink about. The singers
are all greybeards.*

A round, a round, a round, boys, a round![3]
20   Let mirth fly aloft and sorrow be drown'd.
Old sack and old songs and a merry old crew
Can charm away cares when the ground looks blue.[4]

OLD. Well said, old Hearty. And, gentlemen, welcome.

TAL. *Sighs.* Ah!

OLD. Oh, mine ears! What was that, a sigh? And in my house? Look, has it not split my walls? If not, make vent for it. Let it out; I shall be stifled else.   *Exit* Chaplain.

OLIVER. He[5] hopes your pardon, sir, his cause considered.

OLD. Cause? Can there be cause for sighing?

30 OLIVER. He has lost his mistress, sir.

OLD. Ha, ha, ha! Is that a cause? Do you hear me complain the loss of my two daughters?

OLIVER. They are not lost I hope, sir.

---

[1] He is at hand. He is no tortoise.   [2] The singers of a catch or round, a song in which each singer takes up the words in turn.   [3] This song, with music by William Lawes, is in *Catch That Catch Can* (1667), p. 18. [4] Dreary.   [5] Talboy.

OLD. No more can be his mistress. No woman can be lost. They may be mislaid a little, but found again, I warrant you.

TAL. *Sighs.* Ah!

OLD. 'Ods my life! He sighs again and means to blow me out of my house. To horse again! Here's no dwelling for me! Or stay—I'll cure him if I can. Give him more sack to drown his
240   suspirations.

While Oldrents *and* Talboy *drink,* Oliver *takes* Hearty *aside*

OLIVER. Sir, I am chiefly to inform you of the disaster.

HEARTY. May it concern me?

OLIVER. Your nephew Martin has stolen my father's ward, that gentleman's bride that should have been.

HEARTY. Indeed, sir!

OLIVER. 'Tis most true.   *He gives* Hearty *a letter*

HEARTY. Another glass of sack! This gentleman brings good news.

OLIVER. Sir, if you can prevent his danger,—
250 HEARTY. Hang all preventions. Let 'em have their destiny.

Hearty *reads the letter*

TAL. *To* Oldrents. Sir, I should have had her, 'tis true, but she is gone, d'ee see? And let her go!

OLD. Well said. [*Aside*] He mends now.

TAL. I am glad I am rid of her—d'ee see?—before I had more to do with her.

OLD. [*Aside*] He mends apace.

TAL. For should I have married her before she had run away— d'ee see?—and that she had run away—d'ee see?—after she had been married to me—d'ee see?—then I had been a married man
260   without a wife, d'ee see? Where now, she being run away before I am married—d'ee see?—I am no more married to her—d'ee see?—than she to me, d'ee see? And so long as I am none of hers—d'ee see?—nor she none of mine—d'ee see?—I ought to care as little for her, now she is run away—d'ee see?—as if she had stay'd with me, d'ee see?

OLD. Why, this is excellent! Come hither, Hearty.

TAL. I perceive it now, and the reason of it, and how, by consequence—d'ee see?—I ought not to look any further after her. *Cries.* But that she should respect a poor base fellow, a
270   clerk at the most, and a serving-man at best, before me, that am a rich man at the worst, and a gentleman at least, makes me —I know not what to say!

OLD. [*Aside*] Worse than ever 'twas! Now he cries outright.

TAL. I know not what to say, what to say. Oh!

HEARTY. Then I do, sir. The poor base fellow that you speak of is my nephew, as good a gentleman as yourself. I understand the business by your friend here.

TAL. I cry you mercy, sir.

OLD. You shall cry no mercy nor anything else here, sir, nor
280 for anything here, sir. This is no place to cry in, nor for any business. *To* Oliver. You, sir, that come on business—

OLIVER. It shall be none, sir.

OLD. My house is for no business but the belly-business. You find not me so uncivil, sir, as to ask you from whence you came, who you are, or what's your business. I ask you no question. And can you be so discourteous as to tell me or my friend anything like business? If you come to be merry with me, you are welcome. If you have any business, forget it. You forget where you are else. And so to dinner.

290 HEARTY. Sir, I pray let me only prevail with you but to read this.

OLD. Spoil my stomach now, and I'll not eat this fortnight.

He reads aside

HEARTY. [*To* Oliver] While he reads let me tell you, sir. That my nephew Martin has stol'n that gentleman's mistress, it seems, is true; but I protest, as I am a gentleman, I know nothing of the matter, nor where he or she is. But, as I am the foresaid gentleman, I am glad on't with all my heart. Ha, my boy Mat, thou shalt restore our house.

OLIVER. Let him not hear, to grieve him, sir.

300 HEARTY. Grieve him? What should he do with her, teach their children to cry?

TAL. But I do hear you though, and I scorn to cry as much as you—d'ee see?—or your nephew either, d'ee see?

HEARTY. Now thou art a brave fellow. So, so; hold up thy head and thou shalt have a wife and a fine thing.

TAL. Hang a wife! And pax o' your fine thing, d'ee see? I scorn your fopperies, d'ee see?

OLD. And I do hear thee, my boy, and rejoice in thy conversion. If thou canst but hold now!

310 TAL. Yes, I can hold, sir. And I hold well with your sack. I could live and die with it, as I am a true Talboy.

OLD. Now thou art a tall fellow and shalt want no sack.

TAL. And, sir, I do honour you—d'ee see?—and should wish myself one of your household servants—d'ee see?—if I had but a grey beard, d'ee see? 'Hey!' as old Master Clack says.

OLD. Well, I have read the business here.

OLIVER. Call it not business, I beseech you, sir. We defy all business.

TAL. Ay, marry do we, sir. D'ee see, sir? And a 'Hey!' as old
320 Master Clack says.

OLD. Gramercy sack! Well, I have read the matter here written by Master Clack; and do but bear up in thy humour. I will wait upon thee home. *Knock within.* Hark! They knock to the dresser.[1] I have heard much of this old odd-ceited [2] Justice Clack, and now I long to see him. 'Tis but crossing the country two days and a night's journey. We'll but dine, and away presently. Bear up, I say, Master Talboy.

TAL. I will bear up, I warrant you, d'ee see, sir? But here's a grudging still—   *Exeunt.*

[1] A servant's knock at the sideboard, to indicate that dinner is ready.
[2] Eccentric.

[ACT IV] SCENE 2

[The beggars' camp]

A great noise within of rude music, laughing, singing, etc.
Enter Amie, Rachel, Meriel

AMIE. Here's a wedding with a witness,[1] and a holiday with a
hoigh! Let us out of the noise, as we love our ears.

RACHEL. Yes, and here we may pursue our own discourse and
hear one another.

MERIEL. Concerning Springlove and yourself, Mistress Amie.

AMIE. Well, ladies, my confidence in you, that you are the same
that you have protested yourselves to be, hath so far won
upon me that I confess myself well-affected both to the mind
and person of that Springlove; and if he be, as fairly you
pretend,[2] a gentleman, I shall easily dispense with fortune.

RACHEL, MERIEL. He is, upon our honours.

AMIE. How well that high engagement suits your habits!

RACHEL. Our minds and blood are still the same.

AMIE. I have passed no affiance to the other that stole me from
my guardian and the match he would have forc'd me to, from
which I would have fled with any, or without a guide. Besides,
his mind, more clownish than his habit, deprav'd by covetousness and cowardice, forc'd me into a way of misery, to take
relief from beggars.

MERIEL. From poor us!

AMIE. And then to offer to marry me under a hedge, as the old
couple were today, without book or ring, by the chaplain of
the beggars' regiment, your patrico, only to save charges.

RACHEL. I have not seen the wretch these three hours; whither
is he gone?

AMIE. He told me to fetch horse and fit raiment for us, and so to
post me hence, but I think it was to leave me on your hands.

MERIEL. He has taken some great distaste sure, for he is
damnable jealous.

RACHEL. Ay. Didst thou mark what a wild look he cast when
Springlove tumbled her and kissed her on the straw this morning, while the music played to the old wedding-folks?

MERIEL. Yes, and then Springlove, to make him madder, told
him that he would be his proxy, and marry her for him, and lie
with her the first night, with a naked cudgel betwixt 'em, and
make him a king of beggars.

---

[1] Without a doubt.   [2] Profess.

AMIE. I saw how it anger'd him, and I imagin'd then and before
that there was more in Springlove than downright beggar. But
though he be never so good a gentleman, he shall observe fit
40   time and distance till we are married.

RACHEL. Matrimony forbid else! [*Aside*] She's taken.—But
while we talk of a match towards, we are miss'd within the
bride-barn among the revel rout.

AMIE. We have had all the sport they could make us in the past
passages.[1]

MERIEL. How cautious the old contracted couple were for
portion and jointure! [2]

RACHEL. What feofees [3] she, being an heir of fourscore and
seven years stone-blind, had in trust for her estate.

50   AMIE. And how carefully he secur'd all to himself, in case he
outliv'd her, being but seven years older than she, and what
pains the lawyer of the rout here took about it!

RACHEL. And then how solemnly they were join'd and ad-
monish'd by our Parson Under-hedge to live together in the
fear of the lash, and give good example to the younger re-
probates, to beg within compass, to escape the jaws of justice,
the clutch of the constable, the hooks of the headborough,[4]
and the biting blows of the beadle. And in so doing they
should defy the devil and all his works, and after their
60   painful pilgrimage in this life, they should die in the ditch of
delight.

MERIEL. Oh, but poet Scribble's epithalamium!
        'To the blind virgin of fourscore
        And the lame bachelor of more,
        How Cupid gave her eyes to see,
        And Vulcan [5] lent him legs,
        How Venus caus'd their sport to be
        Prepar'd with butter'd eggs;
        Yet when she shall be seven years wed
70   She shall be bold to say,
        She has as much her maidenhead
        As on her wedding day'.

RACHEL. So may some wives that were married at sixteen to
lads of one-and-twenty.

AMIE. But at the wedding-feast, when the bride bridled [6] it and
her groom saddled it! There was the sport, in her mumping [7]

---

[1] Actions.   [2] The joint ownership of an estate by husband and wife, with
widow's rights.   [3] Trustees.   [4] A parish officer.   [5] The lame god
of fire.   [6] Threw up her head, as in pride.   [7] Grimacing.

and his champing,[1] the crew scrambling, ourselves trembling;
then the confusion of noises, in talking, laughing, scolding,
singing, howling, with their actions of snatching, scratching,
80 tousing [2] and lousing themselves and one another!—

      Enter Springlove, Vincent, *and* Hilliard

But who comes here?
SPRING. Oh, ladies, you have lost as much mirth as would
  have fill'd up a week of holidays.

  Springlove *takes* Amie *aside and courts her in a genteel way*

VINC. I am come about again for the beggars' life now.
RACHEL. You are? I am glad on't.
HILL. There is no life but it.
VINC. With them there is no grievance or perplexity,
  No fear of war or state disturbances.
  No alteration in a commonwealth
90 Or innovation shakes a thought of theirs.
MERIEL. Of ours, you should say.
HILL.   Of ours, he means.
  We have no fear of lessening our estates,
  Nor any grudge with us, without taxation,
  To lend or give upon command the whole
  Strength of our wealth for public benefit;
  While some, that are held rich in their abundance,
  Which is their misery indeed, will see
  Rather a general ruin upon all
  Than give a scruple [3] to prevent the fall.
100 VINC. 'Tis only we that live.
RACHEL. I'm glad you are so taken with your calling.
MERIEL. We are no less, I assure you. We find the sweetness of
  it now.
RACHEL. The mirth, the pleasure, the delights! No ladies live
  such lives.
MERIEL. Some few upon necessity perhaps, but that's not worth
  gramercy.
VINC. [*To* Hilliard] They will never be weary.
HILL. [*To* Vincent] Whether we seem to like or dislike, all's one
110 to them.
VINC. We must do something to be taken by and discovered; we
  shall never be ourselves and get home again else.

     Springlove *and* Amie *come to the rest*

   [1] Munching noisily.   [2] Romping.   [3] A tiny quantity.

SPRING. [*To* Amie] I am yours for ever.—Well, ladies, you have
missed rare sport; but now the bride has miss'd you with her
half half-eye, and the bridegroom, with the help of his crutches,
is drawing her forth for a dance here in the opener air. The
house is now too hot for 'em. Oh, here come the chief revellers,
the soldier, the courtier, the lawyer, and the poet, who is master
of their revels, before the old couple in state. Attend and hear
120   him speak as their inductor.

[*Enter the* Crew]

POET. Here on this green, like king and queen,
    For a short truce we do produce
    Our old new-married pair.
    Of dish and wallet [1] and of straw pallet,
    With rags to show from top to toe,
    She is the ancient heir.

    He is the lord of bottle-gourd,[2]
    Of satchel great for bread and meat,
    And for small pence a purse.
130   'To all that give, long may you live',
    He loudly cries, but who denies
    Is sure to have his curse.
VINC. Well said, field-poet. Phoebus,[3] we see, inspires
    As well the beggar as the poet laureate.
SPRING. And shines as warm under a hedge-bottom as on the
    tops of palaces.
POET. I have not done yet. Now this to incite you to dance.

    Prepare yourselves, like fairy elves,
    Now in a dance to show
140   That you approve [4] the god of love
    Has many shafts to's bow,

    With golden head and some of lead,
    But that which made these feel,
    By subtle crafts, was sure a shaft
    That headed was with steel;

    For they were old, no earth more cold,
    Their hearts were flints entire;
    Whence the steel's stroke did sparks provoke
    That set their bloods on fire.

[1] A bag for provisions.   [2] A gourd used as a flask.   [3] Apollo, the god
of the sun; also of poetry, music, etc.   [4] Demonstrate.

150   Now strike up, piper, and each lover here
      Be blithe, and take his mistress by the goll.[1]

HILL. That's no rhyme, poet.

POET. There's as good poetry in blank verse as metre.   *Music*

SPRING. Come, hey! The dance, the dance! Nay, we'll ha' the
    old couple in, as blind and lame as they are.

          [Bride *and* Bridegroom] *dance*

BRIDE. What, will you so?

SPRING. Well hobbled, bridegroom!

VINC. Well grop'd, bride!

HILL. Hey, lusty! Hey, holiday!

160 SPRING. Set 'hem down, set 'em down! They ha' done well.

GROOM. Ah, ha! I am lustier than I was thirty years ago.

BRIDE. And I than I was threescore past. [*Coughs*] Ahem, ahem!

VINC. What a night here's towards!

HILL. Sure they will kill one another.

POET. Each with a fear the tother will live longest.

SPRING. Poet, thou hast spoken learnedly and acted bravely.
    Thou art both poet and actor.

POET. So has been many famous men. And if here were no worse,
    we might have a masque or a comedy presented tonight, in
170   honour of the old couple.

VINC. Let us each man try his ability
      Upon some subject now extempore.

SPRING. Agreed. Give us a theme and try our action.

POET. I have already thought upon't; I want but actors.

HILL. What persons want you? What would you present?

POET. I would present a commonwealth; Utopia,
    With all her branches and consistencies.[2]

RACHEL. I'll be Utopia. Who must be my branches?

POET. The country, the city, the court, and the camp, epitomiz'd
180   and personated by a gentleman, a merchant, a courtier, and a
    soldier.

[BEGGAR] SOLDIER. I'll be your soldier. Am not I one, ha?

[BEGGAR] COURTIER. And am not I a fashionable courtier?

POET. But who the citizen or merchant?

SPRING. I.

VINC. And I your country gentleman.

HILL. Or I.

POET. Yet to our moral I must add two persons, Divinity and
    Law.

        [1] Hand.   [2] Combinations.

190 [BEGGAR] LAWYER. Why, la you now. And am not I a lawyer?

POET. But where's Divinity?

VINC. Marry, that I know not. One of us might do that, if either knew how to handle it.

SPRING. Where's the old patrico, our priest, my ghostly father? He'll do it rarely.

1 BEG. He was telling fortunes e'en now to country wenches. I'll fetch him.   *Exit.*

SPRING. That patrico I wonder at; he has told me strange things in clouds.

200 AMIE. And me somewhat that I may tell you hereafter.

SPRING. That you shall be my bride?

AMIE. I will not tell you now.

VINC. Well, but what must our speeches tend to? What must we do one with another?

POET. I would have the country, the city, and the court be at great variance for superiority; then would I have Divinity and Law stretch their wide throats to appease and reconcile them; then would I have the soldier cudgel them all together, and overtop them all. Stay; yet I want another person.

210 HILL. What must he be?

POET. A beggar.

VINC. Here's enough of us I think. What must the beggar do?

POET. He must at last overcome the soldier, and bring them all to Beggars' Hall. And this, well-acted, will be for the honour of our calling.

ALL. A Scribble, a Scribble!

HILL. Come, where's this patrico, that we may begin?

Enter Patrico

PAT. Alack and welladay, this is no time to play!
Our quarter is beset; we are all in the net.

220 Leave off your merry glee.

VINC. You begin scurvily.

SPRING. Why, what's the matter?

WITHIN. Bing awast,[1] bing awast! The quire cofe [2] and the harman-beck![3]

Some beggars run over the stage

SPRING. We are beset indeed. What shall we do?

VINC. [*To* Hilliard] I hope we shall be taken.

HILL. [*To* Vincent] If the good hour be come, welcome, by the grace of good fortune.

---

[1] Haste away.   [2] Justice of the Peace.   [3] Constable.

Enter Sentwell, Constable, Watch. *The crew slip away*

SENT. Beset the quarter round. Be sure that none escape.

230 SPRING. Lord to come with you, blessed master, to a many
distressed—

VINC., HILL. Duly and truly pray for you.

RACHEL, MERIEL. Good your good worship, duly and truly—

SENT. A many counterfeit rogues! So frolic and so lamentable
all in a breath? You were acting a play but now; we'll act with
you, incorrigible vagabonds!

SPRING. Good master, 'tis a holiday with us; an heir was
married here today.

SENT. Married! Not so I hope. Where is she? 'Tis for an heir we
240 seek.

SPRING. Here she is, master. [*To* Companions] Hide yourselves
in the straw, the straw. Quickly, into the straw!

SENT. What tell'st thou me of this? An old blind beggar-woman!
We must find a young gentlewoman-heir among you. Where's
all the rest of the crew?

CONST. Slipp'd into the barn and the bushes by, but none can
scape.

SENT. Look you to that, and to these here.   *Exit, with* Watch.

SPRING. Into the straw, I say.

250 VINC. No, good Springlove. The ladies and we are agreed now
to draw [1] stakes and play this lousy game no further.

HILL. We will be taken and disclose ourselves. You see we shall
be forc'd to it else. The cowardly clerk has done't to save
himself.

SPRING. Do you fear no shame, ladies?

RACHEL. Dost think it a shame to leave begging?

MERIEL. Or that our father will turn us out to it again?

SPRING. Nay, since you are so resolute, know that I myself
begin to find this is no course for gentlemen. This lady shall
260 take me off it.

AMIE. Make but your protestations good, and take me yours.
And for the gentleman that surprises us, though he has all my
uncle's trust, he shall do anything for me to our advantage.

VINC. If, Springlove, thou couldst post now to thy tiring-house [2]
and fetch all our clothes, we might get off most neatly.

SPRING. A horse and six hours' travel would do that.

AMIE. You shall be furnish'd, doubt not.

Enter Sentwell, [Constable,] Watch

[1] Withdraw.   [2] A dressing-room for actors.

SENT. She's scap'd or is invisible. You, sir, I take to be the chief
rogue of this regiment. [*To* Constable] Let him be whipp'd till
270   he brings forth the heir.

CONST. That is but till he stinks, sir. Come, sir, strip, strip.

AMIE. Unhand him, sir. What heir do you seek, Master Sentwell?

SENT. Precious![1] How did my haste oversee her? Oh, Mistress
Amie, could I or your uncle, Justice Clack, a wiser man than
I, ever ha' thought to have found you in such company?

AMIE. Of me, sir, and my company I have a story to delight you,
which on our march towards your house I will relate to you.

SENT. And thither will I lead you as my guest,
But to the law surrender all the rest.
I'll make your peace.

280 AMIE.   We must fare all alike.   *Exeunt.*

ACT V

[Justice Clack's *house*]

[*Enter* Justice] Clack, Martin

CLACK.[2] I have forgiven you, provided that my niece be safely
taken, and so to be brought home—safely I say; that is to say,
unstain'd, unblemish'd, undishonour'd; that is to say, with no
more faults, criminal or accusative,[3] than those she carried with
her.

MARTIN. Sir, I believe—

CLACK. Nay, if we both speak together, how shall we hear one
another? You believe her virtue is armour of proof without
your counsel or your guard, and therefore you left her in the
10   hands of rogues and vagabonds, to make your own peace
with me. You have it, provided, I say, as I said before, that she
be safe; that is to say, uncorrupted, undefiled; that is to say, as
I said before.

MARTIN. Mine intent, sir, and my only way—

CLACK. Nay, if we both speak together, how shall we hear one

---

[1] 'By God's precious blood!'   [2] Justice Clack is reminiscent of Justice
Overdo in Jonson's *Bartholomew Fair* and Justice Eitherside in Jonson's
The Devil is an Ass.   [3] Accusatory.

another, as I said before? Your intent and your only way, you would ha' said, was to run away with her, and that by her only instigation, to avoid the tie of marriage with Master Talboy; that is to say, to shun the match that I had made for her; that is
20 to say, rather to disobey me than to displease herself, wherein, although she did not altogether transgress the law, she did both offend and prejudice me, an instrument, nay, I may say, a pillar thereof. And you, in assisting her, furthering, and conveying her away, did not only infringe the law, in an unlawful departure from your master, but in a higher point, that is to say, top and top-gallows high.[1] I would ha' found a jury should ha' found it so.

MARTIN. But, sir, an't please you,—

CLACK. Must we then both speak together? Have I not borne
30 with thee, to speak all thou pleasest in thy defence? Have I not broke mine own rule, which is to punish before I examine, and so have the law the surer o' my side? And dost thou still persist? Hold your own peace, or as I am a justice of the king's, I will unsay what I said before and set a *currat lex*[2] at you, sirrah, that shall course you up the heavy hill! Oh, is your tongue fallen into your leg now? Do not you know I have acquitted you? Provided, as I said before—Go your way in, and see that the gentlemen who, I think, were got in sack, christened in sack, nursed with sack, and fed up to grey hairs with only
40 sack; see, I say, that they want no sack. My son Oliver, I thank him, has brought me a pair of such guests.

Enter Sentwell

Oh, Master Sentwell! Good news?

SENT. Of beggarly news, the best you have heard.

CLACK. That is to say, you have found my niece among the beggars; that is to say,—

SENT. True, Sir Oliver, I found her—

CLACK. Now if we both speak together, who shall hear one another?

SENT. I thought your desire was to be inform'd.

50 CLACK. I can inform myself, sir, by your looks. I have taken a hundred examinations i' my days of felons and other offenders out of their very countenances and wrote 'em down verbatim to what they would have said. I am sure it has serv'd to hang some of 'em and whip the rest.

---

[1] i.e. top-sail and top-gallant sail, the highest sails.   [2] Lit., 'let the law run'; i.e. to the limits that the law allows.

SENT. [*Aside*] Justice Clack still. He must talk all. His clack must only go.

CLACK. But to the point. You have found my niece; you have left her at your own house, not only to shift her out of her disguise, but out of her shame to come nearer me, until I send
60   her pardon.

SENT. Most true, sir, but the company she was in—

CLACK. Again! Do not I know the company? Beggars, rogues, vagabonds, and hedge-birds.

SENT. But do you know whom or how many we have taken, and how the rest escap'd?

CLACK. A needless knowledge. Why should we take more than herself? Or how could you take those that could escape?

Enter Martin

MARTIN. Sir, the old gentlemen within sent me to wait upon you. Without you, they say, they need not my service.

70 CLACK. Tell 'em then I'll wait on 'em presently.   *Exit* Martin.

SENT. But, sir, we have taken with her such beggars, such rogues, such vagabonds, and such hedge-birds, since you call 'em so, as you never knew or heard of, though now the countries swarm with 'em under every hedge, as if an innumerable army of 'em were lately disbanded without pay. Hedge-birds, said you? Hedge lady-birds, hedge-cavaliers, hedge-soldier, hedge-lawyer, hedge-fiddlers, hedge-poet, hedge-players, and a hedge-priest among 'em! Such we have taken for the principals, but to see how the multitude scap'd us was more sport than
80   pity; how, upon a watch-word given, they in the instant vanish'd by more several ways than there were legs among 'em; how the creeples leap'd over pales and hedges; how the blind found their way through lakes and ditches; how a doxy flew with two children at her back and two more perhaps in her belly,—

CLACK. A hedge-priest have you taken, say you?

SENT. Yes, sir, an old patrico, an ancient prophet, to tell fortunes and cozen our poor country people of their single money.[1]

Enter Oliver

90 OLIVER. Sir, Master Oldrents, in that he enjoys not your company, begins to doubt of his welcome.

CLACK. Who led him into that doubt? I, or you that brought him hither?

---

[1] Small change.

OLIVER. Sir, his own desire and love to you brought him
hither. I but show'd him the way.

CLACK. You reason fairly. Tell him I come.

OLIVER. Pray, sir, be pleas'd to do so, for he says—

CLACK. Nay, if we both talk together,—

OLIVER. Who shall hear one another?   *Exit* Oliver.

100 CLACK. But are there players among the apprehended?

SENT. Yes, sir. And they were contriving to act a play among
themselves just as we surpris'd 'em and spoil'd their sport.

CLACK. Players! I'll pay [1] them above all the rest.

SENT. You shall do well in that, to put 'hem in stock [2] to set up
again.

CLACK. Yes, I'll put 'em in stocks and set 'em up to the
whipping-post. They can act justices, can they? I'll act a
justice among 'em; that is to say, I will do justice upon them;
that is to say,—

110 SENT. Pray, sir, be not severe; they act kings and emperors as
well as justices. And justice is blind they say; you may therefore
be pleas'd to wink a little. I find that you have merry old
gentlemen in your house that are come far to visit you. I'll
undertake that these players, with the help of their poet, in a
device which they have already studied and a pack of clothes
which I shall supply 'em with, shall give your guests much
content, and move compassion in you towards the poor
strowles.

CLACK. But you know my way of justice—and that's a sure
120 way—is to punish 'em first, and be compassionate afterwards,
as I find 'em upon their examination.

SENT. But for your guests' sakes, who, I know, do favour and
affect the quality [3] of actors very much, permit 'em, sir. It will
enlarge your entertainment exceedingly.

CLACK. And perhaps save me the expense of a renlet [4] of sack
the while. Well, sir, for that respect, and upon your undertaking
that they shall please, I will prorogue [5] my justice on the rogues.
And so to my merry gentlemen, whom I will prepare to see their
interlude against [6] after supper; but pray, Master Sentwell, as
130 you have found my niece, look to her and see her decently
brought home.

SENT. In her own best apparel. But you must prorogue your
displeasure to her too.

CLACK. I will do so until my scarce-welcome guests be gone.

[1] Punish.   [2] To provide with material, and to punish in the stocks.
[3] Profession.   [4] i.e. runlet, a cask.   [5] Suspend.   [6] In anticipation of.

Enter Randal

RAN. Sir, my master sends you word, and plainly, that without your company your entertainment stinks. He has commanded me saddle his nags and away tonight. If you come not at once, twice, thrice, he's gone presently, before supper. He'll find an host at an inn worth a hundred o' you.

140 CLACK. Good friend, I will now satisfy your master, without telling him he has a saucy knave to his man.

RAN. Thank your worship.   *Exit* Clack.

SENT. Do you hear, friend? You serve Master Oldrents.

RAN. I could ha' told you that. And the best housekeeper my master is of any gentleman in the county he dwells in, and the best master to a man, as I, the worst of twenty, can say for him, and would be asham'd to say less.

SENT. Your name is Randal.

RAN. Forgi' me! Are you so wise? You are too young to be my
150 godsire, and I hope not old enough to be a witch. How know you that I am Randal? Were you ever at my master's house i' Nottinghamshire, or at Dunghillford, where I was born?

SENT. No, but I have notes [1] to know you by.

RAN. I was never twelve mile from thence i' my life before this journey. God send me within ken of our own kitchen smoke again!

SENT. Your master's steward's name is Springlove.

RAN. Master Springlove, an't please you. There is not an honester gentleman between this and the head of him; and my
160 heart's with him where'er he is. Know you him too?

SENT. Yes, and your master's daughters too.

RAN. Whaw!

SENT. And that they are all from home, your master knows not where.

RAN. Whaw! Whaw! Know you that too?

SENT. Yes, and the two young gentlemen that are with 'em, Master Vincent and Master Hilliard.

RAN. Whaw, whaw again! You know 'em all, I think. But know you where they all are?

170 SENT. Even here by, at my own house.

RAN. Whaw!—

SENT. And they knowing that your master is here, and Master Hearty too,—

RAN. Whaw, whaw!—

[1] Information.

SENT. And yourself too. They directed me to find you, Randal, and bring you to 'em.

RAN. Whaw, whaw, whaw, whaw! Why do we not go then?

SENT. But secretly. Not a word to anybody.

RAN. Mum. Will you go then?

Enter Martin

80 MARTIN. Oh, Master Oldrents's man. Pray let me entreat you into the buttery.

RAN. Will you go, master gentleman?

MARTIN. Indeed, it is my master's desire, and he commanded me.

RAN. Now, when it's supper-time, did he? To fill my belly with thin drink to save his meat? It's the manner in churls' houses. Will you go, master gentleman?

MARTIN. In troth, my master is so merry with yours within—

RAN. Shite o' your master![1] My master's steward's a better man.
90   I'll to him, at this gentleman's house and all the rest. Whaw, whaw!

SENT. Randal, you forget.

RAN. Mum again then. Why, would you not go then?

Exeunt Sentwell *and* Randal.

MARTIN. The man's as mad as his master; the strangest strangers that ever came to our house.

Enter Talboy

TAL. Well, Martin, for confessing thy fault and the means thou mad'st whereby she is taken, I am friends with thee. But I shall never look upon her or thee but with grief of mind, however I bear it outwardly. Oh!

OO MARTIN. You bear it very manfully methinks.

TAL. Ay, you think so, and I know so. But what I feel, I feel. Would one of us two had never both seen one another! Oh!

MARTIN. You speak very good sense, sir. But does my master continue his merry humour with the old gentlemen within?

TAL. Yes, Justice Clack's clack goes as merrily as any.

MARTIN. Well said, sir. Now you speak merrily too.—[*Aside*] But I could say somewhat that would still him.—And for your comfort I'll tell you: Mistress Amie is fallen in love with one of the beggars!

10 TAL. Then have I nothing else to do but to laugh at thee as long as I live. Ha, ha, ha! To let a beggar cozen thee of her! Ha, ha, ha! A beggar! I shall die merrily yet. Ha, ha, ha!

[1] A vulgar imprecation.

Enter Clack, Oldrents, Hearty, Oliver

CLACK. A hey, boys, a hey! This is right; that is to say, as I would have it; that is to say,—

TAL. A beggar! Ha, ha, ha!

MARTIN. Ha, ha, ha!

CLACK. A hey, boys, a hey! They are as merry without as we were within. A hey, Master Oldrents and Master Hearty! The virtue of your company turns all to mirth and melody, with a
220 hey, trollolly, lolly, lolly! Is't not so, Master Hearty?

OLD. Why, thus it should be. How was I deceiv'd! Now I see you are a good fellow.

OLIVER. [*Aside*] He was never so before. If it be a lightning before death, the best is I am his heir.

TAL., MARTIN. Ha, ha, ha!

CLACK. Again, boys, again! That is to say, a hey, boys, a hey!

HEARTY. What is the motive of your mirth, nephew Martin? Let us laugh with you.

OLD. Was that spoke like my friend, Hearty? Lack we motives to
230 laugh? Are not all things, anything, everything to be laugh'd at? And if nothing were to be seen, felt, heard, or understood, we would laugh at it too.

CLACK. You take the loss of your mistress merrily, Master Talboy.

TAL. More merrily than you will take the finding of her. Ha, ha, ha! A beggar! Ha, ha, ha!

CLACK. Can I be sad to find her, think you?

MARTIN. He thinks you will be displeas'd with her and chide her.

CLACK. You are deceiv'd, Master Talboy; you are wide, Master
240 Talboy, above half your length, Master Talboy. Law and justice shall sleep, and mirth and good fellowship ride a circuit here tonight. A hey, Master Oldrents, a hey, Master Hearty, and a hey, son Oliver, and a hey, nephew Talboy that should ha' been, and a hey, my clerk Martin, and a hey for the players! When come they? Son Oliver, see for Master Sentwell, that is no readier with his new company—

TAL. Players! Let us go see too. I never saw any players.

Exeunt Talboy, Martin.

OLIVER. [*Aside*] This is the first fit that ever he had of this disease, and if it be his last I say, as I said before, I am his heir.

Exit.

250 OLD. But is there a play to be expected, and acted by beggars?

CLACK. That is to say, by vagabonds; that is to say, by strolling players. They are upon their purgation; if they can present anything to please you, they may escape the law; that is—a hey!—If not, tomorrow, gentlemen, shall be acted 'Abuses Stripp'd and Whipp'd'[1] among 'em. With a hey, Master Hearty! You are not merry.

Enter Sentwell

And a hey, Master Sentwell! Where are your *Dramatis Personae*, your *Prologus*, and your *Actus Primus*, ha? Ha' they given you the slip for fear of the whip? A hey!

60 SENT. A word aside, an't please you.

Sentwell *takes* Clack *aside and gives him a paper*

OLD. I have not known a man in such a humour.

HEARTY. And of his own finding! He stole it, indeed, out of his own bottles, rather than be robb'd of his liquor. Misers use to tipple themselves so.

OLD. He does so outdo us that we look like staid men again, Hearty, fine, sober things.

HEARTY. But how long will it last? He'll hang himself tomorrow for the cost we have put him to.

OLD. I love a miser's feast dearly. To see how thin and scattering
70 the dishes stood, as if they fear'd quarrelling!

HEARTY. And how the bottles, to scape breaking one another, were brought up by one at once![2]

OLD. How one of the serving-men, untrain'd to wait, spilt the white broth![3]

HEARTY. And another, stumbling at the threshold, tumbled in his dish of rouncevals[4] before him!

OLD. And most suitable to the niggardliness of his feast, we shall now have an entertainment or play presented by beggars.

CLACK. Send 'em in, Master Sentwell.   *Exit* Sentwell.
80 Sit, gentlemen; the players are ready to enter, and here's a bill of their plays. You may take your choice.

OLD. Are they ready for them all in the same clothes? Read 'em, good Hearty.

HEARTY. First, here's *The Two Lost Daughters*.

OLD. Put me not in mind of the two lost daughters I prithee. What's the next?

HEARTY. *The Vagrant Steward.*

OLD. Nor of a vagrant steward. Sure some abuse is meant me!

---

[1] A popular collection of satiric poems by George Wither (1613).
[2] One at a time.   [3] Gravy.   [4] Peas.

HEARTY. *The Old Squire and the Fortune-teller.*

290 OLD. That comes nearer me! Away with it!

HEARTY. *The Beggar's Prophesy.*

OLD. All these titles may serve to one play, of a story that I know too well. I'll see none of them.

HEARTY. Then here's *The Merry Beggars.*

OLD. Ay, that. And let 'em begin.

Enter Talboy *and* Oliver

TAL. The players are coming in, and Mistress Amie and your man Martin are to be actors among 'em.

CLACK. A hey then for that too! Some merry device sure.

A flourish of shalms [1]

Hark, the beggars' hoboys. Now they begin.

300 OLD. See, a most solemn prologue.

Enter Poet, *for Prologue*

POET. *To knight, to squire, and to the gentles here,* [2]
We wish our play may with content appear.
We promise you no dainty wit of court,
Nor city pageantry, nor country sport,
But a plain piece of action, short and sweet,
In story true. You'll know it when you see't.

OLD. True stories and true jests do seldom thrive on stages.

CLACK. They are best to please you with this though, or a hey with a whip for them tomorrow.

310 OLD. Nay, rather than they shall suffer, I will be pleas'd, let 'em play their worst.

A flourish. Enter Patrico, *with* Lawyer *habited like* Oldrents
See our patrico among 'em.

HEARTY. That offered you a doxy in the barn.

PAT. [*To* Lawyer] *Your children's fortunes I have told,*
That they shall beg ere they be old,
And will you have a reason why?
'Tis justice in their destiny.—

CLACK. Justice, ha? Are you meddling with justices already?

PAT. *Your grandfather, by crafty wile*

320 *Of bargaining, did much beguile*
A thriftless heir of half the lands
That are descended to your hands,
And then, by law, not equity,

[1] Medieval oboes.　　[2] Italic type in the Q sets off the speeches of the play within the play.

Forc'd him and his posterity
To woe and shameful beggary.

LAWYER. *That was no fault of mine nor of my children.*

PAT. *But our forefathers' debts and crimes,*
Although forborne till future times,
Are not so paid. But what needs more?
30   *I wish you happy in your store.*

                                              Exit.

OLD. Dost note this, Hearty?

HEARTY. You said you would be pleas'd, let 'em play their worst.

> Lawyer *walks sadly, beats his breast, etc. To him enter*
> Soldier, *like* Hearty, *and seems to comfort him*

OLD. [*Aside*] It begins my story, and by the same fortune-teller that told me my daughters' fortunes, almost in the same words. I know him now, and he speaks in the play to one that personates me, as near as they can set him forth.

CLACK. How like you it, sir? You seem displeas'd. Shall they be whipp'd yet? A hey, if you say the word.

40   OLD. Oh, by no means, sir. I am pleas'd.

SOLD. *Sad for the words of a base fortune-teller?* [1]
Believe him? Hang him! I'll trust none of 'em.
They have all whims and double double meanings
In all they say.

OLD. Whom does he talk or look like now?

HEARTY. It is no matter whom; you are pleas'd, you say.

SOLD. *Ha' you no sack i' th' house? Am not I here?*
And never without a merry old song?

                              Sing

'*Old sack and old songs, and a merry old crew*
50   *Will fright away cares when the ground looks blue*'.
And can you think on gipsy fortune-tellers?

LAWYER. *I'll think as little of 'em as I can.*

SOLD. *Will you abroad then? But here comes your steward.*

                  Enter Springlove *to* Lawyer

OLD. Bless me! Is not that Springlove?

HEARTY. Is that you that talks to him, or that coxcomb I, do you think? Pray let 'em play their play. The justice will not hinder 'em, you see; he's asleep.

---

[1] Many of the speeches between lines 341 and 387 are condensed or paraphrased from Act I and Act II, i.

SPRING. *Here are the keys of all my charge, sir; and*
    My humble suit is that you will be pleas'd
360   *To let me walk upon my known occasions this summer.*
LAWYER. *Fie! Canst not yet leave off those vagancies?* [1]
    But I will strive no more to alter nature.
    I will not hinder thee nor bid thee go.
OLD. My own very words at his departure.
HEARTY. No matter. Pray attend.
LAWYER. *Come, friend; I'll take your counsel.*
                      Exeunt Lawyer [*and*] Soldier.
SPRING. *I've striven with myself to alter nature in me*
    For my good master's sake, but all in vain;
    For beggars, cuckoo-like, fly out again
370   *In their own notes and season.*

        Enter Rachel, Meriel, Vincent, Hilliard

RACHEL. *Our father's sadness will not suffer us*
    To live in's house.
MERIEL.   *And we must have a progress.*
VINC. *Th'assurance of your loves hath engag'd us—*
HILL. *To wait on you in any course.*
RACHEL. *Suppose we'll go a-begging.*
VINC., HILL.   *We are for you.*
SPRING. *And that must be your course and suddenly,*
    To cure your father's sadness, who is told
    It is your destiny, which you may quit
    By making it a trick of youth and wit.
    I'll set you in the way.
380 ALL FOUR.   *But how? But how?*   *All talk aside*
OLD. My daughters and their sweethearts too! I see
    The scope of their design and the whole drift
    Of all their action now with joy and comfort.
HEARTY. But take no notice yet. See a whim more of it.
    But the mad rogue that acted me, I must make drunk anon.
SPRING. *Now, are you all resolv'd?*
ALL FOUR.   *Agreed, agreed!*
SPRING. *You beg to absolve your fortune, not for need.*   *Exeunt.*
OLD. I must commend their act in that. Pray thee, let's call 'em
    and end the matter here. The purpose of their play is but to
390   work my friendship or their peace with me, and they have it.
HEARTY. But see a little more, sir.

            Enter Randal

        [1] Wanderings.

OLD. My man Randal too! Has he a part with 'em?

RAN. They were well set a work when they made me a player!
What is that I must say? And how must I act now? Oh!
That I must be steward for the beggars in master steward's
absence, and tell my master he's gone to measure land for him
to purchase.

OLD. You, sir! Leave the work you can do no better—I can
forbear no longer—and call the actors back again to me.

400 RAN. With all my heart. And glad my part is so soon done. *Exit.*

Enter Patrico

PAT. Since you will then break off our play,
Something in earnest I must say;
But let affected rhyming go,
I'll be no more a patrico.
My name is Wrought-on. Start not, but if you
Desire to hear what's worth your best attention
More privately, you may draw nearer me.

Oldrents *goes to him*

HEARTY. Hear no more fortunes!

OLD.   You shall give me leave.

PAT. I am grandson to that unhappy Wrought-on,
410 Whom your grandfather craftily wrought out
Of his estate; by which all his posterity
Were since expos'd to beggary. I do not charge
You with the least offence in this; but now
Come nearer me, for I must whisper to you.

Patrico *takes* Oldrents *aside*

I had a sister, who among the race
Of beggars was the fairest. Fair she was
In gentle blood and gesture [1] to [2] her beauty,
Which could not be so clouded with base clothing
But she attracted love from worthy persons,
420 Which, for her meanness,[3] they express'd in pity
For the most part. But some assaulted her
With amorous though loose desires, which she
Had virtue to withstand. Only one gentleman—
Whether it were by her affection or
His fate to send his blood a-begging with her
I question not—by her, in heat of youth,
Did get a son, who now must call you father.

[1]Carriage.   [2] In addition to.   [3] Lowly rank .

OLD. Me?

PAT.   You. Attend me, sir. Young bounty then
Dispos'd your purse to her, in which, besides
430   Much money—I conceive by your neglect—
Was thrown this holy relic. Do you know it?

OLD. The Agnus Dei [1] that my mother gave me
Upon her death-bed! Oh, the loss of it
Was my sore grief; and now with joy it is
Restor'd by miracle. Does your sister live?

PAT. No, sir. She died within a few days after
Her son was born, and left him to my care,
On whom I, to this day, have had an eye
In all his wand'rings.

OLD.   Then the young man lives!

Enter Springlove, Vincent, Hilliard, Rachel, Meriel.

440 PAT. Here with the rest of your fair children, sir.

OLD. My joy begins to be too great within me!
My blessing, and a welcome to you all.
Be one another's, and you all are mine.

VINC., HILL. We are agreed on that.

RACHEL.   Long since.
We only stood till you shook off your sadness.

MERIEL. For which we were fain to go a-begging, sir.

OLD. Now I can read the justice of my fate and yours—

CLACK. Ha! Justice? Are they handling of justice?

OLD. But more applaud great Providence in both.

450 CLACK. Are they jeering of justices? I watch'd for that.

HEARTY. Ay, so methought. No, sir; the play is done.

Enter Sentwell, Amie, Oliver, Martin

SENT. [*To* Clack] See, sir, your niece presented to you.

Springlove *takes* Amie [*towards* Justice Clack]

CLACK. What, with a speech by one of the players?
Speak, sir, and be not daunted; I am favourable.

SPRING. Then by your favour, sir, this maiden is my wife.

CLACK. Sure you are out o' your part; that is to say, you must
begin again.

SPRING. She's mine by solemn contract, sir.

CLACK. You will not tell me that. Are not you my niece?

460 AMIE. I dare not, sir, deny't; we are contracted.

---

[1] The metal figure of a lamb with a cross or flag.

CLACK. Nay, if we both speak together, how shall we hear one
another?

MARTIN. I must disprove the contract.

TAL. That is my part to speak.

SENT. None can disprove it. I am witness to it.

CLACK. Nay, if we all speak—as I said before.

OLD. Hear me for all then. Here are no beggars—you are but
one, patrico—no rogues, nor players; but a select company,
to fill this house with mirth. These are my daughters, these their
470   husbands, and this that shall marry your niece, a gentleman,
my son. I will instantly estate him in a thousand pound a year
to entertain his wife, and to their heirs forever. Do you hear me
now?

CLACK. Now I do hear you, and I must hear you; that is to say,
it is a match; that is to say—as I said before.

TAL. And must I hear it too? Oh!

OLD. Yes, though you whine your eyes out.

HEARTY. Nephew Martin, still the child with a suck-bottle of
sack. Peace, lamb, and I'll find a wife for thee.

480 OLD. Now, patrico, if you can quit your function,[1]
To live a moderate gentleman, I'll give you
A competent [2] annuity for your life.

PAT. I'll be, withal, your faithful beadsman, and
Spend my whole life in prayers for you and yours.

CLACK. And now, clerk Martin, give all the beggars my free
pass,[3] without all manner of correction; that is to say, with a
hey get 'em gone.

OLIVER. [To Vincent] Are not you the gentleman that challeng'd
me in right of your friend here?

490 VINC. Your inspection's good, sir.

RACHEL. And you the gentleman, I take it, that would have
made beggar-sport with us, two at once.

MERIEL. For twelve pence a piece, sir.

OLIVER. I hope we all are friends.

SPRING. Now on my duty, sir, I'll beg no more
But your continual love and daily blessing.

OLD. Except it be at court, boy, where, if ever I come, it shall
be to beg the next fool-royal's [4] place that falls.

SPRING. A begging epilogue yet would not be
500   Methinks improper to this comedy.

[1] Calling.   [2] Suitable.   [3] A permit to travel at will; beggars were
ordinarily permitted to beg only within their native counties.   [4] Court
jester.

Epilogue

Though we are now no beggars of the crew,
We count it not a shame to beg of you.
The justice here has given his pass free
To all the rest, unpunish'd; only we
Are under censure till we do obtain
Your suffrages, that we may beg again,
And often, in the course we took today,
Which was intended for your mirth, a play;
Not without action and a little wit,
510   Therefore we beg your pass for us and it.

FINIS

GLOSSARY

The footnotes and glossary do not define words whose meanings have changed little since the seventeenth century or can be readily found in a modern dictionary. Ambiguous, obsolete and cant terms which occur only once or twice in each play are clarified in the footnotes; such words used frequently are listed below.

'a, he, she, it.
affect, love.
an, and, if.
charge, expense.
credit, believe.
cry you mercy, beg your pardon.
discover, reveal.
fond, foolish.
Gramercy, thanks.
happily, by chance.
How! Indeed!
kickshaws, trifles.
likes, pleases.
Marry! Indeed!

mere, absolute.
'ods my life! God save my life!
present, presently, immediate, mmediately.
proper, handsome.
quean, strumpet.
quit, acquit.
'Slife, 'Slid, 'Sdeath, By God's life, eyelid, death.
still, always.
stomach, appetite.
trow, believe.
use, are accustomed to.
well said, well done.